CRACKERS

MERCER UNIVERSITY

MERCER UNIVERSITY PRESS

Endowed by

TOM WATSON BROWN

and

THE WATSON-BROWN FOUNDATION, INC.

CRACKERS

Bill Merritt

MERCER UNIVERSITY PRESS | *Macon, Georgia*

MUP/ P529

Published by Mercer University Press
1501 Mercer University Drive
Macon, Georgia 31207

9 8 7 6 5 4 3 2 1

Books published by Mercer University Press are printed on acid-free paper that meets the requirements of the American National Standard for Information Sciences—Permanence of Paper for Printed Library Materials.

ISBN 978-0-88146-572-3
Cataloging-in-Publication Data is available from the Library of Congress

Also by Bill Merritt

Where the Rivers Ran Backward

A Fool's Gold

To Peggy with the loving heart.

Your life is proof that courage is the virtue that makes all other virtues possible.

Also, I really like your body.

Contents

I

Sometimes I Feel as if I Have Two Hearts

When I was young, the South was going to rise again. Every filling station, every drugstore, every five-and-dime, it seemed, had a rack of decals featuring a Confederate flag over the legend "FORGET? HELL!" And it wasn't just decals. You could walk into one of these places and come out sporting the hat of a Confederate infantryman. Or a cavalry officer. Even a general. Not that we needed visual reminders to know who we were. We were the stuff of heroes.

Of all Americans, we were the most patriotic. Yet our blood was the blood of the only people who ever came close to overthrowing the United States of America—the blood of men who smashed Northern armies at Chickamauga and Cold Harbor, men who marched beside Stonewall Jackson in the Shenandoah, who tore into Yankee shipping from the mouth of the Mississippi to the coast of Burma, and, especially, our blood was the blood of the wild, fierce men who galloped across Alabama with Nathan Bedford Forrest. If things had been a little different, if our leaders had been smarter, if we'd been a bit luckier, we would be a separate people now, living under our own flag. It was all so vivid in our memories, so real, we might have done those things ourselves.

There were eleven Confederate States, and the flag had a star for each one, thirteen stars in all. You can look it up if you want, but you aren't going to find out any different, so you might as well trust me on this.

I used to chalk up those extra stars to thwarted hospitality, a home prepared for the next two states to tread the path of liberty. Now it seems more as if the flag, like the country, had gone a bit haywire trying to present itself with a harmony it did not possess. With eleven stars, the flag wouldn't have come out even.

There was another thing about that flag. It wasn't really the Confederate flag. It was just a battle flag. We all knew that, but nobody knew what the real flag looked like. “It has been suppressed” was all anybody could come up with. The flag for which a quarter of a million of our fathers died had been cropped out of history.

“That’s the way the Yankee government wants it” was what I’d hear on camping trips from older boys. “They don’t care for any part of that flag. We put the scare on them, we purely did.”

The boys told stories about the war and about the chaos that followed. And what we did about it. About nightriders and secret organizations. About acts of charity and acts of violence carried out in the dark because Federal bayonets were too many and too ruthless to face during the day. And how when the time for that was over, our fathers formed up for the last time and burned their robes. Then took an oath to be even more tightly bound together in future emergencies. That was in January, maybe February, 1869.

Late at night, some of the boys would talk about that ceremony and hint that they considered it their duty to stand on their fathers’ oath. Until our time came, we would drink of our heritage and hold who we were close to our hearts, and ready ourselves for our own call to heroism.

2

Sun So Hot I Froze to Death

My family is American, and has been for generations, in all its branches, direct and collateral.

For nine of those generations we lived on the banks of the Tennessee River in Northern Alabama. Our property came to us direct from the king of England himself. We still had the parchment. George II, by grace of God, King of Great Britain and Ireland, Duke of Brunswick-Lüneburg, Prince-Elector of the Holy Roman Empire, Defender of the Faith and Dispossessor of Indians, affixed his royal seal to the parchment, muttered a benediction in German, and ceded the land to us forever.

This wasn't Plantation South, it was republican, yeoman South. Borderline Appalachia. We worked the land ourselves. It was the home of my grandmother when she was a girl. And of her parents, and their parents, and grandparents, and great-grandparents, back through people I know only in stories, people whose flesh is my flesh, but whose names I would not recognize and do not know how to discover, to a time before farms and tidy homes and hardworking yeoman farmers, a time when Northern Alabama was all tulip trees and honeysuckle, rhododendron and azalea and hickory and loblolly pine and mountain laurel, a time when families more ancient than ours lived there without so much as a by-your-leave from a foreign king, and their names are forgotten as well.

It is the place my grandmother's grandmother's grandmother made the world end. It was where my grandmother's grandmother sheltered with two baby girls while she waited for her soldier to slip home through Yankee lines. It was the place my grandmother retreated when her own soldier dropped dead on the commuter train to Chicago and she was left with my ten-year-old father and his two sisters to take care of and nowhere else to go.

My grandmother's grandmother's grandmother didn't mean to make the world end. She was just a little girl who'd heard way too much about God and not nearly enough about eclipses of the sun. Something else she'd heard too much was, "If you can't be still, then you will just have to leave." The progressive young man who ran the one-room schoolhouse didn't believe in corporal punishment. When a child acted up, he just said, "If you can't be still, then you will have to leave," and it worked. The children seemed to think that having to leave school was about the worst thing that could happen and settled right down. Even my grandmother's grandmother's grandmother settled down.

Until the day came she didn't.

Mostly when children are bad, it's because one thing led to another. But sometimes, it's malice aforethought. God takes it serious when it's malice aforethought, and my grandmother's grandmother's grandmother and her friend Becky put a lot of aforethought into what they did the morning the world ended.

What they did was wait for a beautiful spring day. Then they loaded a basket with big chunks of cake, and a pot of jam, and lemonade, and covered it with a cloth and set it inside the door when they got to school.

Somewhere around the middle of the morning they shot each other a look, then knocked their books onto the floor.

And, when they leaned over to pick them up, began to giggle.

Which triggered the thing about "Now, girls, if you can't be still, you will have to leave." The plan went off as smoothly as a well-made shotgun.

They stood up straight and dignified, like queens of some foreign place, and walked over and grabbed the picnic basket and were out the door before the progressive young teacher could think what to do about it. It was the most wonderful, most appalling act any living citizen of Madison County ever witnessed and would have gone down in the history books if God hadn't decided enough is enough and ended the world.

The girls were down by the river, giggling through mouthfuls of cake and spoonfuls of jam, dancing around making fun of the young teacher, when the sun started to go out.

The first thing my grandmother's grandmother's grandmother's mother knew about any of this was when the girls came tearing into the yard crying and promising never to do something like that again, if only

God would light the sun back up. By then the sun was coming out anyway, so the girls knew He'd accepted their apology. But they were Baptists and they knew He wouldn't be near so understanding next time.

⁂

They must have kept their resolution because the world was still here two generations later when the Civil War came to northern Alabama.

My grandmother's grandmother was sixteen. Her husband was off to war, and she was alone with two baby girls when the Fourth Ohio Cavalry set up camp in our yard. My grandmother said their idea was to invade down through Alabama to Mobile and cut the country in two, but after running up against General Forrest, they concluded it was a better plan to go to Chattanooga and try their luck down through Atlanta.

"Sometimes her husband would come slipping through the Yankees at night to bring presents to the girls and court her." That's the delicate way my grandmother put it. "Come Christmas, the captain in charge of the Yankees wrote to his missus back in Ohio to send down china dolls for the girls, and they were the first china dolls anybody ever saw in our part of the country, so our family didn't come away hating Yankees as much as other people did."

One morning my grandmother's grandmother received a formal note from the captain saying, "We saw your young man slipping through our camp last night. He is a fine looking fellow, and we would hate to shoot him, so I am obliged if you would get word to him not to come around again." We always considered that a courtesy, and that's one more reason we didn't hate Yankees as much as other people did. It also may have influenced my grandmother's choice in husbands when the time came.

He was from West Point and the handsomest man, she told me. The problem was it was the wrong West Point: not the one in Mississippi, but the other West Point, the one up in New York.

He came to Alabama wearing a blue uniform, and there were people, and plenty of them, even some in our own family, who didn't have any use for a girl running wild with somebody like that. Two of my grandmother's sisters would not speak to him. Then, when he and my grandmother married, they wouldn't speak to her either. Not for the quarter of a century the marriage lasted, and then not for another quarter of a century after he died of a detached retina on the commuter train.

My grandmother never gave up voting Democrat or worshipping the Methodist god prosperity had promoted our family to. She also never learned to cook, which was an accomplishment for a woman who raised three children and had two husbands. It was not, as you might think in this day and time, a feminist triumph. It was because she never had to learn to cook. Even for a widow raising three children on the thirty-five dollars a week she brought home as a small-town librarian during the Depression, times were so much harder for other people she could always afford a colored lady to sweep out the place and fix her meals.

Being from Alabama, my grandmother got to balance how much of an American she wanted to be with how much of a Southerner. She got to pick the year she was born, too. She was somewhere in her twenties when the income tax kicked in and birth certificates became de rigueur, so she went down to the courthouse and swore out one for herself. At least that's as much as she ever said about it. After she died, it turned out she'd made more than one trip to the courthouse and had a pile of birth certificates attesting to whatever age she needed to be at the time.

Along with a casual attitude toward birth certificates, she had a talent for happiness. All her life she would refuse to discuss politics. And when she talked about Yankees, it was the captain in the yard with his note she talked about, and the doll he gave her mother, not the other things she must have heard while she was growing up.

My grandmother's grandmother might well have known Emma Sansom; their farms weren't all that far apart. Regardless of whether Emma ever met anybody in our family, I'm sure my grandmother heard a lot of stories about her. Everybody in Alabama knew about Emma and the two thousand Yankee soldiers who came racing along the road in front of the Sansom farm trying to get away from General Forrest. By the time the general himself rode up, the Yankees were on the other side of Black Creek and the bridge was in flames. That's where Emma came in. She knew another way across.

General Forrest didn't have time to saddle a horse for her. His blood was up, and Yankees were slipping through his fingers. He swung

Emma up behind him just as Mrs. Sansom stepped out of the farmhouse, a fierce widow determined to raise her daughters Christian, yelling at Emma, but at the man with her as well, "Emma, what do you *mean*?" Then at the general, but at Emma, too, "Sir, my child cannot thus accompany a stranger!"

"Do not be uneasy, madam. My name is Forrest, and I will be responsible for this young lady's safety." Hearing that name ended the matter in the mind of any Southerner. It was as if Sir Galahad himself and all the knights of the Table Round had appeared in a cloud of dust to save the country.

The next few moments were the most exciting of Emma's entire life. The general spurred his horse, and the three of them raced along a tangled ravine, crashing through undergrowth until they came to Black Creek, and she told him, "I think we had better get off as we are now where we might be seen."

He lifted her to the ground and together they crept through cannon and rifle fire while she pointed out the ford.

A Minié ball hummed and crashed into a tree beside her head, and the gray knight stepped between her and the enemy, tipping his broad-brimmed hat. "Madam, I am glad to have you for a pilot, but I will not make a breastworks of you." Then he lifted her back onto the horse for another wild chase along the bottom of the ravine until they were beside her mother and little sister.

Half an hour later, the artillery was up, gray cavalry was across Black Creek, the Yankees were routed, and the knight, the Avenging Sword of the Lord God Almighty Himself, or so it seemed to Emma, was slashing at their going until they ran to ground at Day's Gap, just outside Rome, Georgia. Two thousand Federal troops taken prisoner by six hundred gallant Rebels. The Yankees never had a chance. For generations, while girls in the North played with dolls, their sisters in Alabama played Emma Sansom.

My grandmother would have, too. But when it came to choosing a heritage, she chose the Colonial Dames, thereby becoming grandmother to both the Daughters of the American Revolution and the Daughters of the Confederacy. As time passed and her childhood became more distant, the stories of Emma Sansom must have come to seem like something out of King Arthur, a fairytale for children, to be treasured up in her heart, but nothing for a grown woman to dwell upon.

Grandfather had been a careful planner, and before his retina came loose, he invested half his savings in blue-chip stocks. The stocks were tied up in a trust my grandmother couldn't get at because ladies had no talent for finance. The other half he left her as play money, which she invested in Coca-Cola on the grounds that "People will always like this stuff." The stock doubled and split and doubled again. Dividends from Coca-Cola supplemented her job at the library and saw her, my father, and my two aunts through the Depression.

When I knew her, she was living in Atlanta, sliding into a dignified old age in a comfortable three-bedroom apartment, traveling when she wanted, doing as she pleased, and every year having more money in the bank than the year before, courtesy of the Coca-Cola Company and her own down-to-earth common sense.

3

Suspended Above the Land, with Flowers

The family wasn't in Alabama anymore.

The land that had been our refuge for nine generations, through good times and war, through poverty and wealth and Depression, through back-breaking labor and enemy occupation, the home of our fathers and of our imaginings, of our longings and our memories, had been confiscated by the army while Dad was off to the Second World War. The place of our leavings and our comings home, of our gaudy triumphs and private sorrows, of our courtships and christenings and marriages, the place we raised our children and comforted our old people, the land where our parents were buried, and too many babies, was now used to brew up phosgene and chlorine gas, and our family was scattered. Of all our generations, mine was the first never to see the land. I tried to visit it once, but the army wouldn't let me in.

I was born during the last months of my dad's war, in the most American of places to be born, in Walter Reed Hospital, run by the same army that took our land, in a hospital that welcomed my mother into its maternity ward—and my wrinkled, squalling self into this world—because my father had put on his father's uniform and was now an officer in that very army.

When the war was over, my parents migrated to Atlanta, thereby promoting themselves in the eyes of man by becoming courtly Georgians and in the eyes of God by joining the Republican Party and the Episcopal Church.

Atlanta had a baseball team, the Atlanta Crackers, and when the bats were connecting and the pitchers were blasting strikes past teams from Charlotte and Durham and other Southern cities cast out from major-league baseball, we were all Crackers. It was years before it dawned on me that when some people heard the word Cracker they thought of things other than minor-league baseball.

Years after that, when the favorite epithet of people who did not know us was to call us racist, it dawned on me what that baseball club had in mind. You want us to be Crackers? By god, we *will* be Crackers, and see what you can do about *that*.

There was another team in town, a team that used the same ballpark as the Crackers, and they weren't our team. They were the team for Altantans who'd not only been excluded from major-league ball but from the minors as well. They were the Atlanta Black Crackers. Whatever the thinking behind that name may have been, it's way too complex to decipher from this distance.

My parents weren't looking for a place to live when they moved to Atlanta. They'd had too much of place by then, along with the poverty and memories that went with it. They were looking for a non-place where they could forget the past and get on with their lives. What they found was Buckhead.

Buckhead is an extravagance, a delusion, a physical amazement—mile on mile on mile of wide lawns, of enormous brick homes and straight Georgia pines. An antebellum theme park of architectural details tacked onto houses built in the twenties. White columns supporting tiny roofs over front stoops, screen porches in place of rambling verandahs. Long, sinuous driveways winding like carriage paths across shaded parkland.

Come spring, the place floats away on a foam of blossom, a riot of wisteria hanging in soft, purple masses. Carpets of jonquil. Hedges of azalea and rhododendron. Masses of pinks and purples, fields of yellow and white. Cushions of reds and violets and oranges until the whole thing seems as unreal and as unmoored from the earth as a Hollywood sound stage, from which it is not too different.

But under all that, and behind it, the land remained. And what had happened upon the land. You could hear it in the names. The street that ran along the edge of Buckhead, along the flank of Peachtree Creek, where the Battle of Atlanta was lost, the street Dad and Mom retreated to from the too-much-history of Depression childhoods, was Peachtree Battle Avenue.

The name Buckhead is redolent with unexplained etymology. I used to imagine a lone trading post set among the pines, a deer head nailed over the door. Or, perhaps, earlier than that—a deer head marking the clearing where the trading post would someday be built. Or even more ancient. A shamanic site—a place of ancient forest gods, of rituals and animal deities, as forgotten now as the people who once knew their mysteries. Pleasant things to imagine as long as you kept your mind on deer and not the other, darker meanings suggested by the name.

The attorney general lived on our street. We were proud of that.

Like successful politicians all over Georgia, he had been in office since the memory of man ranneth not to the contrary, and he held the best interests of our state close to his heart. He once expressed those best interests in a speech before the Georgia Peace Officers Association entitled "The Ugly Truth about the NAACP."

Oddly, for a speech about a black civil-rights organization, he didn't mention race. It was the Communists who ran the NAACP he worried about. He knew Commies ran the NAACP because all but one of its founders had been the children of abolitionists. There it was, the assumption that underlay Buckhead thinking: people who didn't approve of slavery could only be in the pay of sinister foreigners out to destroy the United States.

For the sake of our attorney general, it should have stayed the fifties forever. During the fifties, Eugene Cook was exactly suited to the times.

There was another place on our street, and we kids were proud of it too, in a creepy sort of way. Everybody said it had been a meeting hall for the Klan.

There weren't any Klansmen when I lived in Buckhead. The fact is, there weren't any Klansmen anywhere, not after that cold winter's ceremony in 1869 when they burned their robes. And the people who pretended to be, we learned to hold in contempt. They'd been conjured into existence in 1915 by a dentist who'd spent too much time watching *Birth of a Nation*, looked at his aging father, experienced a Greatest-Generation moment, hiked up Stone Mountain, and burned a cross. A lot of disaffected boys showed up to watch, and the dentist, recognizing a good thing when he saw it, went into the mail-order haberdashery business supplying robes to people who were willing to make fools of themselves by insulting the memory of the grandfathers they thought to honor.

The Klan house was an odd stucco structure, the only place in all those miles of movie-prop Southern that wouldn't have looked Southern to a Yankee movie director. It was mock Colonial Spanish, and in the backyard had a large, concrete-lined hole filled with charred timbers and scorched bits of roofing tile. The story among the kids, probably encouraged by the maids, who would have talked about such a thing while our parents were busily keeping their mouths shut, was that that particular hole had once been an underground chamber where people met to play Klansman until, one night, the cross got out of control.

There were other houses, too. Creepy in a genuine way. Huge, gloomy places surrounded by acres of dark pines and unkempt, overgrown bushes shielded from view by high walls. You could catch glimpses into these yards out on West Paces Ferry when somebody left the gate open. The houses of Old Atlanta money, of people with nothing to prove, people who didn't plant magnolias and dogwoods, didn't lay out fields of jonquils and rhododendrons for public view, people who didn't care to show themselves at all. Places as isolated and cordoned off from life as the private psychiatric hospitals their owners frequented.

In a lot of ways, the places were exactly that, cocoons for those so rich and so isolated they had lost any kind of contact with reality. One English Tudor-style mansion hidden out of sight on seventeen acres of some of the most expensive real estate in the South belonged to Robert Maddox, superannuated banker and former Atlanta mayor, who startled his family over lunch one afternoon with a discovery he'd made about the chauffeur. "I have an announcement to make," he said. "Vernon can read." His chauffeur was Vernon Jordan.

Nearby, an entire block was fronted by a wall twelve, maybe fourteen, maybe sixteen feet high so that when you drove past all you could see on the other side were the tops of pine trees. Nobody knew what else was behind that wall, because the gate was always closed. A lady lived there, so the story went, a horrible caricature of a woman raising a son by herself. Riding in the backseat along West Paces Ferry, my little sister, Anne, and I would give a shudder when we passed that wall, as if the ghost sealed inside might slip into the car before we could get by.

What had become of the boy's father wasn't part of the story, but what happened to his sister was on everybody's lips. The boy had killed her. Expensive lawyers got involved and trumped-up psychiatric examinations, and by the time it was over, the shooting had turned into an accident, the mother had locked the gate forever, and she and her son had degenerated into strange, ghoulish recluses who never again showed their faces.

4

The Grapevine Line

The masons who built the houses had been colored, and when the twenties turned into the thirties and life became tougher, they'd been gerrymandered out of the few jobs that remained. By the time our family moved to Buckhead, the sons of those good, Southern artisans tended our lawns, and their daughters cleaned our homes and cooked our meals and looked after our children, of whom I was one, my little sister, Anne, was another, and Marti hadn't been born yet. Nobody would admit it, but they were much more like us than we were like the people hidden away on West Paces Ferry.

The buses they came in on, and took home at the end of the day, and gossiped together on, were called the Grapevine Line. When a couple of the wives down the block stopped showing up at the grocery store, none of our parents knew they had run away together until the maids told them. If someone had a problem with the bottle, they'd learn about it from the lady shelling peas in the kitchen. When a debutante's Grand Tour of Europe involved a swing through Florida for a live birth, Mary knew.

Mary James was the finest example of a Christian I ever met. She didn't preach, she never judged nor had a bad word about the sins of others. She just lived her faith, moment-by-moment, content that the Lord would provide. Her sorrows were her own, and her joy was for the world. Mother hired her when she was fourteen, and she had a gorgeous voice.

Mary spent her days singing in our kitchen and her evenings and Sundays singing in church. As she grew into a woman, her voice matured and became more powerful until Jesus filled our home. She was also very fond of her stories.

For Mary, soap operas had been placed upon this earth by a Loving God, and what the Good Lord hath provided, it was not Mary's place to cast aside. She honored her Creator by keeping the television running all day. To someone who spent ten or fifteen hours a week on the Grapevine Line, never-ending sagas of white women bedding their daughter's fiancés, embezzling money from orphanages, and poisoning their husbands must have seemed ripped from the headlines.

Mary had the same birthday as my grandmother, and for years she would call when the day came and wish her well, and my grandmother would wish Mary well, and they would chat a bit, then not talk until they were a year older and Mary called again.

As far as I could tell, Mary didn't want to be white. She knew she was made in God's image, and that was okay by her. She didn't even dream about becoming desegregated. Things were the way they were, and that was okay by Mary, too. She didn't hold resentments, even when the resenting might have helped change what she resented. She just wanted to be what my grandmother was automatically: a Southern lady.

Mary was gracious when the time came to be gracious, and she expected people to be gracious to her when the time came for that. She didn't want to change society, she just wanted respect. That would have been such an easy thing to give, respect. And we were fools, all of us, for not offering it in the fullest measure.

When I was in kindergarten, Br'er Rabbit was my literary beau ideal. He talked back. He spent a lot of time outdoors, and he did what he pleased. Except for the outdoors part, Br'er Rabbit was everything my parents never wanted me to be. I learned about him from Uncle Remus himself or, Joel Chandler Harris having shuffled off to that great slave cabin in the sky, the next best thing. His son who lived next door to my grandmother.

Jake Harris was an old man, impossibly old from what I remember, and skinny the way old men are skinny, and wore brown because he spent a lot of time in the garden. He gave me a copy of his daddy's book, inscribed with the words:

> Possum sittin' in de simmon tree
> Rabbit on de ground

Rabbit say, you son of a gun
Throw dem simmons down

I couldn't see what that rabbit wanted with persimmons. I'd bitten into one once. It had fallen in the woods behind our house, and it didn't taste one bit good. Pecans I could have understood. Throw dem pecans down would have made perfect sense. But simmons?

That poem seemed like a literary message, filled with metaphor and secrets about life and the Old South, if only I could puzzle them out. The kind of thing I would understand when I was older.

Well, I am older, and persimmons haven't gotten any tastier and the poem doesn't make any more sense. Sometimes I think Jake didn't understand it either, but he was pretty sure it must mean something and was doing his part to pass it along to a new generation of Georgians to worry over. Other times, I suspect he'd just come in from chopping down a persimmon tree and that was the verse that was running through his head.

The crèche Mother set out at Christmas was another thing I didn't fully understand. She'd place it on the mantle next to the bronze baby shoes, but no matter how many figurines she added, it never seemed complete.

Hark, the Herald, was there. I recognized him from the big swans' wings and the scroll unfolding from the trumpet in his hand. Seraphim and Cherubim were fluttering around. I knew about them from Sunday school. We didn't have a Sidorhim, but we weren't supposed to. He wouldn't have arrived yet. That's all I knew about the Sidorhim, that and he was late. And that he was some kind of child angel. And that he was more than just one of the faithful. He was special enough to have been invited by name: "Oh come, all ye faithful, come Little Sidorhim." I was of an age when I got most of my eschatology from songs.

Round John Virgin was who I worried about. He was one of the big three, Round John Virgin, Mother and Child, and we should have had one. I knew about the Trinity from Sunday school, and you needed all three to get into heaven. Maybe Round John got knocked over one

Christmas and rolled away. I imagined he looked like Tweedledum and Tweedledee with one of those Cub Scout hats they wore in *Through the Looking Glass*. I promised myself that when I grew up, I wouldn't be so slipshod in matters of doctrine.

Mother had camels and donkeys and sheep and kings bringing Christmas presents. There was something strange about those presents. Any kid would want gold. But frankincense and myrrh? They were a puzzle, but not nearly as puzzling as Orien Tar. What kind of country needed three kings? And who was home taking care of business while these guys were running around visiting crèches?

Baby Jesus was a king, too, unless he was a shepherd. Theology ran both ways on that. The king part featured in a lot of songs. But there were sheep in the crèche with him, and I knew enough about metaphor to know sheep stood for Christians. Mother was a Christian, and sometimes when she answered the phone, she'd say, "This is the Sheep." At Sunday school they even had a portrait of Jesus dressed up like the Good Shepherd with a little lost lamb in his arms. The lamb, the teacher explained, wasn't a lamb at all. It was a Christian in sheep's clothing being welcomed back into the fold so Jesus could slay a fatted calf in his honor.

One day I answered the phone by saying, "This is the Sheep," and Mother corrected me. I was a boy, and when somebody asked to speak to me, I was supposed to say, "This is he." Religion was as hard to understand as persimmons.

I have long been attracted to the notion there was something disreputable about Mother's family. Something We Do Not Talk About.

Part of this is pure romance, based on a remark from Mother's aunt Ruth. The one time I asked about their family, she turned away, all save the lone remark, "They showed up out of the mountains selling medicine from the back of a wagon." Selling medicine out of the back of a wagon was almost as good as pirates, and a patch better than an attic filled with tintypes and family bibles. But it was a peculiar vagueness on my great-aunt's part, especially where history was concerned.

Ruth was a genuine early twentieth-century feminist, a professional woman who never married. When I knew her, she was old and dumpy and white-haired. She wore a lot of black and purple and lived in a downtown apartment filled with relics of the past—but not her past. Atlanta's past.

Great-Aunt Ruth had run the Atlanta Historical Society for what, to my childish mind, seemed like centuries. She was the closest thing to an academic the family ever produced and had once been elected Woman of the Year. She was also a romantic.

I remember sitting on the overstuffed couch in her apartment after Alan Shepard went up for his first suborbital hop and came down with the remark, "Boy oh boy, what a ride." Or maybe it was, "Man oh man, what a ride." The *Atlanta Journal* reported it one way, the *Constitution* the other. Aunt Ruth told me she didn't know what Mr. Shepard had said, but she preferred to believe it was, "Man oh Man." "Man oh Man" sounded more manly.

There was something very Southern in all that—in a genuine self-sufficient woman generations before such was held to general esteem—a woman tough and resilient and still, somehow, feminine and admiring of masculinity.

Mother did pretty much as she damn well pleased, and like Aunt Ruth, she enjoyed being feminine. She had the body to pull it off, and sometimes would return from an expedition downtown flushed with pleasure that construction workers had whistled at her. I've never quite known what Dad made of that, but for me, all of Dad's relations with women remain a mystery.

Mother may have gotten her romanticism and her idealization of masculinity from Aunt Ruth or from growing up in the South. Or from being young when the world blew up and all the eligible men put on uniforms and marched away. She once told me that it was the uniform that first drew her to Dad.

They met when he was working at the Pentagon, and she admired him for arranging such an important place for himself so young. She admired my uncle for what he did to earn a Navy Cross on a submarine a thousand miles behind Japanese lines. And she admired all the other men who went off to fight—or even stayed home to serve. She even romanticized Dad's desk job in ways that would never have occurred to me.

To Mom, going to work every day at the Pentagon in times of war with enemy saboteurs lurking and German bombers out there over the Atlantic somewhere was a dangerous thing to do and one more example of Dad's courage and honor.

When they had people to dinner, she would introduce the men by telling me what they did in the war. "He flew fighters over Italy," or "He was in New Guinea with MacArthur." Not that General MacArthur would ever have known who the man in our living room was, but having served with MacArthur was as impressive an accolade as Mother could imagine.

Once, she introduced me to a one-armed man who'd missed the war entirely, in one way, and experienced it more intimately than anybody else Mother knew, in another. He and his wife had been touring Tokyo on December 7, 1941, and had spent the whole war in Japanese prison camps. He'd come home without the arm, and she hadn't come home at all.

Aunt Ruth came pretty close to being Mother's real mother. Not that Mother hadn't had a mother, exactly. Mother had had a very pretty, slender mother in a flapperish sort of way. The thing was that Mother's mother—like Ruth—was born too soon. Only in Lillian's case, the too soon didn't have anything to do with the role of women in genteel society. It had to do with modern medicine, the lack of which forced my mother to spend her teenage years raising her little sister and caring for her dying mother.

The Depression wasn't easy on anybody, but I think it was particularly tough on Mother, having to be everybody else's mother when what she really needed was one of her own. College must have looked like a refuge, at least before she went.

She was sixteen—having not only been uncommonly responsible around the house but in school as well—and hated college. At a stroke, it changed her from a grown woman to a naive girl in a society of adults.

The way Mother handled things was the way she handled most things. She put her mind to becoming the most socially dominant lady on the planet, and by the time I came along, she'd pretty much pulled it off.

Dad was on the road a lot for work, or, considering the work he did, the backroad, and he knew the hidden tracks and pine forests of the rural South as thoroughly as any bootlegger. Summers, when we headed down to Florida, he took us over routes you had to use a magnifying glass to find on the map. The Studebaker would bump along in the heat and dust, and Anne and I would go to sleep in the backseat, which may have been the point, and the trip took two days.

When we reached the coast, we'd leave the asphalt and crunch over roads paved with oyster shells. It was dazzling sometimes, the July sun dancing off the shells. And shadowy other places, the roads hung with Spanish moss and lined with live oaks and dark, water-filled ditches and dancing colored children, four, five, six, seven years old, who would see a car full of white people and go into jigs as we passed.

Dad would toss a handful of silver out the window, and from the backseat, Anne and I would watch as the nickels and dimes bounced into the oyster shells or splashed into the ditch and kids scattered and dove to retrieve them. Seeing those kids made me feel soft, like a sheltered city boy surrounded by life I knew nothing about.

When we stopped for gas, Anne and I spent what nickels Dad had left on an ice cream or on a Coke, but not an ice cream and a Coke. By historic ill-fortune, Mother had been raised by a dentist, and she put her foot down about two treats in one afternoon. Oral hygiene was never far from her consciousness.

With her dad to back her up, Mother didn't just follow the American Dental Association guideline and take us for a checkup every six months; three times a year she plopped us into her daddy's chair. You'd have thought with all that good dental care my teeth would have been in pretty good shape.

You'd have thought wrong. Dr. Garrett couldn't look in my mouth without turning up a cavity or two nobody had ever heard from before. He said it had something to do with Coca-Colas, and his Coca-Cola theory became the basis of a doctrinal dispute that presented serious medical and moral issues on both sides. On the one hand, my father's mother was a living example of the blessings Coca-Cola had bestowed, not only onto the world at large, but onto our family in particular. On the other hand, and often that hand was in my mouth, there was my mother's father.

We kids knew who was right, and we had the weight of medical opinion to back us up. On days we were feeling weakly, Mother would call Dr. Muse. He'd motor up to our house, open his black doctor's bag, pull out a wooden tongue depressor, make us say "Ahhhhhhh," write out a prescription, and Dad would climb into his Studebaker and drive down to the drugstore.

The druggist would see him coming, step over to the soda fountain, draw off a medicine-bottle full of Coca-Cola syrup, and hand it to Dad. This was the pure elixir itself. No carbonated water to thin it out. And no substitutes. No pharmacist on the planet would ever foist off Pepsi syrup. Something like that would cost him his license. The very idea was...well, it was nauseating. Imagine drinking Pepsi undiluted from the chemical works or wherever it is Pepsi comes from.

When Dad arrived home, he would hold the bottle up to study the label and learn how many teaspoons to ladle down our throats, and how often. And a day or two later, we'd rise from our beds revived. Not to mention, refreshed. In the circumstances, Dr. Garrett never had a chance.

Still, he knew what he knew, and there was toughness to him. Life and sloppy oral hygiene were things you stood up to. And pain was an opportunity for moral development. As far as Dr. Garrett was concerned, pain was like crabgrass. Everybody was afflicted by it, but you didn't have to pay any more attention to it than you chose. And he provided all eight of us grandchildren with plenty of moral development. He didn't use Novocain.

What he did use was his dental assistant's arm. He would invite us to squeeze it as hard as we could when the drill began clawing its way into a nerve. What the dental assistant thought of this arrangement was never disclosed, but her morals must have been among the most highly developed in the South.

We were a people of martial virtues, we Southerners, and when my thrice-yearly non-martial response to having my teeth drilled began to prove a threat to the masculinity of our nation, Mother took matters in hand and read me about Dick Whittington's Cat. I don't remember much about Mr. Whittington, or even what he was doing with a cat. I'm not sure Mother ever finished the story because we got sidetracked discussing London. I was still young enough that the whole concept of London was foreign to me, and Mother left the room and came back with a map of the city, framed and suitable for hanging over my bed. Which she did, and which remained hung over my bed until I went away to college.

The map was one of those tourist maps with little drawings of buildings such as St. Paul's Cathedral and Westminster Abbey arrayed picturesquely in the margins. At the bottom of the map was the legend: WE WOULD RATHER SEE LONDON LAID IN RUINS AND ASHES THAN THAT IT SHOULD BE TAMELY AND ABJECTLY ENSLAVED.

Tamely and abjectly enslaved? What the heck was that?

That was Sir Winston Leonard Spencer-Churchill, whom I hadn't heard about, either. But, in matters martial, he was top of the line. Looking back, I'm pretty sure that whole Dick Whittington business was a setup and Mother's real purpose was to get me to go to sleep every night with those words hanging over my head.

Afternoons when Dr. Garrett finished grinding away and I staggered out of the chair, pale and shaky and in the early stages of clinical shock, he would feed me the usual line about avoiding Coca-Cola, and because I had actually lived through the proceedings, would pour a few drops of mercury into an envelope and give it to me to play with. Dr. Muse presented us with lollipops after he gave us shots, which was a point in favor of Dr. Muse, but you had to be related to a dentist to get mercury.

In the backseat on the way home, rolling beads of liquid silver around in my palm, watching it pull apart and then fuse back together, then dripping it into Anne's ear and squinting down inside to see if it had turned shiny in there, like the insides of the sterling-silver straws my parents used when they drank juleps, was one of the high points of my childhood. It was as much fun as those machines they had in shoe stores where you wiggled your toes like a dancing skeleton while the machine blasted x-rays through your feet and into the DNA of your descendants, yea, even unto the seventh generation.

Dr. Garrett was dignified and white-haired and soft-spoken and a staunch supporter of the medical establishment. He had once been president of the American Dental Association, and as far as he was concerned, herbalists and chiropractors and patent-medicine enthusiasts were no better than carnies. The only times I ever saw him angry was when the conversation turned toward alternative medicine.

Mother picked up the torch and spoke against it every chance she got, explaining how even if the stuff didn't kill you on the spot, you were going to die from it anyway because you'd be putting who-knows-what worthless something into your body instead of seeing a real doctor and getting real medicine, which, in this day and age, with all the modern wonder drugs, would set you right in no time.

She and Dr. Garrett were so hot on this issue it makes me wonder whether there was something in their own past involving a wagon coming out of the mountains they never revealed. Or maybe, when I think about it, it had to do with both of them watching helplessly for years, trying desperate cure after desperate cure, while Mother's mother slipped away to tuberculosis.

Long before it became the new black, Grandmother was into pink.

In summer, she dressed in pink silks. When winter came, she dressed in pink woolens and wore a pink overcoat. Sometimes she would step out in salmon, but that was only on festive occasions when she was feeling especially light-hearted.

The canopy over her four-poster bed was pink, she had pink slips on her pillows, her comforter was pink satin, and her bathrobe was pink, as were her slippers. In the bathrooms, which she called commodes, she had pink sachets, and in spring her apartment was filled with pink azaleas. The ceilings were light pink, the walls rose colored, and the carpets Iranian shot through with pink floral motifs. All her Christmas decorations were pink, as were the lights on her tree.

The tree was pink too, a natural fir, seven feet tall and weighted down with pink flocking, as if it had been caught in a cotton-candy blizzard. I think it's one of the reasons her maid spent so much time in the kitchen. She didn't blend with the motif.

When we would arrive on Christmas morning, the only things in sight that weren't pink were Aunt Berta and Sis Anne. They were dressed in black, as if they were a pair of matched widows, but they weren't. It had taken fifty years to forgive my grandmother for running off with somebody from the wrong West Point, but they'd come around. Probably because they had never married, and Grandmother was the only remaining family to spend Christmas with. "Can't marry this one," Aunt Berta would say when a young man came courting. "He's a pharmacist, and I just can't see how I could be married to a pharmacist."

"Can't marry that one," Sis Anne would say. "He's a Baptist, and I could never marry a Baptist."

"Choosing a husband is like riding through the woods looking for a switch," Uncle John would say. "Don't pick this one because it's too skinny. Don't pick that one because it's too short. Pretty soon you're going to be out of the woods, and there won't to be any switches left not to pick."

Uncle John was Uncle John Sanford, and he'd married Aunt Eudora. Doughy, the grown-ups called her.

When John asked for her hand, he'd set his sights high, as he did for everything throughout his long life. At the turn of the last century, Eudora was the warmest, liveliest, funniest, prettiest girl in Madison County. All the young men wanted to dance with her and sit on the porch with her, and when the time came, most of them wanted to marry her. But it was Uncle John who ran away with her heart.

Uncle John wasn't a pharmacist or even a Baptist. He was from Missouri, and he sold feed from the back of a wagon. He didn't seem to have a lot of prospects in 1899, but he promised Doughy that if she would have him, she'd never work again. The fact is, she hadn't worked to start off with. The idea of keeping it that way must have appealed to her because she said yes.

When John Sanford came into the family, he brought something with him we didn't have: a history of slave-owning. His grandfather had also been named John Sanford, but the Supreme Court botched the spelling, like they did everything else about the case when, in 1857, they decided *Dred Scott v. Sandford*, returned Dred Scott to his master, declared that the Federal government didn't have the power to prohibit slavery in the territories, and set the country down the path to Civil War. Not that Uncle John ever owned slaves, he came along too late for that. But had they been available, he would have picked up a few.

John Sanford was a powerful, hard man. It might have been something in his genetic makeup, although I think growing up selling feed from the back of a wagon at the end of the nineteenth century may have contributed to it. Around the time he married Doughy, he went to work for Armour & Company and was there when Upton Sinclair wrote *The Jungle*, exposing what happened in meatpacking in general and what went on at Armour in detail.

Uncle John had a knack for feed and for animal products, and he fit right in at Armour. When I knew him, he had risen to president, where he devoted considerable energy to solidifying his presidency by harassing his second-in-commands to death through overwork and fear.

Uncle John kept his word to Doughy, and then some. He hired a household staff and banned her from the kitchen and from housework of any sort. And using the same ruthless talents that led him to the top at Armour, made it stick, even through the years she was raising Cousin John.

Cousin John was the apple of Doughy's eye. He was her first child and her only son, and with no other household duties, she lavished her domestic attentions upon him. The warm, lively girl who had been so popular when John Sanford came courting became the lively young mother who adored her child.

By the time I knew her, Aunt Doughy was not young and not lively and had not seen the inside of her own kitchen for half a century. When her cook called her to dinner, she would inquire, politely, "Ida, what is on the menu tonight?" She didn't even know what ingredients were in the house because Uncle John got up at four every morning, drove to an all-night grocery, and did the shopping.

We kids called her Aunt Dodo, and she lived up to the name. With nothing particular to occupy her thoughts or her efforts, she had slumped into...if not premature senility, a kind of permanent vacation of the mind, so that she never quite knew what was up.

When we visited, we'd trip over lumps in the carpet because she believed that beneath the carpet was the very spot to store the wads of cash Uncle John lavished upon her. And that the backs of curtains were the safest place to clip her sapphire broaches and ruby stickpins.

There was a tax issue involving the land in Alabama, and Uncle John was thc right guy at the right time to deal with it. The issue was that family resented having to pay taxes on the money they received when the army forced us to sell them the land.

Payment had been held up for a decade while Uncle John kept telling the court the army wasn't offering enough money, and judge after judge agreed with him and sent the matter back to the army to try again. Then, when everybody finally did agree on how much, it turned out the family didn't own the land. The fifth sister, the one who wouldn't marry a Baptist, owned it. All of it. That's not how my great-grandfather's will said it was supposed to work, but that's the way it shook out when the army researched the title.

As a spinster, Sis Anne never had much to report in the way of income. She paid her taxes and that was that, as far as the family was concerned. Convenient for us. Sis Anne paid a lot less in taxes at her rate than all five of the sisters would have paid, had they owned the land together.

There was a seven-year statute of limitations on tax fraud, and as the years began to run, Uncle John became meaner and more nervous, he slept less, paced around the living room more, and drove a whole new generation of underlings to early graves. It was like having a mob accountant in the family.

Dad spent a lot of his professional life visiting feed mills and fertilizer factories and other places that used the chemicals he sold. Sometimes he would take me along. I'd plop into the front seat, and he'd hand me a map and declare me Navigator, and I'd feel important, even though Dad knew perfectly well how to get where we were going and I couldn't read yet.

We would study the map and calculate that the little mill town, or wherever we were headed for, was a hundred and fifty miles from the motel we'd spent the night at. Dad's Studebaker would do sixty, easy, and I'd count on my fingers and figure we could go straight there by lunch. But if we tried that, we were going to go hungry.

This was before interstates, and there was no straight there, anywhere. And sixty miles-an-hour was an academic theory that didn't have anything to do with the real world, because the load of hay, or whatever we found ourselves stuck behind this time, wasn't doing more than about fifteen. Then we'd come to a town and have to slow down from that and work our way around the bronze Confederate Soldier standing guard in the square before we could speed back up to fifteen and head off to the next town. Confederate soldiers were like baby shoes. They'd bronzed a lot of them back in the day and placed them around squares all over the South so we'd remember the way things used to be.

Often as not, Dad's business would take him into the woods. We would drive through forests of loblolly pine redolent with the smell of pitch, the bark peeled from one side of every tree, the bare trunks scored in a herringbone pattern like sugar maples or rubber trees, and the sap collecting in buckets. The turpentine workers were colored, and a few white, in overalls. Lean, as I remember, and not looking like the sorts of men we saw in Buckhead. There was nothing pretend-nostalgic about these guys or the land they lived on. They were the real thing, poor and tough.

At the still, Dad would get out and introduce me to the foreman, and we would shake hands. Dad and the men would call one another Sir, then they would laugh and joke a bit. Maybe discuss the weather, or something to do with the price of supplies, or a funny story involving a mule who'd been bringing in a cartload of resin. Different stories, different people, different places, but all, now that I think about it, part of the same greeting ritual. The grease to reestablish personal...if not friendships, exactly, then...relationships between men of such wildly differing experiences. For somebody with a Harvard MBA, Dad was very good at this. Most Southern men are, I think.

Sometimes the conversation would turn to politics, but Dad never took the bait. Common feeling didn't run that far. These men were Democrats, and life had not been easy for them, and their views on who should be in office and how things should be run weren't hard to guess. We were Episcopal and we were Republican, which put us on the far left of legitimate social and political thought.

Once, in North Carolina, I think, we drove out into a pine forest filled with choking clouds of burning sulfur. The trees were wilted and dead, stripped of their needles like leftover Christmas trees in July.

Further along, they were just bare stobs—peeling bark and broken ends of branches covered with white and yellow crust.

Then the trees were gone entirely and the ground was crunchy from whatever had condensed out of the air. Dad pulled up to a sulfuric-acid factory and I spent what seemed like all afternoon sealed in an overheated Studebaker trying not to breathe the fumes that were eating the chrome off the bumpers.

When Dad came back, he told me how one of the workers had fallen in, and by the time they could fish him out, all that was left was teeth. It was a great story and gave me the shivers. And made me wonder how quickly I'd be able to scramble out if I fell into a batch of sulfuric acid. I'd always been good at shooting up onto the side of the pool so, if it had been me I'd have....

"Don't you try it," Dad said. "Old Ferguson was a champion swimmer. And champion swimmers can pop out of the water like penguins. And he never had a chance. So don't you go and...."

As a cautionary tale, it was first-rate, and right there in the Studebaker, I made up my mind never to fall into a tank of sulfuric acid and to pay close attention to my balance when I walked along the board or whatever it was that crossed over the top.

I don't know where Dad came up with the idea for rosin-baked potatoes. They're not part of any culinary tradition I ever heard of, and I never knew anybody else to cook them except once, and that was a neighbor on Christmas Day evening in New York who didn't have any more sense than to try it in the fireplace.

The idea seems like something Dad might have picked up at a turpentine works from men who grabbed a few potatoes from the garden, then headed into the piney woods to tend a big copper still of boiling pine-tree resin. Come lunchtime, they could tap off a bucket of molten rosin and then plop in the potatoes.

Or it may have had to do with a bottle of bourbon and a bet. Bottles of bourbon and a bet are always a good guess when Southern men are involved. Wherever Dad got the idea, he showed up one Saturday with a hundred-pound sack of rosin and one of the big, black cauldrons witches use, although I never had the impression witches spent a lot of time boiling up potatoes.

When he cut open the sack, the rosin that spilled onto the driveway may have been the most beautiful sight Anne and I had ever seen. Gorgeous, hypnotic, fist-size amber chunks that broke the sun into shards, fairyland gemstones shimmering light from the inside. We could gaze into a piece for hours, turning it over like a never-ending kaleidoscope. Sometimes we'd swear our friends to secrecy, show them a bit of rosin, and whisper that we were fabulously wealthy. They would believe us.

Mother was suspicious about experiments involving boiling rosin and banished the project to the far reaches of the yard. Then ordered Anne and me to stand back while Dad fired up the grill. After that, we waited a long time. Rosin takes considerable heating before it melts.

Once the lovely amber had turned molten, Dad dipped in a long wooden spoon. When he pulled it out, the liquid that came with it hardened into a thick, glassy coating.

Mother took one look at that spoon and ordered us kids further back. "You know those bugs that got froze up in amber? Well, that's what will happen to you if that pot falls over. There won't be anything for it but to stand you in the museum for the rest of your lives and charge people admission to come see you."

"Hmmmm," Dad gave us a speculative look. "Wonder how much we could charge," and Anne and I shrieked and fled to another part of the yard.

The truth is, if molten rosin had spilled, it would have done a lot more than just encase us for future generations of museum-goers. It would have exploded like a flamethrower the moment it touched the coals. For something cooked on an open fire, rosin was crazy flammable.

When Dad speculated the rosin was ready, he lowered in potatoes with the wooden spoon. They sank out of sight, or so he said. Anne and I were nowhere near close enough to see for ourselves. That business about being stood in a museum for the rest of our lives seemed pretty boring.

After the potatoes floated to the surface, Dad ladled them onto a set of old plates Mother donated for scientific purposes. By the time we got them to the table, the rosin had frozen into a half-inch shell we had to smack loose with a mallet.

I can't say they were delicious, but they weren't bad. They tasted exotic, in a piney sort of way, and even Mother had to admit the process was pretty spectacular. Anne and I liked that part. Adored, actually. No other kids on the planet, as far as we could tell, ever got rosin-baked potatoes. We became instant allies with Dad, and when he would come down to breakfast of a Saturday, announce that he felt like cooking out and ask what we wanted, we'd jump up and down yelling, "Rosin potatoes! Rosin potatoes!"

Mother never had a chance on that, and while Dad heaped charcoal onto the grill, she would sigh and pull out her oldest set of plates, the ones with petrified gobs of rosin Mary hadn't been able to chip loose still clinging to the porcelain.

5

Up North, with the Green Witch

For almost two years we were exiled to a tiny house in Pelham Manor, forty-five minutes by commuter train from New York City. It was a spooky thought for an eight-year-old, but when I looked out the window, it was hard to escape the realization that every house in every direction as far as I could see was filled with Yankees, just as if such a thing were perfectly normal. We were up north because Dad had taken a step up in life, traded in the Studebaker, gone to work for an outfit based in Greenwich, Connecticut, and been promoted into an Oldsmobile sort of guy. The idea was for him to learn how the company worked then come back to Atlanta and head up their Southeastern division.

The thought of a place named Greenwich must have struck his fancy because, after dinner, Mother would migrate to the living room to play with our newest, littlest sister, Marti, while Anne and I ran upstairs and jounced on our beds until Dad tromped in and swatted us. And we knew the time had come for the Green Witch.

We couldn't get enough of her. The Green Witch was better than pirates. She was better than selling medicine out of the back of a wagon. She was better than rosin pots. The Green Witch was the prime mover behind hurricanes and fires and explosions. She was the source of mayhem, the cause of children running off to join the carnival, and the reason ships disappeared at sea. The Green Witch was a storm trooper against calm and reason and social order. She was, I imagine, the part of Dad that he kept nailed inside a box so he could survive in the world of grown-ups. At night, he would prize loose a board or two and let Anne and me peek inside at the burning eyes and the wild hair flying loose around the green neck.

I think he especially liked the part about the green neck because the neighbors imagined our necks were red. Racist, Southern trash come to live among them, which aggravated Mother. Mother held the same opinion of white trash as the neighbors did, and she wasn't any more racist than they were, just a lot less sanctimonious about it. But surrounded by all those folks seeing nothing but Faulkner characters, well, worldly as she was, Mother didn't have any choice in the matter. It wasn't long before her drawl deepened, her mannerisms became broader, and she'd turned into the very caricature of the queenly Southern matron. And that, of course, involved flaunting colored servants. I think even Mary and Walter played it up a bit.

When we moved north, they followed in their car. And since we spent the night in Washington on the way, my parents arranged a treat for them. After lifetimes as colored people in Atlanta, a night on the town in DC would be liberation indeed.

Dad slipped Walter a wad of bills, told him we'd see them in the morning, and headed back to our motel for a quiet evening of my parents feeling pretty good about themselves. There was no way he and Mother were going into the city. Not after dark. They'd heard too many stories.

Next morning they quizzed Mary and Walter about their night on the town. "Have a good time? Was it fun?"

Well, maybe it was fun, if you considered barricading yourself in a motel fun. Otherwise, not so much. Mary and Walter appreciated the thought. Really they did. But Washington, DC? Not after dark. They'd heard too many stories.

We sold the house in Buckhead just in time, Dad said.

It turned out we weren't the only ones on Peachtree Battle to sell our property. The big, empty lot across from our house, the one that had been on the market forever, finally sold too. To the Hebrew Benevolent Congregation...who wanted to build a synagogue.

I don't think Dad was glad to get out of there because he had anything against Jews. For the more than half-a-century that his life intersected with mine, I never once heard him say anything against somebody because of religion. What he did have something against was plummeting house prices, and he knew a lot about people. They were the ones who were prejudiced. At least, that's what he said. And there may have been something to it.

In Pelham Manor, Mary and Walter stayed in a miniscule room in the basement of the tiny house we lived in. The room opened onto the backyard, so when they came and when they went, we wouldn't have to know. Other people knew, though, and didn't approve. The idea of servants didn't go over big with the rarefied social consciences of our neighbors.

The neighbors couldn't have been too serious about the servant thing. All the houses came with servants' quarters. The part that bothered them was that Mary and Walter lived in the same neighborhood they lived in. Perhaps a nice Irish girl, they thought, now that would be just the ticket. Or Swedish, maybe.

That was the spring the Supreme Court announced that the time had come for all of America's kids, colored and white, to go to school together, which was just fine with the folks in Pelham Manor. In Pelham Manor, there weren't any colored kids to go to school with. It was the South where integration was going to happen, and our neighbors knew it and got to trot out their social credentials whenever the subject came up. Except where Mary and Walter were concerned.

Mary was young and fertile-looking and Walter was about as vigorous as a man could get, and you know how those people are, it's only a matter of time before...well, you know.

Mother was never one to lie passive in the face of a social challenge, and being thought a redneck was challenge indeed. So when it came time to line up a substitute dentist for us kids, she pulled one of her classic bits of social jujitsu and discovered a dentist living right in our neighborhood. There was no way the Toothachers could keep being snotty to our family when Mother brought them so much business, and so frequently. And with a name like Toothacher, the new dentist was pretty much guaranteed not only to attend to our oral hygiene, but to our moral development as well. Like a lot of things Yankee, Mother misgauged the subtleties of the situation. Dr. Toothacher used Novocain.

The social part worked out fine, though. Anne made friends with the little Toothacher girl, which not only increased our standing in the community but years later did its bit in turning a newly reattached John Wayne Bobbitt into a porn star. Dr. Toothacher had x-rayed Anne's mouth and knew that, in the incisor department, baby teeth were all she was ever going to have. The buds for her grown-up teeth weren't there.

One evening, while Anne was spending the night at the Toothachers, she and the Toothacher daughter got into a tug-o-war, Anne bit into the nightie they were tugging on to get a better grip, Young Miss Toothacher gave a mighty heave, and Anne's incisors popped onto the floor. Dr. Toothacher popped Anne into his car, drove her to his office, popped her into his chair, and re-popped the teeth into her mouth—where they began happily growing again, as if nothing much had happened.

In the medical world plenty had happened, though, and Anne's teeth were the first successful example of a reattached body part ever to take root. Doctors around the world became stimulated to try similar reattachments of their own, and by the time Mrs. Bobbitt wielded her knife on the sleeping John Wayne, surgeons had become skilled in reconnecting body parts much more sensitive than baby teeth.

In the as-yet all-white grammar school I attended, I spent a lot of time missing social cues of my own.

Recess I probably could have figured out, if I'd actually had any practice in attending recess in Atlanta, but since I hadn't, I had no way of comparing. In Atlanta, when the teacher first handed out homework, I did the obvious thing. I forgot about it. The teacher didn't forget, though, and the next day during recess I was invited to sit at my desk and complete the assignment. I spent the time staring at the big world map next to the blackboard. On the third day I owed two homeworks, both of which would have to be turned in before I could go to recess.

Come April, I owed a hundred-and-some assignments, and all possibility of recess had forever receded below the horizon. If we hadn't moved out of the region, I'd still be sitting at that desk puzzling over the Rorschach shapes of Pacific islands.

The teacher I had in New York wasn't as concerned about homework. What got her juices flowing was ma'am, and she set about to rescue me from a life of verbal submissiveness. "Ma'am," she would yell back. "Ma'am, Ma'am, *Ma'am*," whenever I addressed her. "Don't call me *Ma'am*. You're just as good as anybody else." She was a militant socialist, a philosophy that had not made its way to Buckhead, and she had only the thinnest concept of the canons of respect.

Ma'am was a big, important deal with Mother, too, only the other way around. When I mentioned what happened at school, I had hopes she would pull me out, but all she said was that I didn't have to call anybody ma'am for a few days. The few days lasted half an hour, then one of the neighbors dropped by and Scarlett jabbed me in the ribs to demonstrate our Southernness and address the lady properly.

Recess turned out to be fun. It involved lots of running around and roughhousing when the teacher wasn't looking. One morning, a couple of boys got into a fight while the teacher was looking, and when class started back up, the boys found themselves persons of interest in a session of political-criticism that would have done the Great Helmsman proud.

"You should give them double homework," a girl with pigtails said, thereby proving she knew how wrong fighting was.

"*Triple* homework," a fat little boy, who wanted to squelch the whole idea of fights before he got caught up in one, said. And around our little circle it went. When the consensus had reached twenty times extra homework, it was my turn to up the ante to twenty-one.

To my unformed mind, the premise of the thing was faulty. Boys fought, everybody knew that. And the idea of children voting on how other kids got punished didn't make any sense at all. Grown-ups were in charge of punishment. So I said what somebody should have said from the beginning: "I think you should let them fight it out."

If nothing else, that ended the talk of extra homework. The group criticism came to an immediate stop and all eyes focused on me. "That," the teacher said with socialist scorn, "is how wars get started."

The logic seemed a bit of a stretch, but I didn't get the chance to argue the niceties. The teacher had us take out our songbooks and sing "Tenting Tonight" to impress upon us just how bad wars were, and when the next one gets started, you'll know who to blame.

"Tenting Tonight" is a mournful ballad about weary soldiers camping on a battlefield surrounded by the bodies of their dead and dying comrades. People in the North sang it a lot during the Civil War, and the songbook came with a drawing of a Union soldier standing picket so that even us third-graders would get the picture as to what that song was about.

Something is wrong with this song, I thought. What kind of people would pitch tents among a bunch of dead bodies? And if you've got dying friends out there, why don't you stop singing and go help them? Nobody sang songs like that in the South. Pacifism was another philosophy that had not made it to Buckhead. In Buckhead, we sang "Onward, Christian Soldiers."

Then, to let me show how rehabilitated I'd become by all the musical death and dying, the teacher appointed me to pick the next song. A song, I imagine she thought, of redemption. "Amazing Grace" would have been a good choice.

I chose "Dixie."

And made everybody in the class stand up. "Dixie," after all, was a national anthem. Standing up for "Dixie" was a matter of respect.

So was standing up for myself, which was hard to do in a strange land with nobody to stand beside me.

I think Mother had seen this day coming. At any rate, she'd prepared the ground with deftly chosen bedtime stories. Dick Wittington's Cat had been banished from my bedroom in favor of *The Jungle Book*. After a few weeks of Mowgli and Father Wolf and the Banderlog, the forests of India gave way to soldier stories. In fact, one of the books was called exactly that, *Soldier Stories*. Another was *Soldiers Three*, leavened with a diet of *Departmental Ditties* and *Barrack Room Ballads* in case I turned out to have a poetical streak. By the time I was in third grade, Rudyard Kipling formed a far larger presence in my childhood than he did for any other kid I knew.

Afternoons when I came home from school, Mother would talk about India. Foreign places always attracted her. Then, with thoughts of adventure and glory dancing in my head, she'd ask about my day...which usually involved negotiating my way home through a gang of rat-faced thugs with names even stranger than the Learoyds and Mulvaneys and Ortherises Kipling favored.

Mother didn't appreciate having her son bullied any more than mothers today appreciate it, but she wasn't one to go whining to the authorities. Bullies, like the poor, are ever with us. And if you don't like being bullied, or you don't like being poor, then it's up to you to do something about it.

"You know where this Bruno Handberry lives?" she'd lay five dollars on the dining-room table. In the early fifties, five dollars was a lot of money for a kid. Heck, at a time when the minimum wage was seventy-five cents an hour, five dollars was a lot of money for anybody.

"Yes, Ma'am," I'd nod my head like the good Southern boy I was.

"You put your jacket on and you march yourself over to the Handberrys', or whatever they call themselves, and when you come back and tell me you beat the tar out of that Bruno, you can have the five dollars."

As a moral lesson, it was first-rate. But now that I'm older, I wonder whether there wasn't more to it. Mother had her own bullies to deal with, but being a proper lady, couldn't beat the crap out of them herself. So she did the next best thing and dispatched her son to teach their sons a lesson. A win, win, win all around.

Mary and Walter fitted in fine up North, they just weren't allowed to do the fitting in Pelham Manor. Walter started commuting to Harlem, hooked up with a jazz band, and soon was bringing home as much money as Dad. And having a lot more fun doing it.

Then he was pulling down twice what Dad was making, bought a Cadillac, and began parking next to the Oldsmobile in the driveway.

When Walter started making three times as much as Dad, Dad quit counting. Then, one evening, Mary came in with a recording contract.

Mary James, who'd come to work for us at age fourteen. Mary James, who was marginally literate. Mary James, who sang about Jesus around the kitchen, had now been offered money to sing about Jesus to the whole world and wanted to know whether she should do it.

Whatever relatives she had were a thousand miles away, and Dad was the closest thing to a father she could talk to. Maybe he was the closest thing to a father she ever had, I don't know. When she got her big break, Dad was the one she came to for advice. And permission, I think.

I don't know why he told her not to sign. Maybe he was already disillusioned by what was happening to Walter.

Maybe he had scruples about hiring an Irish maid to replace her.

Maybe Mother had scruples about inviting a Swedish maid into the house.

Maybe there wasn't room for a second Cadillac in the driveway.

Maybe he recognized that what Mary really wanted was to be a Southern lady, and he knew we'd all be heading back to Georgia in a few months, but I doubt it. Of all the things Dad could have imagined Mary being, Southern lady was not on the list. And I'm not so sure even Mary wanted that anymore. By then she wasn't the naive out-of-towner who cowered in the motel in Washington. At least not entirely. By the time she came to Dad, she had seen enough of New York, and guessed enough of its possibilities, that, at the very least, she knew there was another life out there.

What Mary needed was encouragement, and Dad told her she wasn't good enough, that breaking out of the life other people had appointed for her might work for some. It might even work for her husband. But for her, well, in Mary's case, a maid was all she was.

Maybe he genuinely thought he had Mary's interests at heart. The recording industry is famous for the shoddy way it treats the people it makes its money off of. Most likely, Mary wouldn't have been treated any different. Dad was a lot more sophisticated than she was, and he got stung on contracts and fast talk, so what chance did she have?

Maybe not much. But what chance did she have not signing the contract? A life of ironing shirts and sweeping floors and watching soaps as her time on earth ran its course, of singing about Jesus in a kitchen where only my family could hear?

Unless Mary had it right and it wasn't just my family listening to her sing, but Jesus, too. He would have been at her side when Dad advised her to pass up the only real break life ever offered her. And when Dad's time comes to stand in front of Jesus, explaining that bit of advice is going to take some doing.

Labor Day, Dad invited the neighbors for a traditional Southern cook-out.

A lot of them showed up. Mostly, I think, they looked forward to the meal the way people nowadays look forward to sharing a traditional dinner at the house of a Korean friend. What fun, you can just hear our neighbors saying. A genuine redneck barbecue. Let's go! Whatever they expected, I don't think they expected to find Dad on the far end of the yard heating a witch's cauldron.

Or to be served potatoes hotter than the back side of the sun and sheathed in what looked like molten glass. None, I think, associated Labor Day with rosin-baked potatoes. Nor, until that moment, did they associate rosin-baked potatoes with Southerners. The fact is, it was hard to know what to associate rosin-baked potatoes with.

The neighbors liked them, though. They were the kind of ethnic food a sophisticated person could develop a taste for. It was surprising, like showing up at your Korean friend's and manfully taking a spoonful of kimchi, only to discover you liked rotten cabbage.

One neighbor developed such a taste for rosin potatoes he came back for thirds, then took the leftovers home with him. A week or so later he showed up in the driveway and inquired when was the next time

Dad might be preparing rosin-baked potatoes, dropping broad hints that he would like to be included on the guest list.

That fall, Dad prized loose a nail or two from his private box, the Green Witch peered around with fiery eyes, and sent down to North Carolina for a hundred-pound sack of rosin. Then she dropped by the hardware and ordered a witch's kettle and by Christmas had arranged one of the finest presents that particular neighbor ever received.

About eight o'clock Christmas night, we were roused from our end-of-the-holiday stupor by the sound of fire trucks. It was a three-alarmer, and our neighbor's house had gone up so quickly it was as if it had been doused with what the fire chief called an accelerant. The situation had insurance fraud written all over it.

Most of the neighborhood crowded around while the neighbor tried to explain how he'd gotten a rosin-pot for Christmas and couldn't wait for spring, so he'd propped it up in the fireplace. When the coals burned down the pot had tipped over and a sea of molten flame had spread across the carpet. He and his wife and kids were lucky to get out with their lives.

"Say *what*?" the fire chief said. "You were trying to boil potatoes in a pot of...of...?"

"Rosin," the neighbor said in a dull voice. "It was rosin."

"It melts when you heat it up," one of his children left off crying long enough to fill in.

"And it burns," another of his children said.

"Of course it burns," I said. "It's *rosin*."

"*Hush*," Mother said and backed me away from the fire chief.

"Maybe it was the *Green Witch*," Anne piped up in her bossy little-girl voice. "Daddy says the Green Witch..." Mother's hand clamped over her mouth.

"Rosin," the fire chief said thoughtfully. "That's the stuff that comes out of pine trees?"

"Yeah," the neighbor gave a forlorn nod. "Pine trees."

"And just where did you get this...this rosin?"

"Christmas. We got it for Christmas."

"And who," the fire chief, wanted to know, "would ever give somebody a pot of rosin for...?" But we didn't hear the rest of that conversation because Baby Marti started to whimper.

"She needs a new diaper," Mother shooed us toward home. As motherly as Mother usually was, there are those who suspect she'd pinched Marti.

Nobody in our family said so, but in our hearts we chalked up the whole sorry episode to inept Yankees so cocooned in their city ways they didn't have any more sense than to heat rosin in a fireplace. How stupid can you get? We couldn't help feeling a bit smug at the way things had worked out.

Until, a couple of days later, insurance investigators showed up at our house demanding a sample of this...rosin...to see if it really burned as fiercely as our neighbor claimed. Then they tried to confiscate Dad's rosin pot for evidence, but they didn't have a warrant, and by the time they secured one, we were on the way home to Buckhead, rosin pot and all.

To Peachtree Battle Avenue. To the same street we'd moved away from two years earlier, but this time to the more fashionable end. The one that would keep its property values. The one without the synagogue.

Dad's new Yankee money bought us a house on the very block where the attorney general lived and just a skip and a jump from the charred hole where pretend Klansmen set their meeting hall on fire. However that happened, we knew rosin pots weren't involved. Big as those fools were, only a Yankee could be that stupid.

6

Lemon-Pie Memories

Mother had an unpromising relationship with toast.

For reasons that were never made clear, she refused to allow a toaster into the kitchen. Instead, she would get up in the morning, tessellate eight or ten pieces of bread beneath the broiler, fire up the gas, and begin scrambling eggs or boiling grits. She could tell when the toast was ready by the smoke.

She'd scrape the charred parts into the sink, then slather butter onto what was left and set it on the table. I was into my teens before I realized that sinks in other kitchens were a cheerful white color instead of black.

Mother also had a Fiat Spider, which, mostly, she kept in the driveway because, mostly, it wouldn't start.

It was a tiny, blue, bullet-shaped two-seater convertible she would tool around in with the top down and was almost obscenely sporty. If Ian Fleming had had a taste for poorly built Italian sports cars, James Bond would have driven a Fiat Spider.

Summer mornings when she could get it going, Mother headed out to the Capital City Club, sun streaming over the wide-brimmed straw hat she kept tied to her head with a scarf. It wasn't the best club in Atlanta, it was the Oldsmobile of country clubs and suited Dad fine until he blossomed into a Cadillac guy and swore allegiance to the Piedmont Driving Club. Until then, Mother would sit by the pool at the Capital City Club and drink salty dogs with whichever few dozen of her buddies happened to be there that day.

The fact that she didn't arrive in an Oldsmobile was a bit of her social jujitsu. Nobody knew what to make of a Fiat. If society had rigged the game so she couldn't drive a Cadillac yet, Mother would just deal a new set of cards with faces and pips nobody recognized and explain the rules as she made them up.

She claimed she loved to swim, but you couldn't prove it by me. I hardly ever saw Mother actually in the pool. What she really loved was to show herself off in her bathing suit. It was a Jantzen Beach suit and formfitting and very modest by current-day standards, and, on Mother, very sexy by any standards at all. That was a hallmark of Mother's—maybe of all the ladies in the fifties—mixing sexiness into everyday life.

She kept a trunk of memorabilia in the attic, topped off with a sheath of photos. There was a confirmation picture of her kneeling with hands outstretched for her first communion, looking like a schoolgirl who, given the opportunity, could turn very naughty. Mother grew up early, and I can't imagine that look was entirely accidental.

An Easter picture had her full-grown and lounging in front of a huge cross, surrounded by lilies, gazing into the distance as alluring as Betty Grable painted on the fuselage of a B-17, except wearing a chaste, black dress set off by a lace collar. If you were a chaste-black-dress-lace-collar sort of guy, that picture would have been a collector's item.

Once, when she came into the house carrying a load of groceries, a copy of *Nugget* slipped from her hands and lay, cover-up, on the floor while she scrambled to pick it back up before Anne and I saw what it was. Mother planning to enjoy a dirty magazine featuring articles by James Joyce, James Thurber, and Erskine Caldwell, now that was an idea to conjure with.

The way I remember her best, along with the tooling around in the Fiat, is in a pair of slacks and one of Dad's old shirts, painting the living room in the house we moved into when we came back to Atlanta. When school let out for the day I would come busting through the door and there she'd be, brush in hand, dripping lemon-yellow enamel, the ceiling meringue white. All she needed was a graham-cracker carpet and it would have been like coming home to the inside of a pie.

The more Uncle John ruminated upon the consequences of tax fraud, the more he fidgeted, and the earlier in the day he became hungry. The Piedmont Driving Club would have been the solution if it had served dinner before seven, but it didn't.

Uncle John had been a member of the Driving Club out of the box. He was a Cadillac man all the way and lobbied to get himself admitted as soon as he could pay the dues. Then, when he decided he wanted to eat dinner in the afternoon, he lobbied for the dining room to open at four.

No dice. Civilized people don't eat before seven-thirty, and the Driving Club wasn't going to change now. Not for Uncle John.

It would change for the president, Uncle John discovered when he examined the bylaws. The president of the Piedmont Driving Club had the power to tell the dining room when to open, so Uncle John got himself elected president. Then he ordered the dining room to start serving dinner at four.

Afternoons when he was feeling hungry, Uncle John would head down to the Driving Club and dine in solitary splendor while cooks and waiters, busboys and maids, lounged around with nothing in particular to do for the next three hours until the civilized members began to roll in.

I never learned why there was bad blood between Mother and the PTA. "I went to a meeting once," was all she would say. "I'm not going to make *that* mistake again." The consequences of her not repeating that mistake reverberated through my childhood because, at our school, PTA was a moral imperative.

Each class had a goal for PTA membership, and the goal was a hundred percent. Even the kids who lived in shacks with dogs lolling beneath the porches and rusting car bodies in the yard, managed to get their mothers to sign up for PTA. On some nights, PTA must have shared similarities with rescue missions, only I wouldn't really know because I never received any first-hand, insider details of what actually happened at PTA. And whatever class I was in never got to eat the cupcakes, or whatever it was the PTA ladies brought, to celebrate perfect membership.

Civil defense was another moral responsibility. A megaton of Russian-made U-235 going off over our school wouldn't have done anybody any good, but at least we had desks to crouch under. "And remember to close your eyes so the glare won't melt your retinas," the teachers told us. We kids were prepared. It was the adults we worried about; adults didn't have school desks. A post-nuclear world was going to be very different with only kids in it.

As I moved up through the grades, I began to wonder about those desks. Were we the only ones who had them, or had the Russians stolen the secret? I knew they had spies over here. Every now and then Superman would catch one on television. But when we thought about it, we decided the Russians couldn't have the Secret of the Desk, otherwise the desks wouldn't be bolted to the floor to keep them from stealing one. "Do you suppose," Tommy Pearson asked one day during recess, "that the Russians have discovered the Secret of the Wrench?" And we all shuddered at the possibilities.

Like a lot of things we thought of as ours, the Soviets already had the formula. Years later, I met a Ukrainian who'd been in grade school at exactly the same time I'd been in grade school, and his teachers made him crawl under his desk too. Maybe even, when we thought about it, at the exact moment I was crawling under mine, only the bombs that were going to vaporize his grown-ups would come special-delivery on good, American rockets built on our family's land. Or, at least, land that used to belong to our family.

The army never actually poisoned any Germans with the phosgene and chlorine gas they made on our land, but rather than do the honorable thing and give it back once the war was over, they renamed it the Redstone Arsenal and turned it over to Werner von Braun and a crew of the very Germans the gas had been intended for. The same Germans Dad had been in the Pentagon fighting the war against when the army took the land.

Paper-sale was another competition school felt strongly about. The class that brought in the most newspapers got a prize, and the school got the money. I don't know what that prize was, either. My class never got one.

The reason my class never won a paper-sale had nothing to do with Mother. My class never won because...I don't want to put too fine a point on this, bygones should stay bygones and not go trailing along behind you all these years later...it's just that the way the recycling people knew which class brought in the most paper was they weighed it. And Mrs. Bethea's class watered their paper.

Cheated or not, we didn't regret the prize all that much. Paper-sale day was better than any prize. On paper-sale day, parent after parent would pull up beneath the overhang that ran along the front of the school, cast around for which stacks of papers belonged to which class, open the trunk, and start unloading.

We had enforcers stationed by our pile to make sure that every bundle was delivered to where it was supposed to go and not to some other class's pile. And to make sure the bad kids from seventh grade didn't slip over and move some of our pile to theirs. Sometimes I got to be an enforcer.

It was a fifties, one-story, ranch-style school. Modern and functional and brick, and like schools built all over America at the time. There'd been a previous school there, built in the twenties, that was two-story and made of wood, but it burned when the custodian went after yellow jackets with an acetylene torch.

There was no way to teach school with a paper-sale going on. There was hardly even any way to get into school on paper-sale day. You had to thread your way through big, teetery stacks of newspapers, because some parents weren't as good at tying bundles as other parents, and stacks tended to be lopsided and fall over. By midmorning, a lot of loose paper would be blowing around on the North Georgia wind. It was like attending class in a landfill. We loved it.

Things were even better when it rained. When it rained on paper-sale day, we tracked wet newsprint into the school, and by lunch, floors and walls were lumpy with papier-mâché. And if it rained enough, all the papers got wet, the school earned more money, Mrs. Bethea's cheating class lost its advantage, and the possibility of a party, or whatever it was, was thrown wide open.

From the perspective of the twenty-first century, there were a lot of odd stories in those newspapers. One that sticks in my mind was a long front-page article about a homeowner who courageously defended his family from some kind of mass attack one night. The article made the thing sound like *Night of the Living Dead*, a desperate family holed up in the house while hordes of the undead lurched and staggered around the yard. When morning came, a bunch of permanent dead littered the grass. The family was safe upstairs, with the father still crouching behind the bedroom window cocking his twelve-gauge.

What actually happened was just as strange. The zombies turned out to be disgruntled employees, and the plucky homeowner was their boss. At a mill, I always imagined. The homeowner was white and the employees, I'm almost certain from this distance, weren't. Why they chose to take their labor grievances to the other side of town, after dark, probably had something to do with working in a nonunion shop. Unions weren't big in Georgia in the fifties.

It was bad tactics, though, and swung public opinion against them. Downtrodden workers just naturally get a lot of sympathy, even in the South. Even in the fifties. But stirring up trouble on the other side of town after dark, especially if you're dark, too, that just wasn't done.

The papers gave a lot of coverage to election results, although it was hard to see the point. Election results weren't exactly news, and they took up a lot of space. In Georgia, every conceivable government job was elective. Governor. Legislator. Judge. Councilmen. Sheriffs. Clerks, auditors. Administrative assistants, coroners, cronies. Hangers-on. Notary publics, garbage collectors, and the ladies who emptied the sand-filled spittoons in the capitol building, I suppose. An explosion of democracy, and none of it made any difference because none of the positions were contested. One choice, one only, for each job. Always a Democrat and always a person nobody in my family would ever have considered for any job.

I always imagined that when the people at the news desk had a few extra minutes, they got a jump on things by writing up next month's election results. Maybe they even had a file of canned election results they could dip into, along the lines of prewritten obituaries.

The Battle of Atlanta was lost in our front yard. Sometimes when I walked home from school I'd try to picture John Bell Hood's cavalry flinging itself down the sloping, manicured lawns, bursting through wisteria and jonquils, to fall upon the invaders in a fury of gallantry and vengeance and anger that didn't extend the life of the Confederacy a single day.

The folks in the house behind us once uncovered a stand of muskets, Yankee muskets, I fancied, splayed with muzzles together like the spokes of a wheel from where they had been stacked, then forgotten and collapsed—their owners having skedaddled from the fury of Hood's assault. A stand of musketry that, had it been ten feet to the north, would have been in our backyard. Who knew what else lay below that ground?

A stream crossed beneath Peachtree Battle Avenue, encased in a dressed-granite tunnel tall enough for a boy to walk through until it opened onto Peachtree Creek and an entirely different world. A world of poison ivy and blackjack, of broom sedge and briars, biding their chance to reclaim the land they had been cast from. A world that, as far as I could tell, was no different from the way it had been a century before.

Most times, the creek was sluggish and muddy, pools of knee-deep water interspersed with bars of silt covered with the tracks of animals I was too much of a city boy to recognize. Raccoons, I was pretty sure. And possums. Maybe badgers. I wasn't sure badgers lived around there, but I was pretty sure their feet were the right size. In my mind, Minié balls and mortars and gleaming sabers lay just beneath the silt, had I known where to dig. To a boy, it was a wild place.

When Marti got old enough, we'd make our way along the bank together, trying to picture what it had been like when this was all there was. Some days, we would shove through pokeweed ten feet high and blocking the view. The berries had such deep red juice, a juice that stained our clothes so thoroughly we had dreams of making fortunes in the dye business when we got older.

The story was that Mosby's Raiders lived off pokeweed for a year. I couldn't imagine how they managed it, but I always thought it was a good trick to know, in case the Russians came and we had to take to the woods and fight a guerilla war of our own. Peachtree Creek was a private place. Russians, I figured, wouldn't know anything about it.

Sometimes it was hard to distinguish between religion and Coca-Cola.

It wasn't as if we had a lack of options in the matter of religion. There were plenty of sects to go around, most of them Baptist. There were lots of Presbyterians as well, and everybody knew a Catholic or two. There were even Jews in town, but nobody seemed to have actually met any. We'd heard there were Moslems and Hindus in the world, but they lived other places so it was hard to know what to make of the fact.

A lot of folks assumed people cleaved to strange gods because they hadn't had the opportunity to hear the Good News, and it was up to us to bring it to them. The rest were more ecumenical and argued that people are no different under the skin, and if you dig deep enough, every religion points in the same direction.

The more I learned about other religions, the less they seemed to have in common, and the harder that line was to maintain. Hindus hadn't exactly narrowed things down in the One True God department. As for the Moslems, it looked disturbingly like Jesus didn't have a primary role during Friday services. Even Baptists couldn't decide whether God wanted you to get dunked as a baby or after you grew up. Or whether you were supposed to go all the way under or if just a sprinkling on the forehead might do. You get that kind of detail wrong, and you're not going to enjoy the afterlife that's been stored up for you. But something we could all agree on was Coca-Cola. If there was one common theme that drew the whole human race together, it was Coke. You could tell just by looking at the bottles.

Molded into the bottom of every bottle was the name of the city it came from. Atlanta, most times. But Cokes got carried along on car trips, and bottles got switched around. Sometimes you'd get a bottle with Macon on the bottom. Or Valdosta. Once in a long while, you'd get a very romantic, exotic bottle from as far away as Birmingham. Or, even, we'd hear stories, Kansas City. Now there was a bottle to be proud of. A bottle to keep and treasure and show your friends. All the way from Kansas City. Imagine that.

The thing was, you never knew what place you were going to get because you couldn't check ahead of time. The bottles were either sitting upright in their wooden cases or wouldn't roll out of the machine until you dropped in a nickel. Which led to opportunities for crime.

When betting on who would get the furthest-away Coke bottle began to threaten the social order, Attorney General Cook took time off from worrying about Communists in the NAACP, and, speaking ex cathedra from just up the block, issued a bull pointing out that wagering of any sort was a violation of Georgia's gambling laws and was going to lead to prosecution and fines and jail time and public disgrace when we catch up with you.

As kids, it never would have crossed our minds to bet on Coke bottles, but now that the attorney general had called it to our attention, it sounded like fun, in a disreputable, underworld sort of way. So, when no grown-ups were around, and we were sure there weren't any police informants in our midst, we'd convene around a Coke machine in some dark stairwell, pull out nickels, and flirt with lives of crime.

There was another way of betting on bottles, one that didn't even have to involve Coca-Colas, one that was legal and could be much more profitable. You could win the get-a-bug lottery.

Sometimes, it was whispered, a bug would sneak past the rigorous inspection process down at the bottling plant, and if you were the one who found that bug, then you became a plaintiff, and, juries being juries, you could cash in big time.

You can see how a silver-tongued lawyer might persuade a jury that a bug or two might get through the system every now and then. And you could see why twelve men, good and true, might want to send a message to the soft-drink company about how we'd all be better off if the company paid a little closer attention to hygiene. And you can see why the soft-drink company would spend a great deal of money defending this sort of lawsuit. Which brings up the father of one of my friends.

I can't remember what company he worked for. Certainly not Coca-Cola. Maybe Dr. Pepper or RC or one of the other low-rent soft drinks you find in gas stations on rural roads, I don't know. Wherever he worked, he had a mournful, hangdog sort of look that I attributed to the fact that it must be awfully hard to earn a living from an off-brand soft drink in Atlanta. You might as well try selling Japanese cars to Americans, as pull a fool stunt like that.

Everybody knew he'd started out as a lawyer, but what he did now was a lot better paid. He had found a professional niche that, as far as I know, wasn't shared by many other people in the country. He ate the bugs. The idea derived from an experience he'd had in court.

When he'd asked to be shown the bug in question, the plaintiff passed over an empty bottle.

"Why, Madam," my friend's father said, "there does not appear to be a bug in this bottle."

"That is correct," the plaintiff said. "While I was swallowing the drink that came in this bottle, I noticed something crunchy in my mouth and spat half a bug back into the bottle."

"Well then, Ma'am, where is the half you spat back?"

"I drank it," she said.

"You drank it?" my friend's father asked. "You drank the other half of the bug on purpose?"

"Well, not exactly on purpose. But I had paid a nickel for that drink and I did not care to see any of it to go to waste, and the bug just sort of came with it."

That plaintiff went home empty-handed. No bug, no money, was the way the jury saw it.

The boss of the soft-drink company thought about the verdict, and my friend's dad had a new profession. From then on, whenever the company got word that one of its customers had encountered a bug, he would motor out to the customer's home, introduce himself, and ask to see the bug. When the would-be plaintiff produced the bottle, my friend's dad would hold it up to the light and say, "Bug doesn't look so bad to me." Then he would lift the bottle to his mouth, down the hatch the bug would slide, and out the window the lawsuit would go.

Coca-Cola in the right setting not only cured physical ills, it eased away social problems. It's how Mother made amends for refusing to join the PTA.

She'd have my teachers over for Cokes. All of them. Mother kept a list. She would issue formal invitations, and one unholy afternoon, I would come home from school to find every teacher I'd ever served time under sitting in the living room looking stiff, sipping Coke, munching little sandwiches with the edges cut off, and talking quietly.

It was the quiet part that was the scariest. People were never quiet at one of Mother's functions. Guffawing and loud stories and bawdy jokes were the order of the day when Mother gave a party, and quiet didn't have anything to do with it. Quiet meant the discussion had turned serious.

And when the ladies doing the discussing turned out to be your teachers, well, nothing good ever comes of a teacher talking to your mother. But to have the whole posse of them comparing notes, something you did back when you were four or five could start to look like a trend by sixth grade, even something you'd forgotten all about. In fact, given the age of some of those old bats, something somebody *else* did could well get tagged to your account.

"I have been successful in this life," Dad once told me. "And I attribute my success to...."

His MBA from Harvard?

The grit and determination he gained from growing up without a father during the Depression?

The courage it took to stand up to a gang of Gestapo thugs on the docks at Hamburg in the summer of 1936?

The self-confidence from going into the army as a twenty-four-year-old second lieutenant and coming out, six years later, as a lieutenant colonel?

"...my hair," Dad wound up with a flourish. "I have always taken good care of my hair."

He was right. Dad always did take good care of his hair. He combed it and brushed it and took it to the barbershop every Saturday. Dad had good hair, and he always would.

As he aged, his hair didn't turn white. It became blond. To Dad, white hair would not have been a sign of wisdom and experience. It would have announced to the world that he was sliding down the far side of the hill of life, and that was an announcement he did not care to make. Not while he was still an Oldsmobile man.

There was a Cadillac in his future, Dad knew that. But he hadn't risen high enough in his profession to go sporting around in a Cadillac. That would have been getting ahead of himself, and people would talk. Mostly, he was into lawn care.

In our neighborhood, lawn care was high on everybody's list. But Dad was a professional. He sold fertilizer chemicals, and nobody had a lawn like ours. Down near the street, where passing motorists could admire it, the dirt was soft and moist even during the driest months, and the lawn...well, the lawn shone with a vivid, vibrant, maraschino-cherry sort of green. It was a green the AstroTurf people would have patented, if only they had the formula. And their customers would believe the color was believable.

At the Coliseum over in Montgomery, Alabama, the Hillbilly Cat gave his final concert. He'd signed a contract with RCA, and from then on, Elvis would be singing under his real name.

His first record had come out that very day. "I Forgot to Remember to Forget" on one side and "Mystery Train" on the other, and he was looking for his next song, the one that would make him King of Rock 'n' Roll.

That song would be "Hound Dog," which had already been made famous among colored Americans by Big Mama Thornton. She was from Montgomery, so the night the Hillbilly Cat appeared for the last time, he was playing Big Mama's hometown. A decade later, she would have another hit, "Ball 'n' Chain," that went on to make a fortune for Janis Joplin. Big Mama was born colored a little too soon to fully cash in on her talent.

It wasn't just the King of Rock 'n' Roll who was in Montgomery that night. A different King had come to town, the Reverend Martin Luther King, and he didn't attend the concert. He was at church. The Dexter Avenue Baptist Church, just down the block from the First Confederate White House. He was there because, two days earlier, Rosa

Parks had gone to jail rather than give up her seat on the bus to a white man. Dr. King was organizing the boycott that would bring the National City Lines bus company to its knees and break the back of segregation all over the South.

Astrologers would have loved the confluence. On one extraordinary night, in the original capital of the Confederacy, the Civil Rights movement exploded out of the African American community and across the entire country...at exactly the same moment rock 'n' roll exploded out of the African American community and across the entire country.

John Cameron Swayze probably didn't know much about rock 'n' roll, but he told us about the boycott on television between personal endorsements for Camel cigarettes. Mary, I'm pretty sure, discussed what was going on with the other maids on the Grapevine Line. Atlanta buses had the same signs as the ones on the National City Lines, WHITES SEAT FROM FRONT, COLOREDS SEAT FROM REAR. Those signs must have been a twice-a-day irritation for years, and Mary had a very strong opinion about what was happening in Montgomery.

"They carried Miss Parks to jail for not giving a white man her seat." Mary was quite exercised about it. "They throwed a lady in jail for not letting a man have her seat."

What bothered her, it dawned on me when I grew old enough for such things to dawn, had nothing to do with race. Mary was comfortable with the world she lived in. What she insisted on being was a lady. And no lady, anywhere, should ever have to give up her seat to a man. Whoever that man thought he was when he tried to make Miss Rosa Parks stand up for him, he was no gentleman. And Mary resented it.

One lovely April morning Mother scraped the toast into the sink, sprung me from school, and we headed up to Etowah to see the Indian mounds. We rode along two-lane blacktop through beautiful, wooded countryside into the foothills of the Appalachians, the woods broken up by small farms, green with new corn and watered by sparkling streams set all about with ferns.

A lot of history happened up that way. Etowah was a station on the Great Locomotive Chase, the place where three gallant Confederates commandeered the Yonah, then sped along the track behind two dozen Yankee saboteurs fleeing in the General before running them to ground near Ringgold.

Not far away, at Day's Gap, two thousand more Yankees threw in the towel to General Forrest and the six hundred Confederates who followed him across Black Creek.

A generation before that, gold had been discovered at Dahlonega, and the first gold rush in America flooded onto Cherokee land. Whatever the Cherokee thought about the gold, they had the land by treaty, and, being one of the Five Civilized Tribes, did the civilized thing. They took the matter all the way to the United States Supreme Court.

And won. Nobody could come onto Cherokee land without Cherokee say-so.

Then lost before a higher court when President Andrew Jackson refused to carry out the order. "Chief Justice Marshall has made his decision," the old Indian-fighter announced, "now let him enforce it." To make sure Marshall got the point about which branch of government actually ran things, Jackson chained the Cherokees together and marched them down the Trail of Tears to Oklahoma. But all that was no more than last week in the history of the land.

Before stolen locomotives. Before Andrew Jackson. Before, even, the Cherokee. Before history itself, there had been Indian mounds. Nobody knew who built them. Or why. Only that they were old when the Cherokee came to Georgia.

The state kept a little park at Etowah and planted the mounds with grass to keep them from washing away after they'd logged the trees and cleared the brush sprouting from the sides. Mother and I climbed six stories up a set of log steps to the top of the tallest mound.

It was broad and flat on top and much wider than it was high, like a big dance floor. We crossed from side to side and back again, admiring the soft spring colors of North Georgia spread out below us.

It felt high up there, higher than it really was, and Mother gazed into the distance for a long time. I imagine she was seeing Cherokee and mound builders, gold prospectors, and the Yonah pouring black smoke as the heroic Confederates chased down the stolen General. Mother was always on the lookout for a romance.

Somewhere along the line, she got involved with the High Museum.

I'm pretty sure she enjoyed art, but she enjoyed the community of people who enjoyed art more. And, I think, she enjoyed the community of people who knew she enjoyed art best of all. Like most things in her life, volunteering at the museum was win, win, win all around.

The museum was an old house on Peachtree Street that had been donated by a family named, naturally enough, High, and the property ran all the way through to West Peachtree. As prime a piece of real estate as you could find.

I never spent much time at the museum, and I don't think I missed much. During the fifties, the High Museum was not world famous for the quality of its art. What it was famous for was ceiling-high, lushly painted fantasies from the New Testament. Roman soldiers in gorgeous red cloaks lounging at the foot of the Cross. Fancies executed with great care and accuracy and no inspiration at all. Still, they were so spectacular to look at it took a long time for me to understand why they weren't listed in all the art books. I imagine the people who ran the museum felt the same way when they'd picked them up at prices that seemed unreasonably cheap.

Where I did spend a lot of time was on the West Peachtree side, in a ramshackle warren of gray, wooden buildings that, if Sherman hadn't come through less than a century before, you'd have sworn were hundreds of years older than they actually were. It must have been the world's most tumbledown art school, and the buildings were connected by a beat-up set of the endless wooden walkways you might use if you visited a tourist swamp, only not in as good a condition.

One shack was for oil painting, another for print-making. They had one for doing pottery (although I can't imagine the fire department would have allowed a kiln within a quarter of a mile of the place), a shack for watercolors, and one for sculptures. There was an administrative shack with stacks of papers arranged among pans and buckets for when the roof leaked.

Other places I wasn't allowed into, places where secret, grown-up art was committed outside the sight of kids. Those buildings had high windows, but not so high a determined boy couldn't climb up and look inside if he had time and nobody to chase him away, which generally wasn't my case, because people were still there when Dad picked me up in the afternoon.

If you grew up in the South, it was impossible not to See Rock City.

SEE ROCK CITY was on the roof of every barn in Georgia. And Alabama. And Tennessee and both Carolinas, as far as anybody could tell. And, even, some birdhouses. In the face of something like that, our parents never stood a chance. There was no way they weren't taking us to Rock City.

The place is situated HIGH ATOP LOOKOUT MOUNTAIN, as the signs pointed out, perched on one of the half-mile-tall cliffs that ring Chattanooga on three sides. Lookout Mountain is a natural fortification and a meteorological phenomenon.

Humid air from the Atlantic sinks partway into the valley before settling onto the cool air below, forming a layer of mist in an otherwise clear sky. In November 1863, the Battle Above the Clouds took place there. Three brigades of Rebels held off three divisions of Yankees. And then counterattacked. We were proud of that.

When we went to see Rock City, the Confederates had been replaced by goblins. And fairies. And a six-foot Humpty Dumpty making its way along the Enchanted Flagstone Trail, a dicey undertaking for an egg navigating a path chiseled into the face of a cliff. Rock City is Geology Improved, courtesy of the guy who invented miniature golf.

They had the Needle's Eye, which grown-ups had to turn sideways to get through, and Fat Man's Squeeze, which just about everybody had to turn sideways for. They had glens and grottoes and a swinging bridge over a deep gorge, which was just the place to jounce up and down and scare the people following behind us. At Lover's Leap we could look out upon seven states—that's the motto of Rock City, SEE SEVEN STATES FROM HIGH ATOP LOOKOUT MOUNTAIN—but it was awfully hard to make out which state we might be looking at.

From Rainbow Hall, we could definitely see Chattanooga. Chattanooga in green. Chattanooga in red. Chattanooga in violet. Chattanooga in every sort of color through the green and red and blue and violet and orange and yellow windows. There was even a pane of ordinary glass where we could look upon Chattanooga as it really is, but nobody much did that. Nobody came to Rock City to see things in their true colors.

After Rainbow Hall, the trail crossed over the lip of High Falls, which is a pretty impressive bit of engineering when you consider that High Falls, like the gnomes and the fairies, was added by the miniature-golf man.

The trail wound its way through Goblin's Underpass and beneath Thousand-Ton Balanced Rock, which we hurried past, and then, safe on high ground, turned and watched, hoping the rock would become unbalanced and roll over somebody.

After that, artificial caves with stalactites pasted to the ceilings, along with coral. And gnomes and elves on trapezes and leering at us from rock shelves: twisted, bloated old-peoples' heads stuck onto children's bodies. They were freaky and wonderful and scary and shimmering with fluorescent paint. Acres, it seemed like, of glowing characters escaped from their fairytales and wandering the dark.

A dish running away with a spoon. Witches and Little Miss Muffet, a kid stealing a pig, and the voices of children singing nursery rhymes over loudspeakers. Everything except any mention of what happened on Lookout Mountain ninety-five years before. I used to think that was a shame.

Now, it seems to me that a phosphorescent princess biting a radioactive apple is a much better thing to be remembered for than twelve hundred scared, starving boys trying to defend their country from ten times as many invaders, invaders better armed and better equipped and better fed. Boys who had been sent up there for what purpose? To prolong a war that was already lost? There's nobility in that. But foolishness, too.

That miniature-golf guy had it about right. If you're going to deal in fairytales, it's best to paint them up in glow-in-the-dark colors so you don't forget it's make-believe.

I loved the mountains in North Georgia. They were ancient and beautiful, the trees huge and impossibly old. Rhododendrons the size of mountain laurel, and laurels as big as oaks—refugees, it seemed to me, from the beginning of time. I'd take friends up there, and we could walk for days and never see another person. Back then, nobody used the Appalachian Trail much, and when we spent the night in one of the concrete-floored lean-tos the Forest Service set up, we'd have to kick the leaves out before spreading our bedrolls.

We packed a lot of grits, ground from dried hominy corn. We carried other food, too, but twelve- and thirteen-year-old boys aren't much at cooking, grits were easy to carry and about as simple to prepare as hot food could get, and water was never a problem. The woods were wet and we would drink straight from streams tumbling over rocks. Sometimes entire cliff faces would be dripping with moisture and we could press our mouths right against the ferns and mosses.

The Appalachians aren't all that high, as mountains go, but the walking was steep and rough, and even healthy boys aren't eager to haul more than they have to. I carried a thin sleeping bag and a rectangle of canvas I could stretch over a log or tie to a couple of trees to make a shelter for the nights we didn't use Forest-Service lean-tos. Parched corn, a bit of canvas, and a bedroll—I felt like a Confederate infantryman on his way to defend Chattanooga. We were going to show those Yankees a thing or two, we purely were.

The higher peaks were bare rock where, on summer mornings, Shelby Lewis and I, or Buddy Wilcox and I, would climb right through the clouds and gaze out over ridge after ever-bluer ridge extending to the curve of the earth. With the switchbacks and the slopes, the ridges and the streams to cross, what seemed a dozen miles on the map could feel never-ending on foot. One stretch, one very steep stretch, led up and over a mountain. We knew where the top was, we could gauge it from the sunlight sifting through the trees as we stumbled up the slope. Willing ourselves to keep climbing. To make it to the summit. Where we could rest and enjoy the view and congratulate ourselves on our fortitude, and it would all be downhill.

When we finally did make it to the summit, the whole glory of the mountain opened up in front of us. We weren't on top at all. We were on a footstool, a way-station on the route to the real summit looming over us in the distance.

An hour or so later when we were up there, we got our first look at the actual mountaintop still hundreds of feet higher. And then again, forty-five minutes after that.

We struggled to another plateau and another, as we worked our way up a giant staircase, the summit forever higher and forever out of reach. "And now," I could almost hear the spooky, deep voice of Rod Serling telling unseen watchers, "the story of two boys trapped forever in a loop of their own devising. Submitted for your consideration on The Twilight Zone."

School integration rocked along in Buckhead with the same deliberate speed it rocked along in Pelham Manor, and for the same reason. There weren't any colored kids to integrate with. The threat was in the air, though, and when it came time for me to go to high school, my parents announced I would be attending Westminster, the oldest and most exclusive private school in the city. Getting there required a long, annoying car ride, but Mother was up to the challenge, dipped into her bag of friends, put together a carpool, and off I went in the morning.

She and Dad wanted me to get a good education is how they put it, and I'm sure they meant it. But they were bounded by the horizons of their generation, just like we all are. I think they were ashamed, though, and never in my hearing said anything against colored people. It is, as I now know from having had children of my own, the only way to stop that kind of disease. The virus is spread by mouth, and as long as you keep yours shut, you can protect the next generation from becoming infected.

They were right about Westminster, I did get a good education. The only problem was there was a religious component to that education that didn't fit with any theology that had been current on these shores since the sixteen hundreds. The headmaster was a Baptist of the fundamentalist kind who give water a bad name. He was an ecumenical Baptist, though, and made a point of hiring as many Calvinists as he could lay his hands on. Not Presbyterians, mind you, hard-core seventeenth-century Calvinists, who did everything except shave their heads and wear buckles on their shoes and shoot Indians with blunderbusses.

Predestination was at the top of the things the Calvinists thought God wanted us to believe in, and it even made sense in a crazy, logical, totally amoral way. God knows everything, they told us, including whether you're going to get the big thumb's up at the Pearly Gates or the switch pulled on the trap door. He's known since before he built the world, and there's nothing poor little insignificant you can do about it.

So...the idea began to percolate into our thirteen-year-old minds...it doesn't make any difference to God what we do while we're down here? For budding theologians, it was a liberating thought.

There was a catch, though. God might not care whether you drank beer or your hemline came above your knees, if you were a girl, or you killed people, but Westminster had rules. Actually, I'm not sure they had a rule about killing people, but get caught doing either of the first two things, and no matter which way you're headed after you die, you'll be heading there with a lot of colored classmates because you definitely weren't going to be graduating from Westminster.

If you were only suspected of those things, you were given a trial, but it was the sort of trial that hasn't been favored in the West since Torquemada yanked one-too-many arms loose from its socket. You were put to the question in front of your teachers. And the headmaster. And a sinister-sounding outfit called the Student Honor Council, supported by God and Jesus and other holy powers hovering around your head to make sure you told the truth. Then, when you did, it was off to public school for you.

That put a strain on our Jewish classmates because, we were led to believe, certain Hebrew celebrations involved sipping wine, and no dispensation was given just because you did the sipping at home. Or with your parents' blessing. Or as part of an ancient ritual that ran much deeper than anything Mr. Johnny-Come-Lately Calvin ever dreamed up. So, on mornings after Jewish holidays, the teachers would hover around, trying to sniff the breath of the Jew and a half who attended school with us.

Westminster had a three-Jew rule. That was how it proved that it wasn't just a place for Society kids to escape modern society. Since the girls were sequestered hundreds of yards away in a building of their own, that left us boys with one and a half Jews to be multicultural with and made the mornings after Jewish holidays easy to monitor.

I don't know whether our teachers hit the bottle in private, but sex was something they spent a lot of time thinking about. In bible class, Mr. Patton treated us to lurid speculations about what the Prodigal Son had been up to while he was running through his inheritance. From there, he would arabesque into gruesome details about how painful it was for the Virgin Mary to give birth, what with her maidenhead still blocking the way. Mr. Patton was also the biology teacher, so he knew what he was talking about.

At carefully monitored school dances, chaperones would interrupt couples for indulging in what they referred to as a vertical execution of a horizontal desire. *Vertical execution of a horizontal desire*, we thought. *So that's how it's done.* You get horizontal and do the twist with each other. It is, when I think about it now, as good a description of the sex act as anybody is likely to come up with.

When the administration realized that the girls were naked under their clothes, they issued a fiat: no girl would be allowed to attend class wearing culottes.

"Say what?" scores of girls wanted to know. "Culottes are a species of baggy trousers. In culottes, a girl is far more modest than she would be in a skirt."

"In culottes," the administration replied, "a girl can sit in positions she would not be able to sit in if she were wearing a skirt."

"If she were sitting in a position she couldn't sit in if she were wearing a skirt," the girls tried to reply, "she wouldn't be *wearing* a skirt." But logic had no place in a discussion of that sort.

The synagogue that had been reducing property values across the street from where we used to live was bombed.

It wasn't the first explosion to take place in the bottomlands of Peachtree Creek. It wasn't the biggest, and, given the odds against the Confederates in the summer of 1864, it probably wasn't even the most pointless. The explosion didn't even hurt anybody. It did some property damage, but that was it.

They tried a man for it, but he was acquitted when his lawyer turned the courtroom into a carnival. After the verdict was read, the lawyer went to jail for contempt of court and the man sued the Atlanta chief of police for false arrest.

Nobody ever learned for sure if he was the one who planted the bomb, or why, but it's hard to escape the feeling it had something to do with anti-Semitism. So, Dad might have been right about what other people were prejudiced against when he announced we'd sold our house just in time. At the very least, having a terrorist bomb go off across the street is the kind of thing that really will depress property values.

As the seven-year statute of limitations for tax fraud began to run down, Uncle John slept less and summoned his underlings in the middle of the night to discuss nothing very important more, and his health began to go.

It didn't go completely, just in spurts. He'd catch cold when everybody else caught a cold. And a month later, when nobody had a cold, he'd catch cold all over again. And sore throats and flus and bronchitises and various degrees of pneumonias.

One Thursday, when the maid was off and he was laid up, Aunt Doughy began speculating about what was in the kitchen.

The more she speculated, the more curious she became until the time came she crept over and cracked the door and peeked in.

When nothing dreadful happened, some of her girlish spunk began to return and she swung the door all the way open and stepped inside.

She recognized things in there. The sink wasn't all that different from the one she remembered growing up. The stove wasn't all that different either. Uncle John saw no reason to go wasting money on modern luxuries if only the help was going to use them. Doughy went over and turned a knob and blue flames sprang up.

She could cook something, she knew she could. Her husband was sick, and she could fix him something. After fifty-some years of marriage, it was her turn to do for him.

Tea, she thought. John would like tea. So she hunted around until she found a saucepan, carefully measured out a cup of water from the sink, and placed the saucepan on the burner. Then she set out to find tea.

Tea bags didn't start showing up in stores until after she'd been banished, both from the stores and from her own kitchen. But she knew what they looked like. Over the years, she'd been served thousands of cups of tea.

It took some doing, but she found the tea bags in a little red box next to the coffee. She put one in a cup then poured in the hot water. It sputtered on the hot metal of the edge of the saucepan, and because it had been boiling while she hunted around for the tea, only half-filled the cup.

Undaunted, Doughy heated a new cupful of water, poured it into a clean cup, and dropped in a fresh teabag. Then carried it upstairs to John, so pleased with herself she almost tripped over one of the wads of money bulging beneath the carpet.

When she handed him the tea, he turned pale, his flu replaced by apoplexy, shooed Doughy out of the room, reached for the phone, and called his grown children for a family meeting. He was furious.

"You know full well," he told his children, "that your mother is never to set foot in the kitchen. I expect you to see to it that *nothing* like this happens again."

On December 19, 1959, the Last Living Confederate Soldier died. His name was Walter Williams, and he'd been a forage master with John Bell Hood. I wasn't clear on what a forage master did, but if he'd been with

Hood, there was a fair chance he master-foraged in my yard. I regretted not knowing about him while he was alive. I would have liked hearing what our place looked like a hundred years ago.

Being the Last Living Confederate Soldier had been à la mode for the better part of a decade. Before Williams answered that final bugle call, the previous Last Living Confederate Soldier had been one John B. Salling, who'd died in May. Prior to him, the Last Living Confederate Soldier had been William Lundy, who passed on in September 1957, preceded in death by Thomas Riddle, who'd died in April 1954, and before him, William Albert Kidney, who died in June 1953. Previous to Kidney, a column of at least six other Last Living Confederate Soldiers extended back to Felix M. Witkowski, who, as far as anybody can tell, was the Original Last Living Confederate Soldier. He departed camp on February 23, 1952, setting a fashion trend during the Eisenhower administration that ran parallel to hula-hoops and coonskin caps.

Somewhere along in there, or maybe a bit earlier (a lot of Confederate records didn't survive the war), the real last living Confederate Soldier really did die. Their numbers had been dwindling for years. As they passed, the struggles and hurts they embodied became ever more distant from the lives of those of us who followed until, by the time I was in high school, the memories had become as artificial as the last living soldiers themselves, the hatred had almost drained away, and we were beginning to grope toward the light in matters racial. It was fitting it should happen when the World War II generation was coming to power.

In their war, they weren't only the winners, but the moral victors, too. Now that we weren't in the wrong anymore, we could aspire to the right.

Dad could strike a match with a bullet. In addition to riding with George Catlett Marshall the mornings he'd been stationed in Washington, Dad had been on the army rifle team. I'm not entirely clear why Westminster had a rifle range, but it did, and the fact didn't seem strange to anybody.

Dad would clip a match to the wire we hung targets from, then return to the firing line, sprawl out in the prone position, sight in, and squeeze the trigger. When he did it right, the edge of the bullet would skim along the head of the match and the match would burst into flame.

Rifle practice counted as athletics, which was lucky for me. I'd given football a whirl but had no talent for it. The coach had a theory that it's not the size of the dog in the fight, it's the size of the fight in the dog, which just went to show that the coach had never been a dog in a fight. To prove his point, he called me up as the living embodiment of all the skinny dogs, handed me a football, and told me to run it past Mosby Cantrell.

Mosby was no ordinary dog. Mosby was the kind of dog who stalks between the fences in prison-camp movies. Mosby weighed more than twice as much as I did, worked out with weights, and had been shaving since third grade. There was no way I was going to run a football past Mosby Cantrell.

So I did the obvious thing. When Mosby erupted out of his three-point stance, salivating and making snarling noises as if he'd discovered an escaping airman, I tossed the ball onto the ground and yelled, "Fumble!" Then stood grinning while Mosby rolled around in the dust. Mosby Cantrell was not bright.

Neither was the coach, and he didn't have a sense of humor, either. The whole team got an impromptu lecture about moral fiber and, "What you have seen here today?" After that, spending my afternoons at the rifle range was just the ticket.

Sometimes Dad would reinforce the firearms part of our heritage and take me hunting. On the way, he'd tell stories about how his grandfather used to ask his grandmother how many guests she'd be serving at dinner, and when she answered, "There will be ten of us," would drop twelve shotgun shells into his pocket and mount up. If he couldn't get ten birds with twelve shots from the back of a horse, he didn't deserve them.

Unfortunately for family tradition, suburban Atlanta was not rural Alabama, where quail and dove lurked in every field. When Dad wanted to go hunting he had to drive us to a farm where the owner picked up extra cash as a guide. To be sure he had something to guide us to, the farmer would buy hand-raised quail and set them out in a field. The next morning he'd lead us to where he left the quail, they would explode into the air, and we'd shoot. At least, that was the plan.

The problem with the plan was that the quail weren't in on it. Also, the quail weren't wild. When we slipped up on them, shotguns cradled in our arms, out would tumble quail like happy puppies, nuzzling our ankles with expectant looks on their faces. Spending a night in the wilderness had left them hungry and frightened and they were glad to see us.

The farmer would kick at them to try to set them flying, and every now and then, one or two would hop into the air. Then circle back and land at our feet. Sometimes we had to swat at them with our shotguns to keep them from perching on the barrels.

One afternoon Dad got involved picking up an important agriculture-chemical person at the airport and was hours late fetching me from art school. While I waited, the other kids went home, shadows lengthened, lights came on in the ramshackle buildings, and the tumbledown walkways grew more tumbledown.

Suppertime came and went, and a group of adults showed up for evening class—laughing and talking and cadging cigarettes before disappearing into the secret, grown-up art shack none of us kids was allowed into. Long before Dad arrived, it had gotten too dark for anybody to notice a boy climbing up for a peek through the high windows.

It was a warm evening, the windows were open, and the air smelled of cigarettes and turpentine as I took a slow gander at the life model the grown-ups were painting.

In a time before the Internet, or *Playboy*, or at least before respectable convenience stores started leaving *Playboys* on the shelves where kids could thumb through them, pretending to be deciding whether they wanted to buy this month's *Ladies Home Journal*, a single peek through that high window answered a lot of questions. And art...well, to this day, the visual arts have been an especial interest of mine.

The week I turned sixteen, a girl and I celebrated by hopping into Mother's Fiat and driving north to discover where Roswell Road went. Up into North Georgia, I imagined, into the foothills of the Appalachians, to the land of sturdy mountain folk. People like my people, Scots-Irish descendants of the first settlers, still almost pioneers themselves.

It was a long drive for somebody with a newly minted driver's license, first through expensive suburbs, then deep, shadowy woods and down the long slope to the single-lane trestle bridge over the Chattahoochee, where we had to wait for a car coming the other way before we could cross. Then up the bluffs where the Yankees had formed up before invading Atlanta. On past the Lockheed plant, where they were churning out airplanes to drop atom bombs on the Russians, and to Alpharetta, the home of one of the distant football teams we played in high school. We'd make cow noises when they came onto the field so they'd feel at home.

After that, burned-out fields and sagging fences and leaning barns and desolate red clay to the very country so many people had fled to Buckhead to escape. Until, surprise of surprises, Roswell Road led to Roswell. We rounded the town square and kept going.

Just outside Cumming, we came to a lane of enormous hickory trees spreading over the road. And a beat-up wooden stand selling ice cream. The woman inside was as beat-up as the stand, and so bitter she might have lived on that land for two hundred years, witness to every dispossession and every crime that had ever taken place. And, in her long life, had enjoyed but a single satisfaction she could call up and admire on a bright April day.

"Reckon why they ain't no niggers here?" she asked. "You seen our sign on the way in? Black Man, don't let the sun set on you in Forsythe County?"

She was a woman filled with resentments of things she had not seen and evils not done to her. "Sign got it right, it purely did," the old lady chuckled. "See them trees?" she waved a withered hand toward the hickories. "That's why they ain't no niggers in Forsythe County. Strung them all up. Won't so long ago, neither."

I never discovered what that old lady meant by not so long ago, but as my own days stretch further behind me, the past seems closer. Now a decade gone feels like last Thursday, and a century something I can hold in one hand. My hope is that her own decades had crowded up so close that the thirties were just last week. And the 'teens not much longer ago than that, and none of what she so gleefully recounted happened anywhere near my time on this earth.

All the times I have recounted this story, nobody has ever admitted knowing what took place in Forsythe County, or when. And I have never really tried to find out. All I care to know, I learned that afternoon over a double-dipped butter pecan.

In a fit of enthusiasm, Buddy Wilcox bought a mail-order rowboat. It came in a big, flat cardboard box.

Inside were a couple of brass oarlocks and six pieces of plywood: two sides, two seats, one stern, and one bottom. The bottom was cut into a curve some wag at the boat factory imagined Buddy could warp the sides around, then nail on. This might have been plausible if Buddy had been six strong men and his toolbox had included a hydraulic press. But he wasn't, and it didn't, and Buddy, being no fool, gave the boat to Shelby and me.

We weren't six strong men, either, and every time we tried warping the sides in place they sprang loose in our hands. Finally, we just forced them around, inch by inch, and pounded in nails. When we were finished, we had a boat of sorts. But not the sort of boat anybody who knew anything about boats would ever take out on the water, because we'd given up trying to make the sides fit around the bottom and just hammered them on, leaving a couple of inches of bottom sticking out in a shelf around the outside.

After squeezing in about a case of caulking, the thing was watertight enough so that if we carried along a bucket and bailed continuously, we could stay afloat. The next weekend, Shelby and I became the first people we ever heard of to navigate Peachtree Creek.

We bailed our way past Bobby Jones Golf Course, through wild tangles of vines, and into shadows from trees leaning over the water, then beneath huge branches we imagined dripping with snakes poised to drop on us. Every now and then, the wildness would be broken by little patches of lawn, flowers sometimes, and once or twice, cast-iron benches. Whose backyards these were, we had no idea. Toward the end of the afternoon, Peachtree Creek emptied into the Chattahoochee. Broad and green and inviting. Shelby and I were enamored.

A couple of weeks and a crate or two of caulking later, we set out down the Chattahoochee. The Chattahoochee is as lovely as it sounds, pure mountain stream, cool and deep, fast moving, with just enough white water to give us something to do beside bail.

I have never learned what that name means—it always sounded Cherokee to me, something along the lines of "The River of the Musical Waters," but what do I know? It could be "The Sewer the White Fools Drink Out Of." Or maybe it isn't Cherokee at all. Maybe when the Cherokee moved onto the land, they inherited the name from earlier inhabitants and never knew what it meant, either. For that matter, maybe it isn't even Indian. Maybe it derived from a Name-That-River contest held by the first white settlers. Or, could be the first white settlers weren't English. Maybe they were Serbo-Croatian and the name means "Death to Muslims" in the old country. What it means now, to me, is "The River with the Musical Name," and that's just fine.

The day was hot and we splashed water over ourselves and sometimes jumped in and drifted along beside the boat. Then climbed back in and lay in the sun to warm back up. Even when the river ran through the middle of the city, you couldn't see Atlanta at all. No buildings, no smokestacks. No lights, no traffic. It was easy to imagine ourselves high in the mountains. Or on uncharted water a couple of centuries ago. There was just enough left of the way things had been to let us imagine how they once were.

Westminster was on a big, wooded tract of land and some time during the fall of my junior year, a naked guy began popping out of the trees and scaring people. We called him Norman. Norman the Nude.

A naked guy hanging around a school would have been scary in any circumstances, but a naked guy hanging around a school that did not acknowledge nakedness raised the administration to a fever of hysteria that ran all the way down to the football team. Every time somebody spotted Norman, or thought he spotted Norman, or wanted to get out of tackling Mosby Cantrell, the naked-guy scare would go out and the team would give a roar and charge into the woods and start beating the bushes for naked people.

Norman always seemed to get away, though. Maybe it was the roar that tipped him off. At any rate, football players weighed down with helmets and shoulder pads and shin guards were no match for a terrified man tearing barefoot and bare-genitaled through briars and poison ivy. Months later, after the police staked out the woods, they caught him. Or at least they hoped they'd caught him. By then, word had gotten out, and the woods were hopping with copycat Normans strutting their stuff. And, if the stories I heard were true, with one or two young Christian girls who'd taken to wandering through the trees trying to see for themselves what all the shouting was about.

Westminster was lucky it had a football team to go chasing after naked guys. But then a foolish consistency hadn't proved to be much of a hobgoblin when all thirteen members of the varsity squad were caught with beer in their hands. Sin-and-go-no-more, at least not to beer parties, is how the headmaster and the teachers and the Student Honor Council put it when they decided to let the football team stay in school. That was the rule where drinking and football were concerned.

"Don't graduate" was the rule a few years later when Werner von Braun's daughter got caught in a motel the night before graduation. I never heard there was a guy in the motel with her. If there was, he was probably her old man, and he would have been in the next room. Werner von Braun was scheduled to give the commencement address at Westminster the next morning.

No skin off my butt, is how young Ms. von Braun felt about being expelled, and come fall, trooped happily off to the college she'd already been admitted to.

Find yourself another speaker is the way her daddy put it when the administration wanted to know why he hadn't shown up at the commencement ceremony. I've got better things to waste my time on than talking to a bunch of religious fascists, although I'm not sure he expressed himself exactly that way, and returned to Alabama and hammering out rockets on our family's land.

That summer, we vacationed on Grand Bahama Island. It was fun for a lot of reasons, but partly because getting there involved airplanes.

There was a doctrinal dispute in our family concerning air travel. Aunt Tootie and Uncle Matt wouldn't go anywhere they couldn't get to by Pullman car, possibly because Uncle Matt had spent the Second World War in charge of an anti-aircraft battery and developed the opinion that planes are apt to be blown out of the air at any moment. Christmas and Thanksgiving and every other family occasion, they would caution the rest of us against flying.

My parents didn't look at it that way. Dad took the plane when he wanted to go somewhere he couldn't get to by Oldsmobile, but for Mother, flying was more than transportation. Planes were things of the spirit. For Mother, all the world lay just below the horizon, and in an airplane, she could go see for herself the wonders she'd only read about growing up in Depression-era Georgia.

What, exactly, my parents were up to in the Bahamas that July, they never said—something to do with Calypso music and rum and maybe, if my intuition is correct on this—roulette wheels. Whatever it was, they had my blessing, just as long as they didn't want to do it with me.

For a teen on the loose, Grand Bahama was a kind of paradise. Afternoons, a gang of us would troop onto a small boat and sail off over water so clear we could pick out each bit of coral, each flashing scale on every fish gliding below. The bottom seemed so close it was if we could reach down and grab a handful of sand.

One time the middle-aged skipper tossed a rope over the side and dragged up a bucketful of tiny, brightly colored shells. When we jumped into the water, he spilled the bucket over us, and the ocean exploded with bubbles as we snatched at the whirling purples and reds and creamy whites. But we never caught any. Every shell we tried to grab slipped through our fingers—until they were all deeper than any of us could swim. The bottom that looked so close from the boat was forever beyond our reach.

Colored people were different in the Bahamas.

For one thing, they were blacker. There hadn't been the same fraternization between the races as you saw in Georgia.

For another, they didn't talk like colored people. They talked like aristocrats. You heard somebody behind you, you'd swear you were in the presence of an English lord. Or maybe an Oxford don, but when you looked, he would be a hotel clerk or maybe a policeman, tall and black and very elegant in his tropical uniform. In that company we were the ones, me and my sisters and our parents, who'd learned to talk in the South, who sounded like colored people.

There was a bar in the hotel where we stayed, and I was old enough and male enough to hang out down there, sipping rum drinks with coconut milk. Or maybe pineapple juice. And listening to the band. And my sisters weren't, which made the experience all the more enticing. And the songs they weren't allowed to listen to, the more memorable. One was the "Big Bamboo."

The Big Bamboo grows long and tall. The Big Bamboo pleases one and all. It didn't take Sigmund Freud to tell you what that song was about

There was another song, *Well is left, right, in front and behind me, Chinese baby calling me Daddy.* Wasn't much question what that song was about either. The man singing it was just about as dark-skinned as any human on the planet, and his lover, she was black like Tar Baby, the song said so. Half black as those kids were, all the man singing in the bar could see—all any man would have seen, most likely—were the Chinese bits.

Chinese? I didn't notice any Chinamen on Grand Bahama. There may have been some, I'm pretty sure I didn't meet everybody, but why Chinese?

Now that I'm older, I believe the Chinese part made perfect sense. Even those Bahamians, dignified and self-confident and remote from the history we all tried to ignore back home, knew who was sitting in the bar and what opinion some of us held of mongrelizing our genes. The idea of Chinese wouldn't raise any hackles on our part, and the singers tailored their lyrics accordingly. When I think about it today, I wonder what they sang in the places tourists never found.

Grand Bahama is flat and sandy and dotted with scraggly bushes and scrub trees, just the place to rent a bike and go exploring, which is how Anne and I wound up pedaling past a bleak concrete-block structure on July 21, 1961.

Nowadays, it's the kind of place you'd expect to find a few tons of cocaine cooling its heels before boarding a private flight to the Everglades. Back then, it was something much more special. It was a NASA tracking station. And at the exact moment Anne and I pedaled up and stopped, Gus Grissom was coasting 118 miles overhead, while the *Liberty Bell 7* broadcast the news—broadcast, when we thought about it, right through Anne and me—to that very tracking station. While fractions of a second later, the station rebroadcasted the news back through us to Cape Canaveral and out to the rest of the world. To this day, I can't but think that, for a few moments, Anne and I were an intimate part of the space program.

And there was something else. The Mercury rocket that blasted Gus Grissom into outer space had been built on land that once belonged to our family. To a sixteen-year-old with stars in his eyes, the family came out way ahead on the trade.

The morning didn't last. Anne was fourteen, and a girl, and, therefore, my responsibility. And, since she was a girl, *her* responsibility was her hair. When her hair had had enough of the sun and salt air, she turned back and I had no choice but to follow her.

Sometimes Baptist girls will surprise you. I took one to the Fulton County Fair.

The fair had come to Atlanta, as it did every year. But the year I was sixteen, the fair took on new possibilities. For the first time, the fair wasn't going to involve riding in the backseat of Dad's Oldsmobile, then having to gauge my movements to avoid bumping into him and Mother until time came to meet them beside the Ferris wheel, or the two-headed-calf, or whatever, and go home. The year I was sixteen I drove down to the fair on my own.

Or, at least, without parents. A girl was on the seat next to me, and this wasn't one of those bucket seats they put in cars nowadays to keep hormones chastely separated. Dad's Oldsmobile didn't even have seatbelts, so she could sit just as close as she wanted with no moral misgivings. She did, and I had a buzz on the whole evening while we drifted around the midway dripping paint onto whirling disks, tossing darts at balloons, and howling at Wolf Woman.

The girl must have been feeling pretty good, too, because when the fair shut down for the night we lingered, watching people close up their booths. As the lights switched off, the carnies, who'd looked exotic when they were yelling at us across a crowded midway, began to seem sinister, part of a strange world I knew nothing about.

Meanwhile, trotting along at my side, my date was still chipper. But, then, she had somebody to protect her. As we tried to find our way to the gate, it dawned on me that not only was she expecting me to do the protecting, but whatever trouble we'd get into would most likely be aimed at her. Not to put too fine a point on it, but a cute, lively girl crossing an empty fairgrounds made a much more inviting target than I ever will. I wanted to get her, and me, out of there.

We found the gate and headed into the parking lot, but what had been a sea of automobiles a few hours earlier had turned into a huge emptiness running, it seemed to me, to the vanishing-point in three directions. A few cars were still there, dotted around, but none we could recognize.

We hiked across what felt like miles of asphalt, checking the shadows between streetlights and the places between the remaining cars, trying to discover where we'd left ours. By then, I wasn't feeling buzzy anymore, and my date was walking closer as if she, too, had figured out she might be the target of choice in our little group.

As we searched, the last of the cars pulled out, the streetlamps flicked off, the little pools of yellow light evaporated, and, still, Dad's Olds wasn't anywhere to be seen.

Neither was a phone booth, and by then, two sets of parents were waiting up, wondering how we planned to talk our way out of it this time.

What seemed like hours later, a dim pair of headlights began working its way toward us. Whoever it is, I thought, I sure hope it's the police.

The headlights pulled to a stop in front of us.

The door opened, but in the glare we couldn't make out who it was. At least not very well, not any more than to make out that it was a man.

And he was colored.

And he wasn't the police.

For an instant it crossed my mind that if I took off into the shadows, he'd go for the girl. But I was new at this dating business, and I wasn't sure I'd ever get another chance, so I stood my ground and waited, my date squeezing my arm like she knew, just knew, I would take care of her.

"You children best get in here," the man said. "Ain't safe out here this time of night." Then he switched on his sign. He was a cab driver. "Probably left your car in the East Lot. I'll carry you over."

East Lot, I thought. "There's an *East* Lot."

"Yes, Sir," the cabbie said. "You think South Lot is big, you should see the East Lot."

"I can't pay you," I said. "Spent all my money at the fair."

"You ain't gone owe me nothin'," the cabbie said. "Just don't like the idea of children out here this time of night."

He was right about the East Lot. If South Lot had been a dark, carless sea, the East Lot was the vast, empty Pacific. Even riding around in the cab, even with no other cars there to confuse the search, it still took a while to find ours. But there it was.

By the time we spotted it, a third car was out there with us. Riding around looking for something. It began following the cab.

"Thanks," I said when we got out. "Thank you very much. You saved our..." Before I could finish, the cabbie popped into reverse and was out of there.

We got into the Olds and tried to leave. But the third car had pulled in behind us, trapping us against the curb, headlights dazzling through the back window and off the rearview mirror so that I had to duck my head to keep from being blinded.

"You rode with that nigger cabbie?" a voice next to the window said. I nodded, but it wasn't a question. This time, it really was the police.

"We gone get that boy," the policeman said. "Can't have no nigger cabbies picking up white people. Cost him his license. Maybe a month or two in jail, dependin' on who he turns out to be."

"He was just helping us," I said. "We lost our car and..."

"Came out in South Lot, did you?" the policeman said. "People do that all that time. That's why the cabbies cruise around out here after closing. So they can pick up some extra change."

"It wasn't like that," my date said.

"Won't like what? Little Missy," the policeman said, "what you think your mama gone say when she finds out you rode in a car with a nigger?"

"I think Mother is going to be pleased as punch I got home safe and that cab driver, if she had his number, she'd call him up and..."

"Don't you worry about that, Little Missy. We got his number. I'll be runnin' him in in a few..."

"It wasn't like that," my date tried again. "We weren't fares. We didn't pay him any..."

"Now let me get this straight," the policeman paused as if the notion of a cabbie giving somebody a ride for free was something he had to grapple with. "You tellin' me that nigger just picked you up and drove you all the way around from South Lot because he has a good Christian heart and never once asked you for money?"

"That is exactly what I have been trying to tell you, lo these many minutes, officer."

"That true?" he turned to me. "That nigger just up and give you a ride for free?"

"You got a bible in your car?" I asked. "I'll swear on that."

"I've got one right here," my date said and pulled out the New Testament she kept in her purse. "I swear on this holy book, so help me God, and may my soul rot in eternal damnation if I should lie, that cab driver rode us all the way around from the other lot where we got lost and brought us to our car here, and never once did he ask for payment."

"Only payment that good man wanted was the riches stored up for him in the Kingdom of Heaven," I started to say, but didn't need to. The swearing on the New Testament had already performed its miracle.

"That New Testament say anything against kissing?" I asked as the policeman drove away.

"I don't believe it does," my date said.

"No need to look too close," I said. "I am willing to take the word of someone as educated in these matters as yourself."

It turned out she was more educated in some other matters than I was, too, but we didn't have the chance to do much about it that night. Right then, our mission was to get her back to her parents before they started calling morgues and trying to remember exactly what their little girl had been wearing when she left the house. And what kind of car her kidnapper was driving.

That fall, Dad took me hunting with the men.

At the cabin we stayed in, the farmer-turned-hunting-guide had a wife who made you realize the unfairness of life. "You know that Europe place?" she demanded.

Several of the men nodded. They'd come to know that Europe place a lot better than they would have liked, back when they were trying to do something about that Hitler person. The others had missed that Europe place because they'd been in that Pacific place dealing with those Japanese guys.

"If it won't for Beauchamp," the bitter woman glared at her husband, "I would have been to that Europe place by now." She was skinny and hard looking and perpetually angry.

Beauchamp gave the sheepish, what-can-you-do? sort of smile henpecked husbands give when their wives embarrass them, then turned and left the room and pretended it didn't matter. That morning he'd taken us out for quail, and we'd gotten a deer. None of us had a deer license, and nobody had been carrying anything besides birdshot, but we'd come home with a deer anyway.

"He's got a bottle, you know," the wife said while Dave Dillard set out the poker things. "Just you watch. That fool'll be drunk before this night is over. Won't for him, I'd have been to that Europe place twice by now." It was as if the ice cream lady out on Roswell Road held the same travel ambitions as Mother.

"She must have been a looker," Dixon Rawlins said, and he might have been onto something. At least it would explain why Beauchamp married her. That and her daddy's farm.

"It's her place now," Munford Black pulled up a chair. "Beauchamp can't dump her. Gotten too old to start a new line of work."

"Hardest way I know to earn money," Dad shuffled the deck, "is to marry it."

"Amen, Brother," the men raised their glasses in agreement. From the kitchen we could hear Beauchamp's wife yelling at somebody, although there wasn't anybody back there to yell at.

"How you want to split up the deer?" Munford Black asked.

"Don't need any," Dad said. "You boys go on and divide it up the way you want."

"Dixon, you got space at the ice house," Dave Dillard said. "Why don't you have one of your people cut it up and we can come by for the meat."

Dixon Rawlins nodded, then tapped the deck, indicating he didn't need to cut the cards. Dixon Rawlins owned an ice factory.

That morning we'd been unloading our shotguns when a deer ran up and jumped into the trunk of Dave Dillard's car. Dave slammed the lid just as a pack of hounds came loping down the road, followed by three out-of-breath hunters. "Any you boys seen a deer go by?"

"No," Dixon Rawlins said, "can't say it ran past here." By then, the dogs were leaping onto the bumper.

"Me neither," Dave Dillard said, "no deers I can see." He had to raise his voice to make himself heard over the baying and the scribbling from the dogs trying to dig their way into the trunk. And from the thumping from inside.

"Maybe it went that way," Munford Black pointed across a millet field. Strictly speaking, you weren't supposed to shoot birds over millet. But if you didn't see to it the birds had some reason to be there, they wouldn't be. Even birds that come in boxes will up and fly away if they can't find anything to eat.

"I thought I saw something run by," Dad pointed at a stand of pines. "Could be over there." By the time the hunters dragged their dogs away, the car was bouncing up and down.

Killing the deer hadn't been much trouble. Munford Black just pulled out his knife and slit its throat. The practiced way he did it, it was pretty clear he'd done something like that a time or two on that Iwo Jima place.

I didn't get to watch, and they should have shooed Dad away, too. He'd never seen something die before, not up close. The combat he'd been in was over by the time he arrived in that Okinawa place, and the deer looked him in the eyes as Munford Black pulled back the head. There'd been a lot of blood. Munford shrugged, and wiped the knife on a spare rag, and said something that sounded like Semper Fi, and that was it.

That night around the poker table they got into the bourbon.

Then they got into the war stories. The stories were funny and a lot of them seemed to involve homemade liquor, usually brewed from army-issue fruit salad, or a stash of brandy liberated from its German captors. Somebody asked Munford Black about what happened on Iwo, but he wouldn't say. "Haven't had enough bourbon to go talking about that." He raised his glass.

Then he turned to Dave Dillard. "What about those two whores you met in Paris? You never told us about them."

"Three. There were three of them."

"Three?" somebody whistled. "*Three*?"

"And they weren't whores. They were school teachers."

"Teach you anything interesting?" Munford Black poured about six fingers of bourbon into Dave Dillard's ice-tea glass.

"Maybe," Dave Dillard took a long pull from the glass.

"I've got a couple more bottles in the car," Dixon Rawlins said and started to get up.

"Bourbon isn't going to do it," Dave Dillard said. "What happened is kind of personal, if you take my meaning, and I'd..."

"You telling us," Dixon Rawlins sat back down, "you're not close enough to your own buddies to say what...?"

"I'm saying, a man can be too close to anybody," Dave Dillard said, and the other men nodded, knowing it was true. Some things a man kept for himself, or he wasn't a man.

"You tell Lydia?" Dad asked.

"*Hell*, no," Dave Dillard said and took another long pull from the ice-tea glass. "And I'd take it as a personal favor if none of you gentlemen happened to mention anything about it in her presence, either."

"You mean you're not even close enough to your own damn wife to tell her what went on in...?"

"I mean, a man can be too close, to anybody," Dave Dillard said with finality. "Even to his own damn wife."

"Here, here." Munford Black lifted his glass.

"*Amen*, Brother." Everybody raised their glasses. A man could definitely be too close to his own damn wife.

It's how you learned to be a man, from other men. And not just for me watching from the sofa, but for all the guys sitting around the poker table. Becoming a man is an ongoing project. And the only people who can judge your success are other men.

The following winter, I was dozing my way through history class when actual history interrupted. An announcement came over the PA system that, because of an event of national importance, we could forget about books and, for once, just pay attention to what was going on in the world. The principal put the microphone next to the radio, and we sat there for a frozen afternoon listening to reports from the Cape.

An attitude control jet had clogged 162 miles up, and a switch in the heat shield broke, and John Glenn might be in orbit forever, gasping out his life as his air turned foul and his power failed. Engineers scurried around Houston working slide rules and mocking-up different ways to get him back, and they came up with a doozy—a plan as daring and scary and as necessary as bellying a shot-up fighter onto the deck of a carrier. They left the retro-pack in place while the Friendship 7 bored into the atmosphere.

Everything went dead for fifteen minutes as plasma blocked the radio waves and we waited at our desks.

Waited for...we didn't know.

For radio signals that would never come maybe.

For word the retro-pack had flown to pieces and torn up the capsule.

That the whole contraption had become unbalanced and some part other than the heat shield had slapped into the atmosphere.

Or the parachute had ripped off and the Friendship 7 had screamed down into the Atlantic and buried itself in abyssal mud.

Even now, after sitting though the real thing, even after reading about it in the paper the next morning and, again, in Tom Wolfe's book, and seeing it in the movies after that, even now when I am very sure I know how those particular fifteen minutes came out, I can still feel the catch in my throat and the tears in my eyes as the radio crackled back on...and God-Speed-John-Glenn parachuted to a gentle splashdown.

School stopped again, three months later, for another event of national importance—when the pitch horizon scanner pitched out on the Aurora 7, and then so did the automatic reentry controls. And Scott, Trust-the-Force, Carpenter had to land the thing by hand. And came within an ace of punching a hole through the deck of the aircraft carrier waiting to pick him up—scoring the closest thing to a bulls-eye landing of any space shot, ever—one small step for mankind in the war against machines.

Ten days after that, Mother and a whole generation of fine, bold women burned alive in a chartered 707 that went down outside Paris. That was, I suppose, the great watershed in my life. It changed a lot of things—not the largest of which was Christmas gatherings, where we had to be cordial to Uncle Matt and Aunt Tootie while knowing Mother had done the right thing being on that airplane.

7

Mr. X Owes Me an Apology

It's hard to get a handle on from this distance, but my sisters and I grew up in a world before pizza. We first learned about it on Mary's day off.

Maids got Thursdays. That was the rule all over Atlanta. Maids worked Saturday, so they got Thursday off. Which meant that white ladies got one weekday a week to express their domesticity by cooking for their families. I don't know where Mother came up with the idea of serving foreign food, but the travel bug had bitten, and Thursdays we expanded our horizons by eating like foreigners. A different foreigner each week. Which is how we discovered pizza. We ate it with knives and forks by the light of a candle stuffed into a straw-covered Chianti bottle.

We had chow mein on the Thursdays we were exposed to the mysteries of the Orient.

And strange, pale sauces on French Thursdays. Looking back, it's a good thing Mother didn't have a clear idea what British people eat or we'd have been treated to spotted dick and blood pudding.

Somewhere along in there, she parlayed her love for exotic food and her yen for travel into a sweet deal involving the Atlanta Art Association and American Express. If she could fill a Boeing 707 with her friends, she'd get a free pass to Europe. Or anywhere else, I imagine. But Europe it was, because they have art in Europe.

With Mother on the job, flying to Europe on a chartered 707 became de rigueur down at the Atlanta Art Association. And since a 707 won't hold any more than a hundred and thirty or a hundred and forty passengers, filling one with her buddies was a snap.

In no time, she was spending afternoons and evenings sitting on the floor, arranging a hundred-and-some packets of travel information. When the time came, we drove her to the airport and off she flew. That flight was a big deal, and even Mayor Hartsfield came out to wave goodbye.

A month later we were watching as her plane touched down. She'd had a great time. Later, she told me, flying back from Europe was the happiest she'd ever been. That when the day came, she'd like to crash into the sea on the way home from a lovely trip.

She also wanted a Viking's funeral where we'd push her body out to sea in a burning ship. Probably at sunset. It was hard to see how we could manage something like that if she'd already crashed into the sea, but never mind. Mother didn't really expect a Viking's funeral, but she did think it would be a classy way to go out.

One of the first things she did after returning home was buy a subscription to *Grit and Steel*, and soon, magazines on cockfighting began showing up at our house. Travel had expanded her cultural horizons, and it wasn't long before she had a little coterie of friends drinking Coca-Colas and discussing the finer points of gamecocks with razors strapped to their legs. Also, one assumes, swapping tips on wagering on gamecocks with razors strapped to their legs.

A few months later she was arranging packets for another set of best friends to accompany her to Europe. Husbands were welcome, but not many signed up. They couldn't take the time off from work, they said. And if they could, well, it was a girl thing. Besides, art was involved, and not many Atlanta men wanted to go back to that Europe place just to tromp around a bunch of museums. Especially after all the tromping they'd done seventeen years ago when that Hitler guy was still over there.

Personally, I would have been happy to troop through a bunch of museums, so long as the trooping took place during the school year, and I lobbied for a seat on the plane. It didn't work, though. My grades in Spanish weren't up to snuff. The fact is, my grades in Spanish weren't even up to passing, and I was invited to spend the time Mother was in Europe reflecting upon my academic sins and hitting the books.

That was shortsighted and an example of misguided parenting. An entire month surrounded by actual foreigners speaking actual foreign languages has just naturally got to be more educational than falling asleep over a Spanish book. It was the right argument, but my parents weren't buying. Maybe they really did believe I needed to study.

Or maybe part of the point was for Mother to get away from family, and the getting away didn't involve dragging a seventeen-year-old son along.

Or, now that I think about it, maybe she'd worked hard for months to earn herself a free trip to Europe, and paying to buy a ticket for somebody else just didn't fit the program.

In spring 1962, the world seemed as frozen in time as some ancient land in a fairytale. Robert W. Woodward had been in charge of the Coca-Cola Company for forty years. Eugene Cook, the man who unveiled the ugly truth about the NAACP to the Georgia Peace Officers' Association, had been attorney general my entire life, and some of our congressmen had served in Washington since before the First World War. But there were glimmerings of change. The mayor who'd run our city since the Depression had retired.

We were sad to see him go. William B. Hartsfield had been about as respected, and as old guard, as a mayor could get. And as enlightened. He'd spent his career working behind the scenes, as he saw it, to make Atlanta more welcoming to its colored citizens. Willy B., we called him.

Willy B. was also the name of a high school football player in a cheeky song on the radio that, as far as I can tell, aired exactly one time before being silenced forever. Willy B. the football player was, as the lyrics kept reminding us, six-foot three.

After half a century, it's hard to remember what position Willy B. played, especially since the song got yanked before I had the chance to study it. Whatever it was, when the team found itself in a hole, when it was third and long yardage, the fans would call for Willy B.

Give that ball
Give that ball
Give that ball to Willy B.

And Willy B. would score the winning touchdown. Willy B. was six-foot three.

Then, one fateful Friday evening, the other team trotted out a gorilla, and the fans shouted for Willy B.

Give that ball
Give that ball
Give that ball to Willy B.

But that was easy for the fans to say. Willy B. was the one out there looking at a gorilla, and he had more sense than to try to run past something like that. He did what I did when the coach trotted out Mosby Cantrell. Willy B. tossed the ball onto the ground. Then he walked off the field.

Somebody in authority may have come to the conclusion that that particular song might have secretly been about a mayor who'd made his reputation managing a racially tolerant city, as tolerant as racially intolerant cities in the Deep South got, anyway, through the forties and the fifties, only to catch a glimpse of the sixties barreling headlong at him and concluded it was a good time to call it a game. Not respectful, the somebody in authority thought. And off the air the song went.

Atlanta did the right thing when we found ourselves without a mayor. We elected a new one. A silver-haired aristocrat who was vigorous and in touch with the times. An aristocrat not of the old order, but a new, Atlanta sort of aristocrat. Ivan Allen, who'd made his name in office products. A man too busy to hate. The sun was still in the sky and things were right with the earth.

Mayor Allen had plenty of friends on Mother's plane so, when she and her buddies set out to visit the art capitals of Europe, he came to the airport to see them off.

Five thirty-two a.m., Sunday, June 3, 1962, four minutes after sunrise and the start of a beautiful, late-spring morning in Atlanta. School had let out for the summer, and I could sleep in.

I woke feeling stretchy and good, and rolled back over, looking forward to...I don't remember. I was going to drive Marti to the club, drop her off, and come home. That afternoon, I would pick her up, then all of us would head out to the airport and meet Mother's plane. When school lets out for the summer, planning isn't big on your agenda.

At 11:32 a.m., Paris time, the exact moment I was stretching and going back to sleep, the Chateau de Sully, Boeing 707-328, Air France charter to New York was beginning its take off. Onboard were Mother, ten crewmembers, and one hundred and nineteen of Mother's best friends, including a few husbands and a handful of children. They had, maybe, two minutes to live.

According to the flight recorder, the pilot gunned the engines for six seconds, which gave him time to check the settings and takeoff parameters for all four engines, then applied full thrust and started forward.

The runway at Orly was 10,700 feet long, and the plane rolled straight, accelerating normally. At about 6,000 feet, it reached takeoff speed, and the pilot pulled back on the control column.

The nose lifted but the plane remained on the ground, and for another five seconds, hurtled down the runway, nose slightly in the air. By the time the pilot decided to abort the takeoff, he was doing 110 miles per hour and had less than 3,000 feet of pavement on which to stop the plane. That was nowhere near enough.

He hit the brakes, the tires shrieked, then evaporated.

Smoke billowed from the wheels as he tried to get the flaps up to provide more air resistance. By then, the plane had angled to the left.

Eight hundred feet later, the aircraft veered starboard as he tried to wrestle it back under control. The accident reports say he may have been attempting a ground loop, although it's not obvious what that would have accomplished. He was out of pavement no matter which way the plane headed.

The Chateau de Sully left the runway doing 95 miles an hour, wheel rims gouging trenches into the dirt.

Three hundred feet later, the undercarriage broke loose and the plane smashed along on its belly.

It spun to the left, both port-side engines dragging into the dirt, and fire broke out in the left wing while the pilot tried to aim for the place between the concrete structure housing the landing lights and a stone cottage. There was no way he could do it.

The plane slammed across an access road, the landing gear beneath the right wing collapsed, number two engine broke loose and hurtled along the ground, the plane smashed into the landing lights, then into a hollow and began to disintegrate.

By then, only the fuselage remained intact, skidding down the steep slope toward the Seine, but didn't make it. It slammed into the stone cottage and exploded in a fireball.

This is the official account, but I have heard another version. 707's were new aircraft, then. For that matter, passenger jets of any sort were new, experience at the controls of propeller planes didn't count for much, pilots of all stripes had to recertify, and five Air France pilots had serious trouble qualifying. The one who commanded the Chateau de Sully that morning was one of the five.

I have also heard that he'd been heavy into the red wine. Not the night before, so he was flying hung-over, but that morning, so he was flying drunk, and when he came to the mile point and pulled back on the control column, he forgot to put the flaps into takeoff position.

Not much doubt about the flaps, there are photos to show it.

And when he neared the end of the runway and the plane wasn't lifting, he forgot he was on a 707 and the four big Pratt & Whitney engines were powerful enough to muscle the plane into the air no matter what position the flaps were in, panicked, and tried to pancake back down instead. And shot off the end of the runway and broke to pieces and went up in a fireball.

Whichever way it really happened or, more likely, some other way, it must have been an awfully long couple of minutes for the people on board.

The stretch of Seine at the end of the runway didn't count as the sea, and Mother never quite reached it, but what happened certainly counted as crashing, and it was on the way home from a lovely trip. And a lot of fire was involved, so, I suppose, at least part of the Viking's funeral romance came true.

A hundred and thirty people died at Orly, and for a while, it was the *Guinness Book of World Records*' all-time biggest single air disaster. There was another crash shortly afterwards that killed 129 people and I remember rooting for the survivors to pull through. Not out of any sense of fellow-feeling, but because I wanted Mother's crash to be the biggest and the worst and not shoved aside by some new air disaster.

You would think that when something like that happened you wouldn't have to wait to hear about it. You'd just know. But none of us did, not that beautiful spring morning in Atlanta. My only premonition came hours later when I returned from dropping Marti at the pool.

The sky was a warm blue, broken with puffs of clouds, and she and I rode with the top down in Mother's little Fiat roadster. The floppy straw hat was in the well behind the seats.

Being Sunday, there wasn't much traffic, and I'd spun into the lot at the club, dropped off Marti, and headed home—the whole glorious summer stretching out in front of me. When I pulled into the driveway, Dr. Garrett was waiting.

I could tell something was wrong, and I knew Mother was supposed to be in the air, so what I remember is a premonition of disaster when I saw him. "Something terrible has happened," he said. She hadn't just been my mother, she'd been his daughter, too.

The image of that courageous, dignified old man standing in the driveway, waiting to give me the news, is one of the strongest memories I have of that day. Of all the people who could have told me, he was the one who took it upon himself to do it.

I didn't have the same courage when I turned around and drove back to pick up Marti. I just hustled her out of the pool and sped her home. That's another memory I have of that day, a ten-year-old girl wanting to know what was going on, why was she being dragged away, and me not being able to tell her.

That stuck, that inability to talk about what happened. And it wasn't just me, it was the whole city, everybody we knew, trying to keep on going as if nothing much had taken place. Dad was so stifled he couldn't bear to make the arrangements to have Mother brought home. Then he couldn't bring himself to tell us where she was buried, so it was our cousin Edward who, forty years later, finally discovered her in a little graveyard in Paris. I think she'd like to be there.

Somebody who didn't have any choice but to talk about the crash was the Air France representative at the Atlanta airport. I never spoke to her and I never met her, but she was French, I know that much. I always imagined her as young and thrilled to be working in such an exotic place as Atlanta. What I do know is that she spent the day answering calls from frantic relatives, then searching through passenger lists, to have to say, "I am sorry, I am so sorry. She was on the flight. I'm so sorry."

She had to say it to Dad.

And to hundreds of other parents and children of passengers.

She had to say it to Dixon Rawlins.

And to Munford Black.

She had to say it to Dave Dillard, and to all the other newly widowed husbands who would never have the chance to be too close to their own damn wives again.

Somebody who got to deliver good news was Malcolm X.

"I have good news," he crowed before his god and assembled brethren of the Nation of Islam when he got wind of what had happened. Allah had done a mighty thing. He had "struck down a planeload of Crackers." And then went on to pray to his god to do the same with a planeload of white people every day from then on. Except I'm pretty sure he didn't use the words "white people" when he was supplicating his homemade god. I don't know for sure because I wasn't invited to attend services at the Nation of Islam. Then, again, neither were real Muslims. But it's pretty clear what his sentiments were.

Malcolm X—street hustler, two-bit ex-con, black supremacist, prophet of racial violence, leader in a cult that mocked Islam, pimp, racketeer, burglar, drug dealer, male prostitute, snappy dresser, and 4F army reject, who told his draft board he couldn't wait to "steal us some guns and kill us some Crackers"—didn't have to do any of the actual killing himself. By the time of the Orly crash, he'd found religion and let Allah do the Cracker-killing for him.

8

There Is No Low Point on a Descending Curve

A photo of Mayor Allen picking through the wreckage ran on the front page of every major newspaper in America, the charred tail section of a Boeing 707 looming behind him.

In the picture, blackened bits of jetliner are strewn for hundreds of yards along the bank of the Seine. Nothing is recognizable and nothing is much bigger than a twisted tray table or a smashed piece of carry-on luggage. At least you want to tell yourself it's tray tables and luggage and bits of jetliner, because you don't want to dwell on what Mayor Allen is really looking at. He'd known almost everybody on the plane, and he was there to identify the bodies.

Given how torn up the wreckage was, and the fact that the fire had burned for hours before the rescue crews had been able to get to the passengers, a lot of his friends were still on the banks of the Seine when he arrived. One was the first girl he ever dated.

The picture must have spoken to something in the strange half-person that was Andy Warhol because he traced it, then marketed the tracing as art. He called it *129 Die in Jet*, but his timing was off. If he'd waited a few days, the flight attendant who'd been thrown into the grassy field at almost a hundred miles an hour when the tail section broke off would have had time to die, too, and he could have made even more money. Surely *130 Die in Jet* would have fetched a higher price on the twisted New York art scene.

As it was, Andy Warhol did pretty well off the Orly crash and went on to make a name for himself with a whole line of disaster pictures. Before he finished, he'd cashed in on car accidents, suicides, a tuna-fish disaster, and the electric chair.

Weeks after the accident I received a postcard from Mother, mailed in Rome. I can't wait to get home, she said. I have the most astonishing thing to tell you.

Dad got mail from Italy too. From the proprietor of a furniture store. *Dear Signor Merritt, the letter started out. It is with great sadness that I learned of the accident in Paris and the loss of your beautiful wife. This is to inform you that while she was in my store, she purchased a number of items.*

Mother sure had. A huge dining table, sixteen chairs, sideboards, and cupboards she would never use.

I have held up shipment of these items pending your instructions. If you do not wish to receive them, please to inform me and I will cancel the order and return the payment to American Express.

For the next almost forty years until he died, Dad looked back on that letter as the single decent act to come out of the Orly crash.

A letter arrived for Marti too. This one was mailed in Georgia. It was from one of Mother's friends, telling Marti how much Mother had loved her. And how proud she had been of her. Marti slept with that letter under her pillow all summer.

Those of us who lost only mothers felt like frauds, as if we didn't have the right to be sad. Enough wives had managed to talk their husbands into going it wasn't just mothers, it was fathers, too, friends of ours entirely orphaned with us half-orphans feeling guilty for feeling bad. In some cases, entire households were erased in one terrifying moment at the end of the airstrip at Orly. Seven from a single family at our school. Mother. Father. All five children.

None of us kids handled it well, and the men who'd lost their wives handled it worse. Men who'd lived through war and the Depression, especially Southern men, weren't the sort to feel sorry for themselves. It was good manners, if nothing else, not to inflict your sorrows on other people. Other people had sorrows of their own. After Orly, other people sure did, and nobody talked about what happened.

Not for months.

Not for years.

Not for a generation. A silence fell over Atlanta that nobody broke, at least nobody who was close to the crash.

Two, maybe three years later, I was in the kitchen when the phone rang. One of Dad's army buddies was in town and wanted to get together. Could I let him and Mother know?

Even then, even after all that time, I couldn't so much as say what had happened. I had to give the phone to Mary, and I was amazed by the calm way she just said it. Mrs. Merritt passed away in the France crash, and that was that. It seemed so easy for somebody else to do.

Six weeks after mother burned alive, Allah did another mighty thing. My classmate, my friend, Jimmy Funk was snorkeling beneath a dock and got tangled in barbed wire. It must have been a pretty bad way to go, struggling to reach the air a few feet overhead while barbed wire tore into his flesh. Malcolm X would have been pleased. I found out about it at a party and went home and stared at the ceiling for a long time.

Jimmy was young and decent and, like the rest of us, just beginning to feel the power of his young manhood. What sticks with me most is his voice.

Christmas our junior year, he stood on stage alone, in front of the whole school, and, with no music to accompany him, sang "Good Christian Men Rejoice" in a voice deep and resonant. It was so beautiful and so heartfelt, and Jimmy seemed so vulnerable, so pure, and so open, he might as well have been naked in front of us. A half-century later, whenever I listen to "Good Christian Men Rejoice," it's not the trivial words I hear—*Giving heed to what we say: News! News! Jesus Christ is born today; Ox and ass before him bow; and he is in the manger now*—but Jimmy, filling the school with the promise of the man he was changing into.

I don't know whether he would have made a good Christian man. He might have chosen the path I took. But I'm pretty sure we all lost something the day he pulled on a mask and a snorkel and went to see for himself what lay beneath that dock.

Here's to you, Friend of my Youth. Still with me, after all these years.

࿐

"Get whatever looks good," Dad would tell us when we went shopping. "I don't want to hear there's nothing in the house to eat." And off my sisters and I would scatter, each with our own shopping cart while Dad filled his with necessaries from the list Mary supplied him.

A long time later, we'd form up at the checkout counter, three carts overloaded with factory-generated pretend-foods, with brightly colored cereal and desserts, with marshmallow cookies and candies no mother in the world, and our mother in particular, would have tolerated. It was like living in a sitcom with an out-of-touch father.

Looking back, I'm not sure how out-of-touch Dad was. He was good with kids, and he knew it made us feel special picking out trash food, as if there were an upside to not having a mother.

He used the same psychology on himself, I think. At least, no married man would ever have been allowed to experiment so freely with that *Cooking with Bourbon* cookbook.

"Dad, don't dump *booze* in the oatmeal," we'd all yell when we saw him heading for the stove with a bottle.

"Nonsense, my little chickadees," he would say as he emptied a cup or two of brown liquid into the pot. "Bourbon makes everything better," then jump back as a scalding cloud of alcohol steam hissed into his face. "Besides, you've got those glow-in-the-dark cupcakes if you don't like what I'm fixing."

That bourbon cookbook was nothing if not thorough, and Dad came up with bourbon baked beans, bourbon-braised brisket, bourbon coleslaw, and asparagus à la bourbon. He even spent a Saturday afternoon hand-cranking bourbon sherbet in the ice cream maker. That was one more thing none of the other kids we knew got to do, eat bourbon cookery. It made us feel special and grown-up and queasy, all at the same time.

࿐

Once Dad had things squared away at home, he disappeared into the world of work. Or at least that's where he said he disappeared into.

He hadn't been on the road since we moved back to Atlanta, but now his company was making him travel again. In fact, he travelled so much he decided to hire a governess. Not that I required governessing, at least I didn't think I did, but Anne and Marti needed looking after, so I got caught up in the governess net along with them. Unfortunately for the tranquility of the household, Dad's taste in governesses was as loopy as it turned out to be for women in general.

None of them were Mary Poppins. In fact, the first was more like Lucille Ball, if Lucy had been the Cuban in her marriage. And the whole Ricky Ricardo family had just been murdered by Che Guevara.

With a pistol.

To the head.

At point-blank range.

Comandante Guevara hadn't just been in charge of assuring revolutionary justice, he was a stone sadist who got his rocks off meting out the justice.

Personally. Her stories about what he did to her family have colored my opinion of psychopathic tyrannies ever since.

She was glamorous in a highly sexualized, push-up bra sort of way. And very high-strung, a tornado of energy and wrath, and accustomed to employing governesses of her own so that although she knew what governesses were supposed to do, in a theoretical sort of way, she really didn't have the instincts for the job. What she did have instincts for was flying to Washington. Dad spent a lot of time rescheduling business trips so he could be the governess while she was in DC pestering who-knows-whom to do things we were all better off not knowing what to you-know-who.

One morning when the Fiat started, I took a girl up to Etowah to see the Indian mounds. There weren't many other people in the little park that day, just a lady and her young daughter.

The six-story flight of log steps was as steep as I remembered, and as high from step to step, and Rachel and I were panting by the time we got to the top. It was sunny up there, and the trees around the park in full leaf, and we were alone so that when we stepped back from the edge, the lady and the girl couldn't see us from below. In the summer of 1963, privacy was hard for teenagers to come by, and we saw no reason to pass up the opportunity.

The lady poked her head over the rim just as Rachel was rebuttoning her shirt. Then smiled and turned and helped the girl up behind her. It seemed like a close call at the time, and over the years, I wondered how our lives would have changed if they'd arrived a few minutes sooner. It seemed like the kind of thing that could have gotten Rachel and me immortalized on a blotter at a police station.

Now, I think, not much would have happened. The lady wasn't the headmistress at Westminster. She wouldn't have cared what Rachel and I were doing, as long as her daughter didn't have to see it. Maybe that's why she was in the lead, so she could cover the little eyes following behind her if it turned out we were up to something.

Or that might be wrong. Could be the lady really did think of herself as some kind of moral exemplar and wanted to catch us with our pants down. There were lots of moral exemplars goose-stepping around Georgia at the time.

Or maybe it was the other way around. Grown-up lives meander down paths I didn't know anything about when I was seventeen. Maybe displays of public lewdness were what pulled her chain, and when Rachel and I disappeared over the top, she collected the little girl and headed our way hoping to see what she could see.

But I doubt she was trying to catch us. Most likely, she'd brought her daughter to Etowah the same way Mother brought me and wasn't hoping to discover anything on the top more stimulating than the view.

Whatever she wanted to find, or not to find, it's hard to imagine Rachel and I were the first. Privacy has always been a scarce resource where teenagers are concerned, and that mound had been there a thousand years.

It probably wasn't built with teenagers in mind, but who could tell? Nobody really knew what it was for. The people who ran the park were happiest thinking nothing went on up there, you could tell by the signs—DON'T DO THIS and NO DOING THAT—as if the human effort that went into piling up so much dirt hadn't been for humans. That seemed disrespectful to Rachel and me, and we did our part to keep alive a tradition we imagined had been hundreds of years old when our ancestors first arrived on this continent, that's the way we saw it. Like the stories I told myself about the Confederacy, the things that happened at Etowah weren't much more than what we made up in our own heads.

There was something else that morning. While Rachel's face was turned toward the clouds, mine was aimed at the grass. And in the grass next to her ear was a bit of bone with a couple of molars still in place. I showed it to Dr. Garrett.

"He was about fifty," the old dentist told me, and for a moment, my heart sank. Fifty years wasn't so long ago.

Then I realized that whomever the teeth belonged to had been fifty when he died. Which still didn't explain what they were doing there. I could think of plenty of reasons you might find bones at an Indian mound, but none of them seemed to fit.

If it were a burial mound, the teeth would have been safely underground where I wouldn't have noticed them.

If it had been a place for sacrificing virgins, or maybe unwary people from nearby villages, or just somewhere to offer up the bodies of the dead, there would have been more than that single bit of jaw, and the little museum at the bottom would have said something about it.

I couldn't imagine the Mound Builders ran short on material and were forced to use one of their own graveyards as a borrow pit. Dirt in North Georgia is not a scarce commodity.

I suppose the graveyard could already have been there when they moved to Etowah. But if that were the case, the teeth belonged to somebody even older. Somebody the Mound Builders didn't know any more about than the Cherokee knew about them. In Georgia, the land goes way back.

"We have a sick cow," my buddy Shelby Lewis told the lady at the pharmacy.

"A *very* sick cow," I said, in case she was the kind of pharmacist who was more inclined to believe two liars than just one.

Even with my endorsement, she seemed suspicious. Cattle hadn't lived in Buckhead since Reconstruction. But she sold us the saltpeter anyway. Saltpeter for a sick cow was the magic formula she needed to hear.

Cows were the legitimate use for the stuff, but there was another use, too. A use that every pharmacist, not to mention pyrotechnician, munitions expert, and Boy Scout, knew. Saltpeter was the key ingredient in gunpowder.

Sulfur would have been easy, too, if we hadn't had to buy it from the same pharmacist who sold us the saltpeter. Sick cow she could explain to the Georgia Bureau of Investigation if something went wrong involving the saltpeter she sold us. But sick-cow-plus-sulfur was going to take more explaining than she could manage. Luckily, there was another way. Shelby and I could use sugar.

The mixture wouldn't explode, at least we never could puzzle out how to make it explode, but the sparks were wonderful. Better than sparks, really. Billows and columns and roiling banks of smoke lit from inside by flaming globs of molten sugar. There's nothing like crude gunpowder to churn out romance.

Night was the time to showcase something like that, and we had a lot of night, the summer I was seventeen. When you're seventeen with the biorhythms of seventeen-year-olds, night is almost the only part of the day you ever see. Shelby would wait for the sun to set and his mother to drink herself into a stupor, then slip over to my place, and off we'd go, sometimes exploring Atlanta after dark. Sometimes staging Civil War reenactments featuring a lot of sparks and even more smoke.

My bedroom was an attached garage with an outside door, which was the perfect setup for boys with gunpowder. The only flaw in the ointment was the gravel in the driveway, possibly the noisiest gravel on the planet, which may have been on purpose. And the service .45 Dad brought home from the army. He kept it loaded and handy. Handy when he was out of town, too, it occurred to Shelby and me, for the Cuban fidgeting away the night in the master bedroom. A Cuban who was a lot more high-strung and a lot less trained in firearm safety than even the most manic Southern male.

But we managed without getting shot to death and would slip down to the street in front of the house where, even at two or three in the morning, cars were still barreling past. There were streetlights, but not many, and plenty of shadows. And the drains faced each other from opposite curbs so that if Shelby and I got the timing right, we could set a wall of smoke and flaming fountains of lava popping and spitting across Peachtree Battle Avenue from both sides at the same time.

It was fun for the drivers, too, and they would slam on their brakes and swerve and fishtail along the pavement, sometimes sideways, like Fireball Roberts busting around curves at the Daytona 500.

Shelby had his nights free, same as me. His mom had taken to the bottle, and to her bed, when his dad died and never climbed back out. That happened when he was in second grade. I don't think she went to pieces because her husband passed on, I think she was already in pieces, at least that's what I make from Shelby's dad's dying request.

"Swear you will take care of my children," he made the colored housekeeper swear. "Swear, Nursey, swear." And like somebody out of Hamlet, she did. Which probably saved the Lewis children from lives of crime.

Mrs. Lewis kept a phone beside her bed, and if this had been in the days of speed dialing, the liquor store's number would have been loaded into all ten slots to avoid confusion. Mornings when she was sober enough, she would call the liquor store, then call for Shelby.

He was much too young to buy liquor, and the store was much too under the thumb of the Alcohol and Tax Division of the Georgia Department of Revenue to let him, but Shelby had an interest in getting along with his mother, and the store had an interest in keeping its best customer oiled and happy. So Shelby was the one who came home with the vodka. His mother was under the impression that if she limited her drinking to vodka, nobody would smell it on her breath and discover she was drunk.

One day he came home with a motorcycle.

I never learned where he got it, but he rolled up to the house on a brand-new, used hog he'd bought on a trip to the liquor store, and since he wasn't licensed to drive a motorcycle, he had to keep it out of sight. Out of sight turned out to be in the bushes beneath his mother's window. It was a single-story house, and the bushes were a few feet from her pillow.

She didn't notice something was amiss until the afternoon she was awakened by a thunderous roar and rolled over to see her boy speeding off on a Harley. It got her attention, and the next time she was sober enough to bring it up, she asked him, "Was that a motorcycle I saw you drive away on?"

That was the wrong way to phrase it, because Shelby just asked back, "Yeah. And did you see the camel I came home with?" Mrs. Lewis chalked the whole thing up to the DTs and forgot about it.

One evening, much later than we should have been, Shelby and I were walking along Peachtree Street when an impossibly old man stumbled up to us. He was dressed in rags and stank of beer and could hardly keep to the sidewalk. "There were so many of us," he said. "Why am I the only one?" He'd been at Anzio. The fact is, he'd never left Anzio.

I think Shelby must have reminded him of somebody because he stumbled up and tried to put an arm around him. "Why me?" he muttered.

We just brushed by. He wasn't anybody we knew.

People who came home from war were heroes. They might drink, but it would be in private, and they never told the stories that this old man wanted to tell. The men we knew told stories that were raucous and funny and manly, and Shelby and I couldn't recognize anybody with something different to say.

I've thought about that man a lot since then, wishing I'd had it in me to say something. I don't know what it would have been, how I could have answered his question. Maybe I wouldn't have had to. Maybe all he wanted was for us to listen. But on a warm summer's night when we were seventeen, listening wasn't in our repertoire.

Nights when I was sure Rachel's parents were asleep, I'd tap on her window. Their bedroom was next to hers, but they never heard her drop to the ground.

I don't remember what her daddy had done during the war. Probably not a lot of guard duty, I was pretty sure from the way he never seem to notice what was going on. I do know he'd been a sergeant and, mostly, sergeants don't carry side arms. At least, I was pretty sure they didn't get to carry them home when the war was over.

Nights with Rachel were clear and moonlit and humid, and instead of being lit by sparks of molten sugar, were filled with lightning bugs—so bright and so many, they illuminated whole trees, entire landscapes. Sometimes she and I would slip down to Bobby Jones Golf Course and fool around on one of the greens while the trees along Peachtree Creek flickered with fairy light.

There had been a time when the dark along there was broken by something a lot less romantic than lightning bugs, a time when good Southern boys died defending the scrap of land Rachel and I used as our couch, but I never thought about that when I was with her. Not that summer. Not at night.

Nights that summer, our childhood was falling away, and we were poised on the edge of a future neither of us could quite see.

Fall came, and my sisters and I couldn't get to school because the mothers who drove our carpool had burned up.

To Dad, the Fiat looked less like a way of getting us there than a ready-made excuse for not going. The only solution, other than driving us himself, was to buy us a car.

Dad had an eye for cars and knew Rambler was a good place to look if you wanted one for your teenaged children. With the American, he hit the jackpot. No matter how bad the company I fell into, no gang of drunken yahoos was ever going to pile into a Rambler American and lurch off in search of girls. And nobody, ever, in the history of the world, had tried to drag race one of the things, so he was covered when I went out alone, too. But still, wheels? I would have settled for a Citroen.

No dog comes without fleas, though. My sisters weren't old enough to drive, and the price I paid for the car was ferrying them places I wouldn't have gone on my own. Which wasn't much of a problem where Anne was concerned. For Anne, there was always a boy more fetching than me who was eager to fetch her to one hairdresser or another, then wait outside while she got frosted and snipped.

Marti didn't care about getting snipped or frosted. Marti's hair was long and straight, and all she needed was to brush out the seeds and bits of hay from time to time. Marti's love interest was a lot more focused than Anne's. Marti was into horses. Since horses hadn't lived in Buckhead much more recently than cows, I spent a lot of afternoons driving to faraway places, then waiting for her to toss her barn-covered boots in back and plop exhausted onto the seat next to me.

The whole thing was fun. I was seventeen with a new car and a driver's license and just itching for an excuse to use them. Picking up Marti introduced me to a world I'd never seen, and Marti was a good, if tired, companion.

I never discovered what Dad was doing in Shelby's mom's bedroom. Not what you're thinking, I think. From the way Dad told it, sex wasn't on his mind when he dropped by. But it sure seems to have been on hers.

Now that Atlanta was awash in men whose situation had suddenly become unmoored, every constitutionally unmoored woman began daubing on makeup and doing her nails and perfuming her cleavage in case one drifted within range of her portion of the woodwork. So, whatever reason Dad may have had for being in Shelby's mother's bedroom, Mrs. Lewis was prepared. Odds were, it was going to be a long time before another successful, unmoored man passed that way.

However needy Dad may have been, he wasn't that needy, and when Mrs. Lewis made her move, he started backpedaling toward the hallway.

"Where you goin', Big Fellow?" she asked.

Out of here and far away, Dad wanted to say. *Out of here and far, FAR away.* But he was too much of a gentleman and much too Southern to say something like that, so what he said was, "Out," the same way Anne said, "Out" when she was headed for a liaison she wasn't supposed to be headed for.

"Out?" Mrs. Lewis knew the drill. She had four children.

"Dinner. I have to eat dinner."

"We can eat here," Mrs. Lewis patted her bed. "I'll have Nursey fix something. She can bring it in here and we can..."

"A long-standing commitment. I have to go to..." Here Dad stalled, not knowing where he had to go to. Only that he really, really had to go there.

"Somebody already invite you to dinner?"

"Susan," Dad groped for a name. *That's it.* "Susan. Susan invited..."

"Susan?" Mrs. Lewis thought she knew all the unmoored ladies in town.

"Ison," Dad said. "Susan Ison." *That's it.* "Susan Ison." Aunt Suzy was my mother's sister.

"Well, if it's just family, why don't I come along?" Mrs. Lewis rolled out of bed and stumbled toward the closet. "I'll grab somethin' to put on and the two of us can head over to Susan Ison's and..."

"Formal," Dad said. "It's a formal dinner."

"I've got formal." Mrs. Lewis wobbled a bit as she tossed seriously out-of-style formal wear onto a settee. "I'll just slip into..."

"Formal seating," Dad said. *Yes. That's it.* "Formal seating. Man...woman...man...woman. Can't just toss in another woman...these things take planning."

"Well, give Susan a call so she can get to plannin'," Mrs. Lewis steadied herself against the closet door, then lurched for Dad.

"Don't know the number," Dad said. *That's it*. "I don't know Susan's number."

"I'll look it up," Mrs. Lewis turned and headed toward the phonebook.

If Dad had realized there was a Harley in the bushes, he would have taken it. Instead, he broke several traffic laws, and probably some stock-car speed records involving Oldsmobiles, getting home in time to call Aunt Suzy before Shelby's mother could locate her number.

Life in these United States would have been a lot less exciting if he'd handed his gun to the Cuban and let her do something about Comandante Guevara before things got out of hand.

Che had been a busy boy. He'd found time in his crowded schedule of murdering his countrymen for sport to dabble in international affairs. In October, it came to light he'd arranged for the Russians to station ballistic missiles in Cuba. Which put atom bombs a lot closer to Atlanta than when they'd been in, say, Poland. Close enough, in fact, to drop a megaton or so just south of where we lived. That's what the maps in the papers showed, concentric circles centered in northern Cuba, setting out the range of each kind of missile they had down there.

For people in Atlanta, those circles came as a relief. When the missiles flew, Miami and Jacksonville and Savannah would be radioactive toast. We could write off New Orleans and Mobile. Even Newnan and Peachtree City just south of town, if there was mega-tonnage to spare on not-very-important places. But Atlanta, especially the north side of Atlanta where I lived, was out of reach. What we had to worry about were waves of burned, injured, starving refugees. If we were going to get through this in one piece, it seemed like a good idea to lay in extra blankets and food. And maybe a Geiger counter or two, in case the refugees turned out to be dangerously radioactive.

Nowadays, I think whoever drew those maps was trying to keep us calm. Or maybe somebody in Washington, because those missiles had enough range to take out Denver. Atlanta wouldn't even have required a full load of fuel.

I never found out what papers in other places said about the missiles. Maybe the *Times-Picayune* showed them petering out just short of Port Sulfur down at the entrance to the Mississippi and the *Miami Herald* had them falling harmlessly into the sea somewhere around Key Largo. Too bad for the folks in Key West, but that's what the Overseas Highway is for. Burned, injured refugees? Send them on up. It's October. We've got plenty of vacancies on Miami Beach.

The reason we aren't all glowing like radioactive gnomes in Rock City is because the corrupt Georgia political system saved us. And, most likely, the rest of the world. Carl Vinson, who'd been elected to the House of Representatives by Confederate veterans during the Roosevelt Administration—the Teddy Roosevelt administration—had been in Washington so long he'd already sent Americans to World War I, World War II, Korea, and just recently had authorized advisors to South Vietnam. When the other members of the Armed Services Committee split seven to seven on whether we should invade Cuba, even he, even unreconstructed old Southern hawk Carl Vinson, had finally had enough.

I would have voted against it, but the day came when the Cuban had to go. Or maybe she just flew to Washington and never came back. Either way, Dad had learned his lesson. No more glamorous Latinas for us. This time he showed up with a dumpy old lady who'd made her bones as housemother for a fraternity at Georgia Tech. I never found out why the fraternity let her go, but I think it had something to do with the fact she was a lunatic.

She wasn't the sort of lunatic to put her craziness on display for a prospective employer, she was a lunatic with common sense. Unlike the Cuban, who was basically a sane woman with no common sense at all.

Mrs. Tighe's lunacy expressed itself as a suspicion, some would say clinical psychosis, about the motives and activities of young men. So maybe she wasn't really as loony as she seemed. From what I hear goes on in frat houses at Tech, her fears may have been grounded in hard, unfortunate experience. I first got an inkling of what was in store the morning she announced over breakfast that I was the one who was rubbing the stick on her window.

Rubbing a stick against the window of a sleeping old lady, that's something that would never have occurred to me if she hadn't pointed out the possibility. Besides, it would have taken an awfully long stick. Her bedroom was on the second story, and our house had high stories.

After being accused of the same thing three or four mornings in a row, I conducted a forensic investigation and discovered an ornamental vine running up the side of the house and across her window. Nights could be windy, and it wasn't me who did the scratching. The vine did it.

And the vine kept on doing it, at least when the wind was up.

And when the wind was down, too. From then on, whenever I was out and about at, say, four in the morning, which was considerable, I would give that vine a tug. It made nighttime more cheerful.

Looking back, it may be that the frat boys at Tech drove Mrs. Tighe around the bend, but I have my doubts. I think the fact that she was already speeding into the curve may have encouraged them to give her an extra shove.

Another thing she worried about was salt, which turned meals pretty bland, especially after the fiery cooking the Cuban had ordered up. I don't know whether it was my idea or Marti's, but getting rid of Mrs. Tighe involved one of those round, blue containers with a little girl on the side carrying an umbrella. And hanging around the stewpot when Mrs. Tighe came into the kitchen.

And jumping back and acting sheepish, as if a cup or two of salt had just spilled into the stew.

The fun part was that we got to be righteous and tell the truth about it. We didn't put salt in the stew. We would never put salt in the stew. We care way too much about your health to go putting salt in the stew. You may think you saw us with salt, but don't make anything of it.

The more Marti and I tried to reassure her, the more she...well, let's just say the taxi arrived before dessert. We were rotten kids.

One day, Anne got into some mischief at school and the principal, not knowing Dad had been out of town for weeks on important agriculture-chemical matters, called his office.

And he answered.

Dad came home that night looking guilty and explained that he'd flown back unexpectedly that morning and driven straight to work. It seemed like an odd thing to do since he traveled by Oldsmobile, but I didn't question him on it. I was just glad I wasn't the reason the principal called and began pretending to study Spanish in case what was about to happen to Anne lapped over.

Years later, Marti discovered that when Dad was off on a trip taking care of business, he went into the office every day, just like when he was in town. He didn't come home at night because the business he was taking care of was in downtown Atlanta. Somehow, he'd hooked up with a brothel that took lodgers. Who knew there even was such a place?

I don't know what my sisters would have made of it, but Dad didn't need to keep a secret like that from me. I didn't get to see as much of him as I wanted, and I would have cherished a little quality time together, especially if it involved a brothel. It's a pity to look back from old age and regret missed opportunities like that.

Fall turned to winter and winter to early spring. Eventually, Dad gave up the whole governess thing as a bad idea, dismissed whatever woman was currently nursing private grievances in the master bedroom, and began looking for love from home. Or maybe he just ran out of money. In any event, the company stopped sending him away on business trips, and he began to bring unattached ladies of Good Social Standing right into the house. We would all have been better off if he'd stuck with whores.

Of good social standing they may have been, but of good mental health was an entirely different question. Regardless of the down-to-earth common sense Dad showed with Shelby's mother, there was something about unbalanced women that set his blood to pounding.

If a woman was mildly nuts, Dad would be mildly interested.

If she had some kind of flamboyant personality disorder, he'd have her out to dinner and introduce her to family and friends.

If she was major, screaming, carpet-chewing, out-of-her-mind deranged, he'd have her in bed, if she would go. Dad liked her even better when she wouldn't.

If she was...well, it wasn't long before he wound up engaged to the lady behind the wall on West Paces Ferry, the one who hadn't been seen since the trial when her son murdered her daughter. How Dad got across that wall has never been revealed, but once firmly on the other side, he presented the proprietress with a diamond ring.

The son was still there, and he still had a thing about sisters. Nobody, including our soon-to-be stepmother, ever wanted him to come within shooting distance of another one. And now Dad was planning to turn Anne into one. And so that the son could have some choice in the matter, Marti, too. In fact, the sister he'd offed a few years earlier had been the same age as Marti. And looked like her, too. And had been into horses, which was what triggered the shooting.

Noon one Saturday, Rachel's parents were out for the day, and she and I became foolishly optimistic about what we could get away with. We were in their bed when their car pulled back into the driveway. Her dad had taken ill and they'd come home so he could lie down.

I grabbed my underwear, Rachel kicked the rest of our clothes under the bed, and we were out of there. She to her room to find something to wear, me to the backyard because I didn't have anywhere else to go.

It was March or early April, barely far enough into spring to allow me to say, "Oh, just sunbathing," when, an hour or so later, Rachel's mom poked her head out the door.

"Don't you bother your dad," her mom would yell every time Rachel tried to creep into their bedroom to retrieve my clothes. I think her mom had fun with that, and that-idiot-goy-who-hangs-around-my-daughter became the topic du jour down at the Jewish Community Center. We didn't pay attention to other people's religion at my house, and I hadn't noticed Rachel was Jewish when I first asked her out. With only one-

and-a-half girl Jews at Westminster, the odds of hitting one right out of the box weren't that high.

April dwindled into May. I graduated and summer came.

Summer is the rainy season in Atlanta. The afternoons are hot and very humid. Violent thunderstorms roll in, the day turns black, trees bend in the wind, thunder crashes, windows rattle, rain pelts down so hard you feel like you could drown just trying to breathe, and water runs in great rivers along the streets.

A few minutes later the wind dies off, the storm blows past, the sun comes out, and geysers of muddy water well up from the overloaded storm sewers, turning iron manhole covers into boogie-boards floating an inch or two above the openings for teenagers to hover and twirl upon.

But that summer was different. The rains didn't come and the land dried out. Yards turned yellow and scraggly. The dirt on the little hill leading up to our house became hard and the grass thin. But the patch down near the street was lusher than ever. A deep, soft green. A reproach to the neighbors and a flourishing advertisement for the fertilizer chemicals Dad knew how to wield better than anybody else. Even the soil seemed soft and pliable down there.

Then one morning we woke to find the grass, and the soil beneath it, gone. The beautiful, deep-green lawn, the grass that was soft and green no matter how dry the year or how dead and yellow everybody else's yards had turned, had been swallowed by a huge crater that looked as if a badly aimed Cuban missile had overshot Peachtree City and misfired into our yard, a crater that extended almost to the neighbors' property. And it stank. At the bottom, a dozen feet down, was a foul pool of untreated wastewater.

When you leaned over the edge, you could make out busted tiles from an ancient terracotta sewer pipe. The fertilizer that had made our lawn prosper all those years hadn't come from Dad at all, but from leaking sewage that was hollowing out our yard. The whole thing seemed very metaphorical of something or other.

One midsummer night a couple of months before we headed to college, Shelby and I came to the end of the road of our fascination with homemade pyrotechnics. Or, rather, we came to the end and smashed through the barrier at about a hundred miles an hour and flew through the air and exploded in a ditch.

We'd slipped a wad of unmarked bills to our connection at the pharmacy and come away with an industrial-size jar of saltpeter. Then we'd swiped five pounds of sugar from the pantry, and when night came, slipped into the kitchen and recruited Mother's largest mixing bowl. We were preparing the greatest Civil War reenactment anybody ever heard of. The Battle of Peachtree Battle Avenue right out in front of our house. There was going to be so much flame and smoke even Billy Sherman and his bummers would lose heart and flee back North, where they belonged.

The mixing bowl didn't turn out to be big enough. The mound of sugar and saltpeter heaped up past the rim into a cone like a dunce's cap, which, when I think back on it, might have been a hint of some sort, if Shelby and I had been a little more open to hints.

We stirred the sugar and saltpeter around in the bowl, trying to eyeball whether the white sugar crystals had mixed with the white crystals of saltpeter. We didn't want anything to go awry while we were exorcising Sherman and entertaining late-night motorists.

There was no way to know without testing, so I ladled out a teaspoonful, stepped to the far side of my bedroom, struck a match, and...well, for gunpowder that was notorious for burning unevenly, this set a new standard. It poured out more smoke and spit sparks further than any batch we'd ever touched off before.

A single spark, that's all it took, one spark fizzed across the room and landed on top of the dunce's cap. On the very point of the dunce's cap. It was a shot I couldn't have duplicated in a hundred years. NASA couldn't have done it. But there, at three in the morning on a warm Atlanta night, I did it. I landed that spark exactly on top of about ten pounds of very crude gunpowder.

For what seemed like a long time, not much happened. The gunpowder didn't explode. It didn't even go up in a flash. Instead, the spark just settled in among the sugar and saltpeter, and the top of the cone began to glow. Nothing very alarming at first. At first, there wasn't much more to it than there was to the point of a pencil, if the point of a pencil were spitting flaming lava.

But it was a point that was burning down, and each quarter second, the point got blunter and the number of sparks increased in a geometric sort of way.

Which set off secondary fireworks along the sides of the cone.

Which began smoking and shooting more sparks and setting off...well, you get the picture.

Smoke and flames and burning globs shot out faster and faster until they turned into a three-foot-thick column of sparks and molten sugar I remember in the same part of my brain where I keep the images from the afternoon I stood in downtown Portland, Oregon, watching Mount St. Helens blow.

And mushroomed along the ceiling to the walls and down, dropping burning globs of sugar onto the yellow shag of the carpet while Shelby and I tumbled into the driveway.

When the glowing and roiling died down or, more likely, when the smoke became too thick to see what was going on, we crept back inside to straighten things out before anybody in authority noticed something unusual had happened. I blame what occurred next on out-of-date construction practices.

A modern house would have been more tightly put together, and one wouldn't expect smoke from an attached garage to make its way through a closed door and upstairs and into his sister's room. No, one wouldn't expect that, and Shelby and I were throwing open windows, stomping fires that sprang from the shag, getting molten sugar stuck to our shoes, and leaving more fires, fires shaped like footprints, as we raced around pulling down burning curtains and tossing flaming bedding into the driveway when the smoke alarm went off.

Technically speaking, we didn't have a smoke alarm. But Anne was upstairs and neither she, nor her companion du jour, had been sleeping, and when the light on her princess-set bedside table suddenly went dull from all the smoke, she smelled a rat.

Also, she smelled burning sugar and saltpeter and curtains and shag and bedding and ceiling and wood paneling and shoes, and, well, to hell with what anybody might think about the company she was keeping, began to scream.

Shelby and I didn't hear the screams, we were too busy trying to get the fires out, and do something about the flaming sugar dripping from the ceiling, and air out the room.

Dad did hear the screams and did what any responsible Southern father would do in the middle of the night when a commotion breaks out in his daughter's bedroom. He grabbed his service .45 and lit out down the hall to see about the situation.

I don't imagine anybody got a good look at anybody else, what with the visibility, but nobody needed to see much to know what was going to happen when Dad busted into Anne's room carrying a gun. Especially, Jasper Ruggles.

The first Shelby and I knew something was up, in the upstairs department, was when we heard Jasper's voice. "Ooooh nooooo, Mr. Merritt, don't shoot," then a very hasty and clumsy bump at the bottom of the drainpipe that emptied into the bushes next to the garage. Jasper was so lively in his departure, and from such an old Atlanta family, I naturally began to wonder if his ancestors hadn't had something to do with the stand of rifles that were abandoned in the yard behind ours.

The next morning, his pants and car keys and shoes were still in Anne's room. Jasper didn't live close by, and imagining what he had to go through to get home before the sun came up made me appreciate Rachel's mother and her worldly ways.

Marti was at summer camp when she got the letter telling her she wouldn't be coming home to the house we lived in. This didn't have anything to do with the fact the house had almost burned down. It was because we'd all be living behind the big wall on West Paces Ferry by then.

Dad had jumped the gun with the letter because when he picked up Marti from the bus, he drove her to our place. It turned out there was a little matter that needed to be attended to before the move could take place. The lady-behind-the-wall had to interview her.

On paper, Marti was a good fit and could take up right where the little dead girl left off. Marti could have all her stuff, the lady said. Why, she could even move into her room. The only problem was the boots. Marti hadn't worn boots to the interview, but it didn't make any difference. The lady could imagine Marti wearing boots, and that was enough.

Her son had a thing for girls in boots, and not in a good way. His sister was wearing boots the day he shot her. Finding himself suddenly confronted with a sister in boots, the son pulled the trigger. In the circumstances, what else could he have done?

Or so the lady explained a few days later, when she called Dad from behind the wall and broke the engagement. "I just don't know what would happen if Marti ever came home with boots on. I just don't know." Although, looking back, I'm pretty sure she had an idea.

Toward the end of the summer, Shelby and I took the bus to Acapulco.

Given my track record in the responsibility department, I'm not sure why Dad let me go. Maybe he thought that in the interest of fire safety, we'd all be better off if I spent my last few weeks before college somewhere other than at home. Maybe it wasn't me he was worried about. It could have had something to do with discovering that Shelby spent a lot of time at our house at night—the same house Anne was holding court in.

Shelby was an attractive boy, and if there was one thing Dad did not want, it was being put into the position of having to deal with Shelby's mother. Especially over something like a mutual grandkid. He knew that if I headed off to Mexico, Shelby would go with me. As for Shelby's mother, I'm not sure she ever fully realized he was out of town.

We took the Greyhound. Rode the Dog, as the experienced passengers put it. A lot of them seemed to be old hands at this Dog business, eating out of sacks they'd carried onto the bus. Drinking out of sacks, too. It was a long trip.

We headed down through Newnan and Columbus, then to Apalachicola and along the Gulf Coast, crossed beneath the Tombigbee at Mobile, and on to New Orleans. We sped through the humid, chemical-rich air of Houston, and on the third morning, the Dog came to the end of its leash in Laredo. Shelby and I grabbed our gear and walked across the Rio Grande into Mexico.

From there, it was Autobus del Norte past the rocks and sagebrush of the Chihuahuan Desert, barren and scorching hot. This wasn't one of your modern, air-conditioned imitation jetliners with television sets and stewardesses serving drinks that you ride on during long-distance trips in Mexico now. It was a rattly old rust-bucket of a bus overcrowded with people and livestock and bundles of consumer goods lugged over the same footbridge Shelby and I crossed from Laredo, with nowhere to sit because it hadn't occurred to us there wouldn't be enough seats, and we'd stepped back politely and invited the ladies to climb on ahead of us. A lot of those ladies had small children and a lot more were pregnant.

If this had been a bus in America, we would have stood in the aisle for a long time. But on the Autobus del Norte, we weren't more than an hour into the trip when a pregnant lady on the rear seat, the one that runs across the back of the bus like a sofa, a pregnant lady with a couple of small children, offered us her place. And her children's places, too.

All we had to do was hold the bundles of clothes and whatnots she'd purchased in America. The whole thing seemed odd enough, at least to boys raised in the South, and our Spanish was shaky enough we had trouble parsing what she had in mind. "You mean, you just want us to hold these bags?"

"*Si*, *Señores*. Yes. Yes. Sit right here. Here are the bags, you can put them in your laps. *Aquí*. Sit."

By then, the bus was beginning to slow down, and passengers standing next to us were shifting to keep their balance.

"Right here, *Señores*. If you will please..."

The bus swayed and came to a stop, and Shelby and I had to lurch across crates of chickens to keep from being thrown to the floor. Outside was nothing but scorch and sagebrush and burning rocks and a couple of police cars.

"*Señores, por favor.*" The lady scooped up one of her children and thrust it at Shelby. Then stood and tried to shove me into her seat. Up front, the door opened and a couple of men in uniform got on and had a word with the driver. They were the Mexican Federal Police.

This must have been the lady's stop. "*Vamanos, chicos,*" she said to the children, took back the one from Shelby, and began to make her way to the front of the bus.

It was slow going. She was too pregnant and there were too many crates of chickens and too many people, and she had the children to worry about. Also, she had forgotten her bags. "*Aquí,* Ma'am," Shelby and I both called to the retreating woman as she made her way past the first of the Federales, "You forgot your bags." It was noisy in the bus and she must not have heard. Instead, she kept shoving toward the front. But she couldn't get off. A third Federale was blocking the way.

"These bags belong to that woman?" the Federales who'd worked their way down to our end wanted to know.

"Yes, Sir," I said. "This was her seat right here and she got up and forgot to take her..."

"*Aquí?*" the Federale pointed to the empty place where the woman and her chicos had been sitting.

"Yes, Sir. I mean *sí,* Sir. She was sitting right..." By then there was enough room for a dozen people back there, the other passengers had squeezed so far to the sides.

The Federales explored around the seat, and beneath, and came up with a couple of more bags the lady forgot, then they took her by the elbow and all four, and the children, climbed down and into one of the cars and sped away. Shelby and I finally sat down.

The country didn't get better. Just two-lane blacktop and sun and sage and blazing-hot rocks. Every fifty miles or so, we'd pass through a village as dry and dusty as the land, and more passengers would get off. We didn't see a lot of traffic, just the burned-out frames of wrecked cars on the sides of the road. I wondered what would happen if the bus broke down.

And then it did break down. The transmission made a loud clunk followed by the sounds of parts dropping onto asphalt.

The bus lurched, the driver down-shifted, and we limped along in second for an hour or so until we came to a small dusty town. The driver pulled over, the door sighed opened, and everybody climbed off.

We were going to be here a while. There weren't any other buses to take us deeper into Mexico and the only thing we could do was wait.

And drink Coca-Colas.

A beat-up red cooler stood in the shade of a cantina—*the* cantina—and we all bought one.

Coca-Cola. Hands of friendship between people the world over. A gift from Atlanta to folks everywhere. Common ground between Shelby and me and a busload of Mexicans.

"*Mi puebla*," I tried to explain in my shaky Spanish. "*Coca-Cola venga...*"

"Oh no, *Señor*," an ancient gentleman in a cowboy hat tried to explain back. "This is his village." He gestured to a man in a serape lounging beside the red cooler.

"*Mi puebla...*" I tried again. "*...es dónde esta Coca-Cola...*"

"There, *Señor*," the gentleman in the cowboy hat gestured at the cooler. "There are many more Coca's in the..."

"No," I gestured back. "*Mi Puebla. Coca-Cola es de mi...*"

"No, *Señor*. This is *his* village." By then the man's smile had frozen to his face and he was backing away.

The other passengers were smiling and backing away, too, as if a gang of Federales Shelby and I hadn't noticed was about to start checking around for illegal shopping bags.

"Maybe," Shelby suggested, "this would be a good time to find out where we are." So we grabbed our map and our packs and started walking toward the head of the village, looking for a sign with a name on it. It wasn't a long walk.

"Alto," Shelby said when we got a look at the only sign leading into the village. "We are in the little town of Alto."

Try as we might, we couldn't find Alto on the map, though. We knew Alto was small but we couldn't see why they'd left it off. There wasn't anything else out here to put on a map. Surely if you were dying of thirst in the Chihuahuan desert, you might want to know where to find a cooler of Cokes. Odd they would leave it off. At the time, we chalked it up to lackadaisical cartography.

They can fix buses in Alto, which is something else you might want to know if you ever find yourself rattling along that particular stretch of two-lane blacktop in a disintegrating bus. It took them seventeen hours, and Shelby and I spent the night rolled out in the desert at the edge of town, but by the middle of the next morning, we were on the road again and on our way to Mexico City.

There's a park outside Mexico City called Chapultapec after the Aztec word for grasshopper. It's at the foot of a citadel on top of basalt cliffs, and it's hard not to think of grasshoppers when you go there. Grasshoppers jump off things.

In the summer of 1847 there had been a good deal of jumping off going on up there. Mexico City had been invaded by foreign soldiers, the remnants of Mexican resistance was backed up into the Citadel, and cadets from a military academy, gallant fourteen- and fifteen-year-olds, fought to their deaths or jumped rather than live to see their country surrender to the enemy below.

It was hard to look at the statues of those boys and not think of other boys, of cadets from the Citadel and the Virginia Military Institute, called up to defend their homes, and what they believed to be their nation, against some of those same soldiers. To the people strolling through the park, to the girls walking with their arms linked together as Mexican girls do, to the families with picnics spread out on the grass, Shelby and I would have been the ones in blue uniforms.

They would have been right. Robert E. Lee was at the foot of the Citadel when the last of the cadets wrapped himself in the Mexican flag and jumped to his death. He was an officer in the United States army, then. As were President Davis and T. E. Jackson and Joe Johnston and George Pickett and half of the others who would turn into Confederate generals and give their old comrades such fits fifteen years later.

South of Mexico City was mountains, and the driving was slow. A few hours before Acapulco, the highway fell away through misty switchbacks with cliffs so steep and the valley below so swallowed in cloud it looked as if there were no valley down there at all, as if we were driving along the edge of the world.

The road dropped into the fog and became slick with moisture and doubled and redoubled back on itself in sharp hairpins. The driver didn't give it much respect, squealing around the turns while cars hot-footed behind us, dancing to the outside and back, looking for their chance to pass, then roared by at what must have been a hundred miles an hour.

When we broke out of the bottom of the fog, the valley was covered with beautiful trees and dripping ferns and the darting colors of tropical birds wheeling and soaring through patches of sunlit jungle. I think that's what I remember most about our time in Mexico, those beautiful trees.

When Shelby and I returned to Atlanta, staggering from too many hours folded into uncomfortable seats and hallucinating from too many bus-station peanut-butter crackers, it was to the news that Dr. Garrett had had a stroke. I went down to Grady to see him.

It hadn't been a large stroke, just enough to put him in the hospital. By the time he was ready to come home, he was hit by a second stroke, also small. And then another and another, chipping away at him, keeping him in the hospital for what would turn into half a decade, scattering the wealth he'd worked fifty years to accumulate, making it impossible to provide for his widow, using up his life. In the end, squandering his manhood, plundering his dignity, and leaving nothing for him.

9

Doctrinal Differences

Back in the twenties, tobacco zillionaire James B. Duke paved his way into heaven by bequeathing scads of money to Trinity College in Durham, North Carolina, on the understanding that, one, it would change its name to Duke and, two, churn out generations of Methodists armored in faith against an increasingly secular world. He also decreed that the young-lady students be sequestered two miles away, behind a nine-foot stone wall.

The wall got built, but it was only three feet high, and we used it as a place to sit when we needed somewhere to make out. Urban legend had it that Mr. Duke's executors didn't want any legal challenges, so they built the wall as specified. Only they put it in a six-foot trench.

By the time I showed up, Methodism had pretty much gone the way of the wall, supplanted by more stylish cults. Freud. Marx. Jung. Whatever critical theory was du jour in the English department. One thing everybody was ecumenical about was Coca-Cola. Coca-Cola was evil. And not just your namby-pamby, ax-murderer, serial-killer sort of evil, but deeply, profoundly, genocidally evil. It wasn't war or corruption or thieving governments that was destroying the indigenous peoples of the world. It was Coca-Cola. Coca-Colanization, they called it. Something else they all agreed on was that white people were racists.

I'm not sure what Freud or Marx had to say about racism, but if there was anything besides Coca-Cola those two were united in, it was that America in general, and the South in particular, had been built upon a foundation of racism. And that I, and everybody I knew and loved, was guilty. In fact, if it wasn't for people like me, private property and war and social status would have been consigned to the dustbin of history and peace and good feelings would reign. If only the Little Sidorhim would hurry up and get here, we'd all be living in a crèche.

There actually was a colored student at Duke, but nobody I ever crossed paths with. She was hidden away on the girls' campus, and somewhere around my senior year, got elected Queen of the May, which the people from the North considered a moral breakthrough, and the rest of us thought of as racial pandering...none of us, Northern or Southern, having actually laid eyes on the young lady in question.

Nature doesn't like a vacuum and the more sensitive Northerners, at least the ones with curly hair, began sporting Afros and lounging around the dorms pretending to sing the blues. As the decade wore on, the singing didn't get any better but the Afros kept growing until some were bigger than the one Angela Davis stashed guns inside of.

All that would have come as a surprise to Mr. Duke. He never expected colored people to live on campus. Especially white ones. What he expected was medieval scholars, and he built the dorms of quarried stone three feet thick with narrow leaded-glass windows for shooting arrows out of in case the peasants revolted.

The walls were so solid, and the rooms were so much like caves that the Civil Defense people outfitted them with Federal crackers and boxes of water and declared the whole place a bomb shelter on the off chance the Russians decided to take out the tobacco factories in Durham. For reasons that probably made sense in the twenties, the place came with maids to tidy things up.

Nobody had a clear idea what the maids were paid, but whatever it was, it couldn't have been enough, not with three students shoehorned into rooms built for two. And the three weren't exactly West Point cadets. They were eighteen- and nineteen-year-old boys with the personal habits of eighteen- and nineteen-year-old boys, and the more enlightened residents took time from desecrating the blues to campaigning to get the maids raises.

Uplifting colored maids into strong black women became an ongoing social project, a sort of White-Students' Burden. It was the perfect cause: a conflation of Civil Rights and the old-fashioned job actions their parents reminisced over.

Pretty days, the maids would sit in rows in the quad, their hands folded, and endure speech after speech about Blackness and Womaness from white guys who knew all about standing up to colonial masters and fascists and Ole Massa down on the Duke Plantation. Metaphors tended to get muddled.

As long as you were white and a college student, you were automatically entitled to do that. They ran articles in the student paper to make sure you knew. If you want to tell the maids how to run their own business, we'll put you on the speakers' list.

What the maids wanted out of the deal was more money, and if they had to sit through all this stuff in order to get it, they sat. And exchanged glances among themselves and never said anything, except to other maids.

Even people who made a career of Duke seemed ambiguous about what was going on. One professor got in serious trouble for saying in public what he'd been saying at faculty parties for years. "Teaching at Duke is like casting artificial pearls before genuine swine."

He was right about the swine, at least some of us, if you believed the stories. It's hard to imagine Duke University as a hotbed of Klan activity, but a coolbed it might have been. At least as far as the Kappa Alphas were concerned

They're the Klan fraternity, people would say. And they certainly did seem to have an accumulation of rednecks. In fact, given the demographics of the student body, they'd managed to acquire almost every redneck on campus, and it was worth your life to walk beneath their windows on Saturday night.

Not that the KA's had anything against you, the KA's didn't know you, and gravity didn't have an opinion either way. It's just that the beer bottles and sofas and television sets that came flying out of the windows were going to land somewhere, and if you weren't careful, that somewhere could be you.

Kicking your way through broken glass outside the KA's the next morning, smelling stale beer and listening to the retching inside, it was hard to take the stories about the Klan seriously. The Klan must have had *some* standards. They already had a bad name. Allowing people to think they were mixed up with the Kappa Alphas would have ruined them.

❧

I think that professor overstated where the pearls were concerned. My Spanish professor cast a genuine one at my feet the day he asked us to tell the class what we'd done over the summer.

When I got to the part about Alto, he doubled over and guffawed in a sophisticated, European manner, slapped his knee, and once he'd caught his breath, announced, in as non-patronizing a way as he could manage, that Alto is Spanish for Stop. Shelby and I had walked to the head of town and discovered a stop sign.

The nacre began to wear thin on some of the other pearls, though, starting with the talk in literature class about something called The Human Condition. I tried to follow along, but I never could get a handle on what having a dead albatross around my neck, or jamming a harpoon into a whale, had to do with my situation. It was in the dorms that people said things that made sense.

While the students from the North were busy being poor, black people singing mournful songs, the guys I hung out with were exploring genuine issues of what it means to be human. "If I was a girl," Bo Jenkins popped out with one night, "I'd be a slut," as cogent a statement of the adolescent male condition as I ever heard.

Johnny Yuma mentioned a survey that claimed that the average college guy had had sex with eight women. Then Mike Adair said, "You telling me some son of a bitch out there has banged sixteen girls," and we all sat stunned at the thought. Before we found out who that guy was, stories began making the rounds that sex was happening to ordinary college students in California.

Then we started hearing that it was taking place at other colleges right here in North Carolina, colleges we could have gone to if we'd been a little savvier about the application process.

Soon rumors were circulating that they talked a lot about sex in anthropology class. When the time came, we signed up for anthropology, and it didn't take long to discover that pretty much everybody in the world, except anybody we knew, was having sex all the time.

One day Margaret Mead showed up, and it turned out she'd written a whole book about sex and how good it is for you. Not that any of us needed an important scientist to point out anything so obvious, but it was nice to have official validation. And in the how-much-sex-we-should-be-having department, nobody could validate like Margaret Mead.

Margaret Mead had credentials. She'd been in Samoa watching from behind bushes while the improving hands of unfettered sex turned would-be hoodlums into loving, productive members of society. The only reason crime happened in America was because Americans weren't getting enough action. Who could argue with Margaret Mead about something like that?

With that one speech, she multi-culturefied a whole auditorium-load of randy college guys into future productive members of society on the prowl to spread peace and love all over whichever girl we ran into next. The only thing we needed were girls sophisticated enough to do some spreading of their own. Even if they weren't sophisticated, even if they turned out to have oppressive, patriarchal values linking sex to marriage...or just to guys they actually wanted to have sex with...we had Margaret Meade to bludgeon them into the sack. The problem was, we couldn't locate any.

"They're with the fraternity guys," Bo Jenkins said, and not being fraternity guys ourselves, we nodded in agreement.

The thought of all the sex going on in fraternities changed our opinion of Greek life, and a few months later, we formed ourselves into a loose coalition we called BOG's, for Bunch of Guys.

I'm pretty sure we failed to register as an independent fraternity. I know we never had any wild parties involving naked girls in togas, and we never paid dues. Instead of referring to ourselves as brothers, we called each other cousin, which was the way we wanted it. As a non-fraternity, the BOG's suited us fine and didn't have any long-term prospects at all.

Conversations about race were a lot like discussions in literature class. The less evidence you had for whatever you said, the better. Things no rational person would think had anything to do with race, things like the scientific method, turned out to be nothing more than tools to suppress black people.

Angry Black Men took to parading around on television with their fists in the air, and we were supposed to be afraid of them. Black guys from town watched the same shows we did, "angry" came into fashion, and they started hanging around at night beating up anybody trying to walk back from the women's campus. They really were guys to be afraid of. The obvious thing would have been for Duke to extend the hours the buses ran, but that would have been racist. Everything was racist.

With all that going on, it wasn't long before we'd spot a Yankee coming down the hall and drop into drawls Pa Snopes would have had trouble deciphering. When the Yankee came in earshot, one of us would say something along the lines of, "I ain't no racist."

"I *know* it," one of the others of us would say. "I ain't no racist neither. I got me *no* trouble with no Knee-grows."

"Me neither, Bo," somebody else would pipe up, even though only one person I knew was named Bo and he wasn't usually involved in these conversations. "I'm a liberal where Knee-grows are concerned. I think *everbody* should own hisself a couple." After that, there might be some compliments paid to Leander Perez.

Judge Perez, people called him, was the political boss of Plaquemines Parish over in Louisiana, and the rumor was, he owned slaves. Nobody was sure about the slave thing, because nobody could go look. Apparently there was a law in Louisiana that if a year and a day went by and no members of the public used a public road, then the road stopped being public and belonged to whoever owned the land the road ran across. Judge Perez had the muscle to keep people from driving on the roads, and that was that. They were his roads now.

Outsiders were swarming over Louisiana, just like they were swarming over Duke. But they weren't swarming over Plaquemines Parish. Judge Perez had put out word that he also controlled a couple of old Civil War forts down by the mouth of the Mississippi, and any outsiders who got caught in his parish, well, he'd just leave them in the forts for the mosquitoes to work on.

At times, when the hour was late and beer was involved, it almost came to seem as if Judge Perez was on to something. For even the best of us, it was hard to maintain a moral compass in the face of so much moral certainty.

Summer came, and then fall. Thanksgiving I met Rachel in Lynchburg. She'd taken the train down from New York, where she was in college. We drove to one of the passes in the Blue Ridge, parked at a little turnout next to a concrete picnic table, and hiked back onto the Appalachian Trail. We didn't see a single other person the entire four days.

We found a little meadow with a lush stream splashing alongside a rocky cliff. I stretched a shelter-half over a fallen log, making a lean-to no more than a foot above the ground. A cozy lair, I thought, low and snug, out of sight from the trail, and out of reach of whatever vagrant breezes might happen to swirl down to where we were.

The night was warm and we drank from the creek and roasted steak and corn over a small fire. Rachel didn't have fantasies about being a Confederate infantryman and had brought along luxuries that weren't au courant during the bleaker parts of the Civil War, including a couple of bottles of Greek wine that was so awful it was hard to figure how it had been allowed into the country.

While I tried to choke mine down, she held hers over the fire in a tin cup. That seemed like a bad idea to me. Heating, I thought, would just encourage the flavor. But she being a girl, and being with me, and at night, and in the Blue Ridge, I had no sales resistance. Before long, I tried a sip and...it wasn't bad. Somehow warming had mellowed the wine from corrosive to piquant, in a fruity kind of way with an aftertaste of, I don't know, turpentine, maybe. Whatever, we downed a lot before wriggling into the sleeping bag.

It was quite a wriggle, a one-person bag had been just the ticket all those years I was being a Confederate infantryman. Squeezing two of us in there was a different story, but with Rachel I was happy to give it a try. Then lie paralyzed on my side, squeezed next to her for the entire night. And she didn't seem reluctant to lie on her side all night squeezed against me.

Usually, it's the bad times that linger. Good times speed by. But not that night, and it wasn't just from the sore hips and arms and cramped legs pressed together so closely that neither of us could shift our weight, let alone roll over. After a while the Greek wine kicked in and I had to relieve myself. But wriggling out of the sleeping bag and then sliding from under the shelter-half seemed more like a task conjured up by a psychotic phys-ed instructor than anything I cared to do.

And then there was the matter of naked feet. Our boots were out there in the dark somewhere. And so were sticks and rocks and other pointed things. All in all, it was better to wait for dawn. How much longer could dawn be?

A long time, as it turned out.

Damn long.

And longer than that. But how much longer, we weren't sure. Our watches were outside, too, along with our boots and all our clothes.

The night was quiet. No rustling of leaves, no scurrying of small animals. Just endless, noiseless darkness when, it seemed to us, light should long since have been streaming in.

Finally, Rachel couldn't stand it any longer and tried to sit up and smacked her head against the shelter-half...making a solid-sounding whomp, as if she'd bumped into a low-hanging mattress instead of a thin piece of cloth.

"Snow," she said in a remarkably calm voice, and she was right.

The night had seemed endless because the night was endless. Dawn had fallen hours ago. And snow, lots of snow, had buried the shelter-half and the fire and our watches and our boots and our clothes so thoroughly it was impossible to see where we'd left them.

And given the heated wine and overheated evening before we wriggled into the sleeping bag, even harder to remember.

Sunday morning we descended into Lynchburg. We were wet and cold and tired and, being college students, nearly broke. Then, after I filled the tank with gas and we'd shared a single meal at the Colonel's, we really were broke except for thirty cents.

We waited together at the station until the train came, then I headed back toward Durham through a set of nit-picky tollbooths that required you to stop every few minutes and drop in a dime. I figured I was good for three booths, then I'd have to take back roads.

When I ran out of money, I pulled off the highway, and found... another tollbooth. The avaricious bastards were making me pay to get *off* their road. The attendant waved me around to a place on the far side of the booth where I climbed out of the car, not knowing what was going to happen.

What happened was that an ancient Packard, overloaded with colored people, mother, father, lots of kids, spun by, honking and waving and laughing. I jumped back and waved automatically, courtesy taking over on autopilot, but wishing I'd given them the finger. People making fun of a filthy, wet, broke white boy pulled to the side of the road because he couldn't come up with a fucking dime. The more I thought about it, the madder I got.

"They paid for you," the tollbooth guy said.

"What?"

"You're free to go. They tossed in a dime for you."

It was a sign of how on-edge we all were. How everything, even a spontaneous act of kindness, took on racial overtones. I wish I knew who that family was. I'd like to write them. Not to thank them for the dime, although I'd like to do that, too. But for what tossing that dime made me understand.

Ceci Maddox was the only good argument for Communism I ever encountered.

Like the lady Dad tried to marry, she came from behind a wall out on West Paces Ferry. But Ceci's was the highest-class wall of all. It was the wall around the Tudor-style mansion where Robert Maddox had lived. He was her daddy, and she'd been at the table the afternoon he announced his chauffeur, Vernon Jordan, could read.

Not having accomplished anything other than being a Maddox, Ceci thought of herself in terms of money. And some money was better than other money. In her heart, she fancied she was Jackie Kennedy, only better. Maddox money wasn't déclassé rum-running money.

Unfortunately for Ceci's self-image, she was no longer a Maddox. By the time Dad unearthed her, she was thirty-four years old and had been discarded by three husbands. She also didn't have any money, having been disinherited as too sketchy even for her mother. The only way she was going to get reinherited was to settle down, prove she'd learned her lesson, and lead a stable life.

That's where Dad came in. If you didn't count the business about living in a brothel, nobody was more stable than Dad. A good fourth marriage, at least a marriage that looked good from the outside, and Ceci was back in the chips.

I don't know where Dad met her but, in the Crazy-Lady Sweepstakes, Ceci took all the marbles. She'd studied crazy on a professional level and had it down. Before being defrocked for running off with one of her patients, she'd been a Freudian psychologist. By the time she met Dad, she was just a Freudian, moving through life surrounded by sex and darkness. And she didn't just have a son who would have murdered Marti; when the time came, she took matters into her own hands and tried to kill Marti herself.

She was also a drunk, which she wore as a badge of especial accomplishment, and she wasn't kidding. "I have been an alcoholic since I was fourteen," she would announce whenever there was a lull in the conversation. Then, sometimes, prove it by throwing up on whomever she was doing the announcing to. During the last twenty years of her life, she bragged about how she kept her figure by getting all her calories from alcohol.

Ceci would pass out in unlikely places including, one time, the oven in Cousin Edward's kitchen. Despite being sophisticated people who'd been introduced to all the morally instructive literature aimed at children, Edward and his wife did not do the required thing and slam the door and crank up the heat. It was an unexplainable lapse that would haunt the family for decades.

Ceci tended to dress in fabrics that dripped off her body like some ancient prophetess of Delphi. But mostly she defined her look by whatever she thought would fluster the people who constituted the background actors and bit players in the ongoing drama of her life. If a restaurant required ladies to wear skirts, she'd appear in a beige pantsuit looking like a paratrooperess in the Israeli Defense Force, then complain in high-decibel righteousness when the restaurant wouldn't let her in. Where Mother's fashion mistakes became the *costume du mode* for an entire social set, Ceci's triumphs led to ostracism and talk behind her back. Dad was hopelessly in love.

Semester break, I hopped the Dog to New York City.

The bus set out through pines and leafless kudzu vines as big around as my thigh, past fallow cornfields and empty tobacco patches, to Washington, DC. Then through Baltimore and up the Atlantic Coast. Morning, the sun rose over marshland and grass on the Jersey shore. The place stank of rot and industrial waste, even inside the bus. Outside, fields of storage tanks were connected together by huge pipes like some kind of derelict oil refinery. But the crude oil being processed out there, if that's what it was, wasn't turning into gasoline. The tanks and pipes belonged to a conglomerate that manufactured salad dressing.

The bus pulled into the Port Authority at midmorning, and I stepped off, feeling as out of place as all those New Jersey boys who'd wound up at Duke. I checked into the Hotel Dixie and waited for Rachel to join me. The Dixie may have been the world's tallest flophouse.

I liked the place because of the name and the price, which would have been cheap in Durham. Rachel liked it, I think, because it made her feel wanton and we could do things that even her worldly mother would not have supposed. Unlike a lot of guests, we kept the room for the entire night. Then, for several more nights.

One afternoon we were taking a breather when we passed a newsstand. There, on the cover of every paper, including *The Daily Mirror*, was the news that Malcolm X had been gunned down.

He had, naturally enough, been running off at the mouth at the time. Since his mouth was doing the running off at the Organization of Afro-American Unity, and all four of his assassins were black, I don't think it was Crackers who did him in. Not that some of us wouldn't have liked to take a shot at it, but that particular venue wouldn't have presented much of an opportunity.

In any event, Mr. X caught a shotgun blast at point-blank range in the chest and was approximately dead by the time he hit the floor. Then, to make sure he wasn't just foxing, three more gunmen pumped sixteen bullets into his body.

I knew Andy Warhol read *The Daily Mirror*, and I kept thinking he might want to add a bit of diversity to his oeuvre and do a disaster picture of Malcolm sprawled on the ground. I might have even purchased a copy, but I never heard they became available.

The eulogies said Malcolm had turned into somebody else. That he'd been sworn in as an actual Muslim. That he'd made the Hajj. That he wasn't even Malcolm anymore, but Abdul Rahman Hassan Azzam. A flattery to all the Abduls in the world, one would imagine. And that he had given up crime, violence, racial demagoguery, prostitution, racketeering, and drug dealing, and, at the end, was preaching peace and racial equality and the rest of us should just forget about all those other things he'd done.

Well...maybe. I don't know what Islam's ideas on forgiveness might be. Perhaps you just go humbly to Allah and ask that your sins be washed away. I know that's what Mary James would have done, except Jesus would have been the go-to guy for her. But what did Mary know? She never had anything to be forgiven for. And I don't see how religion of any sort can offer forgiveness for something you do to somebody else. It's the somebody you did it to who has to offer that. And Mr. X, Mr. Little, Mr. Shazzam, never asked me to forgive him. Nor, as far as I know, any of the ones he robbed, or pimped, or sold drugs to, or stirred up hatred against.

As time passes, I find that I wonder if there wasn't more to that X than a mere letter. Maybe by the time he was gunned down he'd tried on so many new Malcolms he'd arrived at Malcolm the Tenth. But that doesn't quite fit. When you add up the titles and emoluments, all the turning tricks for male clients, the drug dealing and thievery and demagoguery and whatnot, you're up to Malcolm the Twelfth, and the algebra doesn't come out right.

Whatever he had in mind, I think the X just about sums him up. When you add together the plusses from one side of a man's heart and subtract out the minuses from the other, it's hard to say what that comes to in any life. With somebody like Malcolm, it's impossible.

Maybe he did change. I know that since his death, he has grown in memory from a hate-filled opportunist thug to some kind of icon for people who never met him and have no knowledge of who he actually was—his venom hosed away by time and his malice turned to racial pride. Maybe that's how it should be. If we don't let the things we hate turn into something else, they stay with us forever.

Eugene Cook, the attorney general who lived up the street, died somewhere along in there, too.

His death was as unexpected as Malcolm's, at least as far as I could tell. Nobody ever mentioned he was sick. Just attorney-general-for-life one day and, boom, dead the next.

He got some play in the papers, and that was it. A new man was sworn in and attorneys went on being generalled. The only people outside his family who knew what really happened were the maids. Attorney General Eugene Cook offed himself in his living room.

I never discovered why, but if the maids didn't know, they probably had a theory. He may have been sick and didn't want to stretch things out.

Or maybe a scandal was about to break, then got swept under the rug to protect his feelings after he was gone.

It could have been he was just depressed and shouldn't have been allowed around guns.

But now that I've gotten old, too, I think it may have been something else. The more decades that pass, the farther the country I live in comes to seems from the one I grew up in until, sometimes, it doesn't seem like the same country at all. I can't help thinking something like that may have happened to Eugene Cook.

How strange the sixties must have felt to someone who once spoke on "The Ugly Truth about the NAACP" to a convention of cops. A man who, I am sure, really did believe the National Association for the Advancement of Colored People was a Commie front.

A man who knew all about abolitionists and their children and the organizations they set up to inflict alien social theories on the rest of us, a man steeped in the resentments of a long-ago past with no feeling for the modern-day resentments that had accumulated around him, even as he imagined the justice he administered was even-handed.

A man who'd devoted his life to keeping the world he loved intact. A man once splendidly suited to his times who felt his times run out on him, until there was no place left for him to be. Even in his own living room.

You had to hand it to Ceci. In the personalizing-her-space department, she was top of the line. When she and Dad returned from their honeymoon, she wasted no time in making our home into her home. First, she hired a crew to repaint the lemon-pie living room in a tasteful cardboard color. Then she gathered up all the photos of Mother and us kids and carried them to the attic and put them in the trunk with the rest of Mother's memorabilia.

Not long after that, she declared the trunk a fire hazard and donated it to the Salvation Army—along with the photos, Mother's high school yearbooks, the newspaper clippings of her birth and confirmation and marriage, her engagement pictures, her scrapbooks, the diaries she kept when she was a teenager, keepsakes from her own mother, report cards, awards, love letters, her wedding dress, and souvenirs from trips with her parents.

It's hard to imagine what the Salvation Army did with that stuff. Sold the trunk for a few bucks, maybe, but they probably dumped it first. Somebody might have picked up the wedding dress to wear to at costume party, but who knows?

Mother left behind hundreds of friends, all of whom had a good word for Dad, and my sisters, and me. Ceci went after them on a case-by-case basis. Throwing-up on their feet or burning cigarette holes in their furniture. When that didn't work, she'd accuse them of something or just be so scathingly unpleasant they wouldn't want anything to do with her or Dad again. Sometimes she'd try to seduce their husbands. That pretty much did the trick.

Aunt Suzy was Marti's godmother. Ceci dismissed her as if she were firing a maid. When Suzy decided that Marti might need the services of a godmother more than ever, Ceci turned her attention to Uncle Robert, but there weren't going to be any seductions in that quarter. He had been one of the truly great tight ends ever to play for Georgia Tech, had plenty of experience with the ladies, took one look at Ceci, and made his opinion vociferously known. So she took a different track. She accused Suzy of trying to seduce Dad.

Dad, who always seemed amazed that any woman would want to go to bed with him without being paid, was flattered. The more Ceci harped on Suzy's evil intentions and the more Dad bought into it, the louder and more aggrieved Ceci became until, finally, it was Dad who told Suzy not to come around anymore.

To prove who was the sexiest lady in the house and, I suppose, because she knew Anne's dates were expecting a little more than a warm handshake at the door, Ceci would crowd them into a corner when they showed up, ply them with kisses, and try to get them to fondle her before Anne came downstairs.

As Anne grew to look more like Mother, Ceci had to do something about her, too. She knew she wasn't going to be able to physically get rid of Anne, so she condemned her to emotional exile by accusing Dad of having an affair with her, then raising such a stink, and for so long, Dad was frightened ever to be alone with his daughter again. One spring break, the stink du jour was the affair Dad was having with Ceci's eleven-year-old son.

The times Dad tried to stand up to Ceci, she'd storm out of the house, storm into a bar, shack up with whomever was handy, and not return home for days. By then, Dad would be so frantic he would have forgotten whatever it was he'd tried to stand up to her about, and just be glad to have her back.

Somewhere in the pinewoods and tobacco patches where folks worried about such things, the perception began to grow that the Ku Klux Klan was losing the struggle for the hearts and minds of the people. Even Superman, defender of Truth, Justice, and the American Way, had turned against the Klan in one of his episodes.

It's those left-wing papers smearing our name, somebody must have said. High time we showed folks what we're really like. And so the local klavern held what they called an open rally in a picked-over cornfield twenty miles outside Durham, and all were welcome.

It was near sunset on a wintry night when I arrived. The field was muddy and spiked with stubble from cornstalks. A couple of beat-up trailers were parked next to a small stage, and in the distance stood a cross that was so tall it looked like telephone poles lashed together. It seemed padded, as if someone had tied pillows, or burlap, around it.

There may have been a few other college students there, I didn't recognize any. Mostly, I imagine, we weren't the ones the Klan was reaching out to. Nobody was wearing masks. Out of courtesy to us guests, I suppose. And because the idea of hiding their faces had gotten a lot of bad press as cowardly. Some of the Klansmen were women, women whose lives hadn't been easy, and their faces showed it. A handful of children were there, being raised in the faith by dutiful parents, and even a baby or two, decked out in baby-sized pointy robes with the red Klan insignia emblazoned on the left breast.

The robes weren't always white, that was a surprise. A couple were red, another deep purple, to show the office of the wearers. My guess is one was a chaplain and the others, most likely, sergeants at arms in case of college boys. Or maybe not. There wasn't any way I was going to call attention to myself by asking.

It took the proceedings a long time to get under way. I think the idea was to give us outsiders the chance to become acquainted with the knights. That's what they called themselves, Knights of the Ku Klux Klan. The evening kept getting colder and I was feeling shy and nobody made the effort to introduce himself. I didn't care to socialize, either. I was there for the cross-burning. A blazing cross, I thought, would be a fine thing to see. But first we had to make our way through the speeches. And those gentlemen giving the speeches, whoever they were in the other parts of their lives, they weren't professors of rhetoric.

Listening to them spew their fantasies across that freezing cornfield, the faces next to me didn't seem hard anymore. They seemed cold and bored, like me, and mostly they just seemed lost. Like people watching the world change in ways that made no sense to them.

They were people who'd grown up on stories about their land being invaded, about heroic ancestors arrayed against impossible odds, about defeat and poverty, of ruined farms, of social chaos. Of twelve years under the bayonets of an occupying army.

And now more bayonets had come down, to Little Rock and everywhere else anybody tried to yell, "Hold." At a time when the nation was learning to celebrate everybody's heritage in the diversity of our great people, their heritage alone was a shame and brought disgrace.

They were a whole class of people, shoved aside and spat upon and called vile names by the rest of the country they still loved. A people whose concerns and fears were never given a hearing. A people who deserved much better. And, when they didn't get it, called up memories of a past that never existed, of bold knights sallying forth to protect their women and their ways of life. Of crosses burning against a darkling sky.

My feet were cold and my back was cold, and the speakers droned on through ancient, crackly loudspeakers, exhorting us to take up arms against Communists, Niggers, and the International Jewish Conspiracy. Communists. Niggers. The International Jewish Conspiracy. The shadow sides of love of country, pride in your fathers, and reverence for your god—the three things the people in that field held most dear.

When the time came to ignite the cross, a hundred knights, maybe more, formed up in ranks, each with an unlit torch, robes glowing in the light from a huge bonfire.

One by one, they thrust their torches into the flames and raised them high. Then to the crackly strains of Tennessee Ernie Ford singing "That Old Rugged Cross," circled around the cross until they were a flickering diadem of torchlight in the night. They raised the torches, as if saluting, then swung them down, just grazing the ground, and back up and tossed them in arcs of blazing light soaring through the darkness.

The cross flared into a thirty-foot high emblem of suffering and shame, as Tennessee Ernie put it. The pillows, or burlap, must have been soaked in kerosene.

There was something about that ceremony, something deep and very moving, something that went back past humans, far into our collective past. Something almost religious. Maybe, even, explicitly religious, with that crackly hymn. Something that touched emotions deeper and more powerful than any rational analysis I could manage.

The night seemed even colder when the circle broke up, and we sidled close to the bonfire. Behind us, chunks of flaming burlap, or pillow, dropped onto the now-frozen ground, and the light from the bonfire didn't illuminate anything. It just made the faces under the hoods seem shadowier.

Semester break, my college buddy, Sam, and I set out from Durham and headed north. We wanted to see what a Yankee winter looked like, and Sam wanted to fly Island Airways.

Sam spent his summers painting stripes down the center of airstrips in South Carolina. Once, when he was riding shotgun in the stripe-painting machine, he and the driver got to discussing girlfriends. Which led to a discussion of coitus interruptus. Which led Sam to remark that there are enough sperm in precoital flow to get a girl pregnant. Which led to...well, if you're ever at a small airport in South Carolina and notice the centerline splattered all over the runway, you'll know a lot more about the intimate sexual practices of the guy driving the line-painting machine than his girlfriend would care for you to know.

With a job like that, Sam had learned a lot about small, local airlines. One of the things he learned was that Island Airways flew Ford Trimotors out over Lake Erie. The islands up there were close together, and the longest leg was eleven miles. The shortest was two. The entire round trip was seventeen miles and took forty-five minutes, including all five takeoffs and landings. No other airline in the world still used Ford Trimotors, and he wanted to fly in one while he still could.

We headed north through the Virginias and then into Ohio and were watching in Port Clinton on the shore of Lake Erie when a plane touched down. It had a motor on the nose and one on each wing, and the fuselage wasn't smooth and rounded the way planes are nowadays. As Sam put it, the wings were slabs and the fuselage was square in section, like a boxcar. The plane looked like it had been designed by an anvil maker and was covered with corrugated iron, like the roof of a shed. The door was next to the tail, and next to the door was a small oval sign, proudly announcing STOUT METAL AIRPLANE CO.

The interior was fitted with wicker seats, control wires ran through the cabin, and this being before terrorism, the pilots kept the cockpit door open for ventilation. The oil gauges for the outboard engines were mounted on the landing-gear struts where the pilots could shine flashlights on them after dark. Back in 1929 when Admiral Byrd flew one over the South Pole, Trimotors had been cutting-edge aircraft.

When the pilots wanted to hit the brakes, they pulled back on a huge lever set in the floor on the same principle, I think, that brakemen use on San Francisco trolleys. When we took off, we could see birds nesting in the trees at the end of the runway, who was fishing off the dock, and what kind of sandwiches they'd brought for lunch.

Back in Port Clinton a very short time later, Sam and I headed north into Michigan through hours of second-growth pines weighed down with snow like department-store-window Christmas trees shimmering in the moonlight. Imagine, we thought, Yankees living somewhere so beautiful. It was a puzzler.

We crossed to the Upper Peninsula, then took the Trans-Canada Highway around the far side of the Great Lakes. The blacktop was reasonably dry, that is until somewhere near Rivière-du-Loup, we passed the snow plow and a sign cheerfully announcing, Most Canadian Roads Receive a Fresh Bituminous Coating Every Summer. On the bottom the message was translated into French.

Farther along, the signs were French with English subtitles.

Then just French.

A couple of evenings later, we were deep into country as rural as any in North Carolina and looking for a place to spend the night. We pulled up at a farmhouse that, as far as Sam could make out from his high school French, took lodgers.

"*Oui*?" a suspicious woman gave us the fish eye through a crack in the door.

"We have come, *Madame*," we tried to explain in French-accented English, "to rent a room for the night, if you *plaît*."

"You are not..." the lady swung open the door for a better look, "...*Anglais*?"

"*Non*, Ma'am," I said, "we *être* Americans."

"*Americains*," Sam corrected. As always, more worldly than me.

"*Bonjour. Bonjour*," the lady threw open her arms as if she were about to give us both hugs. "Come in, Come *in*," she said in perfect English. "My house, she is yours." Then, "I feared you were *Anglais*."

Anglais seemed like a good thing not to be, about then, and I considered taking her over to the car and pointing out the Georgia plates, but there was no need. No English Canadian could ever speak English the way Sam and I spoke it.

In some places, being a white Southerner opened doors. Who'd of thunk it?

Winchester Cathedral was William the Bastard's reward to God for letting him oust King Harold, take over England, and change his last name to Conqueror. God, at least for William, was a cheap date.

For eight hundred years, the churchyard at Winchester had been the go-to place to bury dead people. Rachel and I spent the summer after our junior year digging out the bones so that an archaeologist could get at the foundations of the old Saxon cathedral beneath them.

College students came from all over to help with the project, and because it was the thousandth anniversary of the Viking conquest, science tended to get interrupted by Danes shouting, blowing horns, quaffing mead, and grabbing local women. The people we were digging up probably wouldn't have remembered the Danish invasion in the same joyous way those kids remembered it.

Archaeology is slow digging. We'd work a bit. Somebody would come out and measure what we uncovered. Somebody else would take pictures. Then we'd deliver the skeletons we dug up to the Bone Lady so she could count the sexes and ages and, when she could, what the bones had died of, in a sort of post-mortem medieval census.

Most of the bones didn't wind up with the Bone Lady because she needed a skeleton to work from and, mostly, we didn't dig up skeletons. Mostly, we dug up dirt mixed with pieces of bone. Medieval sextons hadn't cared where the previous residents of the churchyard were buried and just dug through whoever was down there when it was time to make room for the next inhabitant.

In the part of the graveyard reserved for nuns, we found baby bones. No surprise there, at least not for us committed moderns. Once, I struck my pick into the ground and the ground wiggled for yards in every direction. Tens of thousands of bones were down there, jumbled so tightly together there was hardly any dirt. Plague victims, I always imagined.

Besides skeletons and dirt and bits of bone, we disinterred tombs made out of slabs of chalk. When we came across one, we left it alone. By midsummer there were so many unopened tombs the excavation had taken on the aspect of a Mediterranean town with white, boxlike buildings jumbled together.

Who any of the people in the churchyard were, we couldn't tell. They were as gone from memory as if they'd never lived. Farmers, for sure. Merchants. Butchers and bakers. Town drunks, goodwives, and wenches gone wild. Generation upon generation upon generation lost forever. It was hard to shake the feeling that if we could go back in time and cancel out any of those people as a baby, nothing today would be different. The same gentleman would be Lord High mayor. The same bishop would be at the cathedral. Whatever meaning those lives might have had, they had for themselves, alone. And when they ended, their meaning came to an end, too.

I wasn't really cut out for archaeology, and the morning came when the archaeologist took a skeptical look at the place I was working and discovered a pit that went down about fourteen stratums deeper than any of the rest of the excavation, along with a corresponding heap of dirt and bones and who-knew-what-else all piled together in a disorganized and unrecorded mess, and I found myself exiled to digging a private hole next to the wall of the cathedral. The churchyard didn't run all the way to the wall. Over there, I could swing a pick to my heart's content. There wasn't anything there to damage. Except the hermit.

He'd been a public sort of hermit who'd lived in a hut propped against the cathedral. There was an old lithograph showing it. When he died, they'd buried him in the hut, and nobody seems to have thought about him since. Least of all the archaeologist, or he'd have exiled me to some more distant place. Preferably deep into the New Forest where he wouldn't have to deal with me again.

The hermit was right where they'd left him, surrounded by the foundation of his hut. You can see a drawing of that foundation if you check the site report; at least you can see the portion of the foundation that was still there when I got caught tossing pieces of it aside to find out what was underneath. For a while you could have seen most of the hermit, all except the thighbone from his right leg. The thighbone you'd have to go to Buckhead to see. I feel bad about that now. But at the time

I told myself the Bone Lady had plenty of hermit left to work with. And it wasn't like she kept track of which skeleton was which.

Hermit shermit. This was science. When she was done, she tossed her parts of the hermit in with the butchers and bakers, town drunks, goodwives, and wenches gone wild he'd devoted his life to keeping his distance from. And the part that didn't get tossed in, the thighbone, that wound up in a footlocker in our attic along with a bit of jaw and a couple of molars from Etowah. If the hermit was right in his Profession of Faith about the resurrection of the body, he's going to find himself in some surprising company: an Englishman who never heard of North America walking into the afterlife alongside a pre-Columbian Georgian with no clue about Europe. A very modern situation when you think of all the peoples today stirred together like scraps of bone in a medieval churchyard.

Rachel and I bought a couple of cheap French mopeds on the grounds they didn't cost as much as good British mopeds and puttered around Winchester. People who saw what we were riding said we were fools. The license plates said we were fools, too. French fools. FOU 14D and FOU 15D...FOOL 14D and FOOL 15D in English. Toward the end of the summer, we loaded the mopeds onto an overnight train and headed up to Scotland for a couple of weeks.

In Edinburgh, we lied about our marital status, checked into a hotel, and spent a couple of days walking around the city. Then we set out across Scotland, mopeding along two-lane roads, camping beside lochs, and wearing black rubber slickers against the rain. We carried our bedrolls and a shelter-half on the back of the mopeds, toothbrushes, and not much else except an ever-accumulating layer of mud, and we did not fit in. I'd go through some village, pedaling as hard as I could to help the tiny, eccentric French motor turn over, while people gaped and pointed. Thirty seconds later Rachel would pedal by, their jaws would fall wider, and they'd say something like, "Hoot Mon, there goes another."

Ten days out of Edinburgh FOOL 14D and FOOL 15D pulled up to a hotel near Loch Lomond and went inside for lunch. If this had been a hotel in Atlanta—heck, if it had been the lowest-rent diner in Durham—the maître d' would have blocked us at the door. No Shirt. No Shoes. No Mud. No Fools, that would have been the rule. Instead, he seated us in the middle of the dining room as if we were regulars returning after a long absence. The waiter suggested entrees, then nodded in satisfaction at what we ordered. "Excellent choice," the sommelier beamed when I pointed blindly to one of the wines on the list.

After we finished, Rachel and I sat at the table and chatted for a long time, shedding dried flakes of mud onto the ancient hardwood floor, and nobody came by with the check to hurry us along. When we finally did leave, she paused in the lobby to study a photograph of the Queen. Taken in that very lobby. Rachel and I weren't the only ones who got treated like royalty in that hotel. That meal was a lesson in graciousness I have never forgotten.

By the time she and I got back to Winchester, the chalk tombs were standing open and forlorn, like so many empty shoeboxes.

The churchyard was Christian ground, and Christians aren't supposed to include grave goods with the deceased. Still, I'd been sorry to leave town knowing we'd miss the grand opening. I couldn't help thinking about golden chalices and emeralds and rubies an anonymous digger might be able to palm while the archeologist was distracted by treasures heaped in adjacent burials.

It would have been a disappointment. There hadn't turned out to be treasure. Mostly what was in the tombs was skeletons, but sometimes not. Coffins had been there, they found the nails, but the coffins hadn't been occupied. Thoughts of ancient Satanic rituals and grave robbers flitted through our minds. Early medical experiments, perhaps. Not even the archaeologist knew what to make of it. Other graves were even more baffling. In one, they found the hind leg of a horse.

The idea that somebody...any somebody, in times when people believed in hallowed ground, and meat was a luxury...would bury a horse's ass, or even just a half-assed horse's ass...was beyond anything we could parse. Whatever had gone on in Medieval Winchester, whatever it was those merchants and farmers, those butchers and bakers, those town drunks and goodwives and wenches gone wild had been up to, it was stranger and more distant than we were able to imagine.

After Robert Maddox took leave of his inexplicably literate chauffeur and headed off to that great Tudor Mansion in the Sky, Ceci's mother remarried. She lived with her second husband in an enormous house in Gulf Stream, Florida. Or, rather, shared the house with him. He spent most of his time upstairs in his private suite. Their paths didn't cross much.

Gulf Stream is the fancy upper-caste suburb of West Palm Beach, and all the houses are huge. Ceci's mother's second husband's house was the hugest of all, and the property extended from the Atlantic straight through to the Inland Waterway. Her second husband was Harold Johnson, one of the founding partners of Merrill Lynch Pierce Fenner and Bean. The reason it hadn't been Merrill Lynch Pierce Fenner and Johnson was because Harold had been in charge of the European side of the operation.

He'd been in Paris during the thirties, and when the Nazis took over, stayed on, bringing unheard-of profits for Merrill Lynch. When Germany declared war on America, Harold beat feet across the Pyrenees, sat out the fighting in New York, then returned to Paris in forty-four when Ike put him in charge of liberated France. Or, at least, that's how Harold chose to remember it.

After the French government got back on its feet, he returned to New York, but instead of being greeted as a hero for all the money he'd brought in, Charlie Merrill fired him. Harold was in his early forties at the time and worth millions.

What I did not discover until years after Harold died, and then only by accident, was that Charlie Merrill had had good reason to fire him. Like a lot of people who made their nut in Europe in the Nazi years, Harold had been a collaborator.

I don't believe in curses, even curses that run with tainted money, but if I did, the fortune Harold brought home would be pretty good evidence in support. Forty years after that, he killed himself.

Ceci's Mother got the fortune, but she had terminal lung cancer by then, and she, too, died by her own hand.

Then Ceci got the money, and she was the unhappiest person I ever met, except Dad when he was married to her, and both of them died in strange circumstances.

The Tudor mansion where Ceci grew up burned, and the Maddox property got sold to the State of Georgia. The state used it to build the new governor's mansion.

In 1966 another Maddox entered the picture. Lester Maddox, former proprietor of the Pickrick Cafeteria, Home of the Three-Legged Chicken. Maddox would have his cooks sew a third drumstick onto his chickens before cooking them. It was a family-friendly restaurant, with pickricks stored in nail kegs on either side of the large fireplace. Pickricks were what Maddox called ax handles.

When the civil rights movement kicked into gear, a group of demonstrators showed up at the door. Patrons grabbed pickricks from nail kegs and poured into the street to confront them, backed up by Maddox with a handgun. Federal lawyers got involved, and by the time it was all over, Lester Maddox had lost the most famous public-accommodations case in United States Supreme Court history, and rather than integrate, sold the restaurant to his employees. The employees were black.

Lester Maddox became an instant martyr of the segregationist resistance and ran for governor in the Democratic primary in 1966. In ordinary circumstances, he wouldn't have won. The liberal Atlanta press was against him, the old-line Democratic power elite was against him, and enough Democrats in general were becoming fed up with segregation not to want to have anything to do with him. But circumstances in Georgia politics were anything but ordinary. That was the year the Republicans nominated Howard Calloway, and Calloway was a scary candidate.

Calloway was young and vigorous, he'd graduated from West Point, Southerners loved that kind of thing, and he wasn't Ellis Arnold. Arnold was the Jerry Brown of Georgia politics, an ancient, ineffectual retread left over from the forties, who was famous for being the governor who'd added something like ten thousand trivial amendments to the state constitution, and not much else. Most Democrats weren't going to go down and vote for the likes of Lester Maddox, so Ellis Arnold was going to be governor. Again.

He would have, too, except something like a hundred thousand Republicans showed up at the Democratic primary and pulled the lever for Maddox. That was the downside of keeping Republicans out of electoral politics, we all registered as Democrats. Otherwise, we wouldn't have gotten to vote at all.

The plan worked, Maddox won, and the establishment went ape-shit. There was no way that man was going to win the general election. In one of the great cynical moves in the history of American politics, and there have been a lot of those, the liberal Atlanta press and the old-line political elite rallied together and began to tout Ellis Arnold as a write-in candidate. That way, the Democrats who would have sat home could vote their conscience, Arnold would get enough votes to deny Calloway an absolute majority, the election would be thrown into the Georgia House of Representatives, where every single member had been forced to take an oath of loyalty to the Democratic Party before being sworn in, and the Democrats would get to keep the governor's office without anybody ever having to say a kind word about Lester Maddox while they did it.

When he moved into to the governor's mansion on the old Maddox property, the Atlanta papers took the high road and continued to campaign against the man they'd conspired to put into office. Among other talents, Governor Maddox was a trick bicycle rider, and when a photographer caught him on New Year's Eve 1969 sitting on the handlebars and pedaling with his feet, the headline was, "Governor Pedals Backwards into the Seventies."

On another occasion he gave a speech supporting the fine arts, and somebody in the composing room swapped the N and the R and the headline had the Governor in Favor of Fire Ants.

Not long after he and Ceci tied the knot, Dad started finding reasons to travel again, if that's what he was doing.

One Thursday while he was out of town and Anne and I were off at college, Ceci was fixing supper and swinging a large knife. She didn't often have occasion to become involved with food, either as the preparer or the consumer, but it was Mary's day off and Marti had to eat. The indignity of the situation may have affected her mood. But, at least at the start, it was Dad she was angry at. He had done something, or he hadn't done something, and, besides, he wasn't there, and the more Ceci reflected upon the unfairness, the sheer insensitivity of it all, the faster she swung the knife. And, don't you agree, Marti, how horrible your father is?

That one of Dad's daughters might side with her on a question like that seems an unlikely thing to expect, but Ceci was never totally rational when she started dwelling on how mistreated she was, and when Marti didn't agree quickly enough, swung the knife harder. And became more insistent. "Don't you *agree*?"

Marti still didn't answer, and Ceci stopped chopping. And asked again. If there was one thing she demanded, it was loyalty. And Marti wasn't showing enough.

This would have been a very good time for Marti to recognize the righteousness of Ceci's cause, but before she realized her faux pas, Ceci came at her with the knife.

They circled the kitchen a time or two, Ceci slashing at the air and muttering incoherently until Marti dodged for the back door.

And into the car.

And over to Betsey Black's house.

Betsey let her in, they stepped around Mrs. Black, who was passed out on the living-room floor, went upstairs, started their homework, and laughed about who the real grown-ups were in their families. Alcohol was the drink of choice among Atlanta housewives of a certain social class.

"Ceci wouldn't do something like that," Dad said when Marti told him what happened. "Ceci loves you. You are her little cricket."

Cricket or not, some of what Marti said must have sunk in, because for the rest of her high school career, days would come when she'd be summoned to the principal's office and handed the phone. "Ceci is in one of her moods," Dad would tell her. "You need to find a place to stay for the next few days." Just until things blow over. "You know Ceci loves you."

Every cell in Dad's body must have screamed "Halt" whenever he and Ceci tried to have sex. With Viagra still decades away, it couldn't have been pleasant for either of them, and they became regulars at Masters and Johnson. It may have been that Dad was lured into the deal by the possibility of spending time in the loving hands of a sex surrogate, but he would have been disappointed. Treatment at Masters and Johnson was two weeks of talk.

Now I don't know what they actually talked about, but my guess is it had something to do with relaxing and enjoying the moment, with Ceci accusing Dad of being frigid and Dad meekly mumbling that it was true. Then the conversation would spin around to the ways people enjoy being sensual, and dirty movies and books would get involved, and noticing the sensual things going on around you in the environment would come up, and Dad would swear to loosen up and be more open next time.

What I do know is that when I was home from college, he would slip me ten bucks and tell me to go to a bar and pick somebody up, but before I went home with her, to give him and Ceci a call and let them know what we were doing. *Exactly* what we were doing. Ceci, meanwhile, would corner Anne when she came home from a date and demand details about what she and her guy had been up to.

It wasn't until years later that we discovered she and Dad had installed baby monitors beneath every bed in the house they didn't personally sleep in. My bed. Marti's. Ceci's son's. The beds in the guest bedrooms.

It was hard to figure why Dad would want to voyeur on his own children, but it seemed like the kind of thing Ceci would get a thrill out of. Could be it didn't have anything to do with sex, though. Maybe she just wanted to listen in on what people were saying about her.

Or to find out what we were planning so she could do something about it.

Or, and the older I get, the more likely this seems, to discover that we *weren't* talking about her. Ceci was always on the lookout for something to be aggrieved about.

Four-and-a-half years after Mother burned alive, I attended a nun's convention. It wasn't that I had become a nun, or even had thoughts of taking up the habit. It was just that three college buddies and I were spending a long weekend in DC and had blundered into a hotel filled with nuns.

They had nuns in black robes. Nuns in gray robes. Nuns in white robes with white headdresses. There were gray nuns with white headdresses. Gray nuns with gray headdresses. Sporty-looking gray nuns with purple headdresses. Purple nuns with white headdresses. Cream-colored nuns. Beige nuns. Tan nuns. Nuns in every non-color Glidden makes—the sands and oysters and toasts and cobwebs and all the other euphemisms for off-white and stain-brown and mummy-dust that a creative paint company can come up with.

These weren't your daring, movie nuns, either. These were ladies who had been, well...cloistered...for so long they couldn't even step boldly to the back of the big hotel elevators, but huddled in little color-coordinated knots in the corners, too abashed to look sisters of a different color in the eye.

It was a large hotel even by big-city standards, and there were, maybe, twenty-three stories of nuns on a subdued frolic, gliding as noiselessly as so much smoke across the lobby. There was also the usual complement of house detectives, and as far as I could tell, that was it.

Something like two or three thousand nuns, some detectives, and four college seniors sneaked into a room for two.

We would have been better off choosing a hotel with a more diverse clientele because with all those nuns, the detectives knew whom to detect. We hadn't been checked-in fifteen minutes when the phone rang.

On the other hand, choosing a good hotel has its rewards. And we had chosen the best. That's why we were quadrupling up—so we could afford a nice pad. And the pad was nice about it. No recriminations, just a gentle phone call reminding us how pleased they were that we had chosen their hotel and how really happy they would be for us all to be in that room together, but there were certain issues involving fire regulations and could they please send somebody to move a couple of us to a more suitable room where we would be just as happy and a lot more fire-proof?

Well, when they put it like that...

A polite bellhop got two of us safely installed next door, where we flopped on the queen-sized beds and switched on the television and...Gus Grissom and Ed White and Roger Chaffee had burned to death in the *Apollo I* capsule.

Gus Grissom from the *Liberty Bell 7*. Gus Grissom, who'd soared overhead in a Mercury rocket built on my family's land while Anne and I stared across a sun-warmed field toward a cinder-block building on Grand Bahama Island, back when Mom was alive.

Our DC blow-out turned old and sad and, mostly, we just wanted to go back to school and bury ourselves in books and theory and put the nuns and Washington and the feelings behind us. But, of course, we never really could.

A few weeks later, a blizzard came to Durham. And so did Rachel.

Pines bent under the weight of the snow and their tops snapped off, plunging sometimes eighty, sometimes a hundred feet, like darts into the frozen ground, to create a forest of new Christmas trees. Out on the interstate, cars backed up all the way to Raleigh, accumulating on the tops of hills to race down, one at a time, and try their luck, skidding and sliding, at cresting the next hill. It was the snowiest day in years, and a very slow drive in from the airport.

The sun was low by the time we made it to Durham, and I got lost. Rachel's motel was in a part of town I wasn't used to, the paved roads gave way to snow-packed dirt, the tidy suburban homes to shacks, the car skidded into a ditch, and we were stuck.

And then surrounded by a gang of black teenagers who came out of the shadows.

A couple of lanky boys tapped on Rachel's window and said something I couldn't make out. It was the fairgrounds all over again, with me as protector. Then a huge guy tapped on my window and pointed at the road.

He grinned and yelled, and four or five more guys walked to the back of the car, leaned on the trunk, and shoved us out of the ditch. Then came to the driver's side and gave us directions out of the neighborhood. When I offered to pay them, they laughed and danced aside and began throwing snowballs at each other.

It was hard dark by the time we made it to the white part of town and pulled into the snow-covered gravel lot of the cheap place I'd booked. Rachel signed in and we carried her bag to one of the ramshackle, wooden cabins, slipping on snow as we went. Inside was a threadbare bed and a single sixty-watt bulb behind a paper lampshade on the table. I found the electric heater and turned it on. Then Rachel sprawled on the bed, and I sprawled on her. We were glad to see each other and glad to be out of the snow.

We were still in our wet clothes when the phone rang.

It was the manager.

I'd reserved the room under my name, Rachel had signed in under hers, he'd checked, and the names didn't match. We were, the manager suspected, not married, and back into the snow we went.

Divorce her, is what Marti told Dad the nights he came into her room and cried on her bed, needing comfort for something Ceci had done. A tough position for a teenaged girl, giving emotional counsel to her dad when she was supposed to be the daughter.

Divorce her, is what my grandmother told Dad when he came to her apartment in tears.

Divorce her, is what Dixon Rawlins told him. And Dave Dillard. And Munford Black.

But Dad couldn't. He and Ceci had gone to a marriage counselor and made a pact. This marriage was the most important relationship in their lives, they would stick it out. More important than family. Or friends. Or children. And Dad was nothing if not a man of his word.

There was something else that was more important than family, or friends, or children, too, that Dad didn't tell Marti. Or my grandmother. Or Dixon or Dave or Munford. It was a reason none of us found out until after he died. Harold had peeled off four-million dollars of collaborationist money and bought him for Ceci.

If Dad wanted out of the marriage, he had to give it back.

The last spring I was at Duke, the social event of the season was a be-in.

Victimization wasn't just for maids anymore. By the spring I graduated, pretty much everybody was wrapping themselves in the comforting folds of oppression.

We college students were oppressed because...well, because of a thousand things but, basically, because Duke wouldn't treat us like grown-ups, which was probably wise. It told us what to smoke. And who could visit our rooms, and they weren't women. Professors graded our work. They made us wear clothes to class. But now, for a single day, the dusty bonds of paternalism would be loosed.

At the be-in, we could be whatever we wanted to be. And we could be authentic and express whatever political and social thoughts we'd been forced to bottle up all these years. At the be-in, peace and love would rule the world.

Looking back, that whole business about authenticity wasn't as well-defined as the organizers, if you can call them that, imagined. What I thought of as authentic and liberating, somebody else might think of as assault and battery. Which it pretty much was.

The peace and love I wanted to express involved a gorgeous redhead in my Roman History class, and planting a big smooch upon what, I was sure, would be her delighted lips. I spent a large part of the day searching the Sarah P. Duke Memorial Gardens for her, but she may have been tipped off that I was around because I never caught sight of her.

By the time of the be-in, organizing colored people had given way to being against the war in Vietnam. The azaleas and rhododendrons I was beating my way through in search of my willing redhead turned out to be filled with orators declaiming on the evils of the military...unless the military in question was fighting against our military, in which case they were heroic freedom fighters.

There was a lot of bad folk singing, and lots of talk about Comrade Che. There were even a few guys who hadn't had much luck with the ladies posturing about how they were heading to Bolivia to join him in the Struggle. And maybe you should have sex with me right now because, well...the guys would stare into the middle distance "...you never know."

There was a lot of talk about The Masses. The Masses this and The Masses that. The Masses may have included American soldiers, but it was hard to know.

There was one guy, an imposing, bearded fellow with granny glasses I especially didn't like. He would have been a Quaker if he could have shut up long enough to let somebody else become inspired. I'd seen him around for years, especially on rainy days. He was easy to spot because he was sanctimonious about rain, and walked across the quadrangles at his usual leisurely pace while everybody else was fleeing for shelter. I never quite figured out what that was about. Either he wanted to show contempt for the elements in a meditative sort of way, or he had a theory based on the geometry of falling bodies that proved he got less wet if he walked slowly and the rain only landed on his shoulders and the top of his head. Whatever he had in mind, he spent a lot of time shivering and wet. Because of his righteousness, he was a beau ideal to a large selection of the university community, and at the be-in, he was surrounded by acolytes hanging on his every word.

I wanted to hit him in the face with a pie, so I motored into town and bought a couple of cream pies from the frozen-food department at the A&P. I left one next to the pond for my buddies to keep an eye on and headed off across the gardens, other pie primed and ready to launch.

I homed in on the first knot of worshipful followers I saw, and there he was, holding forth on the duty of nonviolence. "Never," he said. "Never under any circumstances should anyone ever lift his hand against a fellow human. No matter what the provocation. No matter what they do to us, we must never..."

That's when I got him, splat in the face.

I hadn't meant to break his granny glasses. The fact is, I hadn't even thought about his granny glasses when I let fly. And I hadn't thought to examine the pie, either.

I should have. The afternoon was warm, but the pie had been in a frozen-food bin not long before, so even though the top of the pie was fluffy, the insides were still pretty solid. Another thing I should have thought was, What is the purpose of pie number two? It just seemed like you should always have some spare ammunition handy. And pies were cheap, so I'd picked up another. Save a second trip to the A&P, maybe.

It did save a trip, but not for me.

Half a-dozen acolytes, fuming nonviolence, followed me back to the pond, and before I had time to settle in and tell my proto-redneck friends what happened, an apostle of nonviolence grabbed the second pie and let me have it in the face.

That seemed unsporting. The very least a pacifist could do is to stick to his guns. I believed in violence, it's the Southern way, so it made moral sense for me to hurl a pie. But he didn't believe in violence, he believed in shaming-thy-enemy when thine enemy doth violence to thee. I was disappointed in him and the thinness of his beliefs. If you can't count on the righteous to be righteous, who can you count on?

As unlikely as it seemed, a new generation of BOG's was following along behind us, which meant we needed a tradition. The night before graduation, we busted into a commons room, toasted each other with wine, hurled the glasses into the fireplace, and passed a very shaky helm to the juniors who would be taking over the non-organization that didn't have a lot of a future and none of us would ever think much about again. Or, so we imagined.

Decades later, *Sports Illustrated* did a cover story on Duke basketball, and of all the people the writer could have interviewed, he came up with a BOG. BOG's. Bunch of Guys. A sort of non-fraternity, as the writer described it, sounding puzzled as to what the BOG's were up to.

No more puzzled than I was. Somehow that loose, non-organized non-organization had managed to survive for decades. More than survive. It had thrived to the point it made the cover story of *Sports Illustrated.* How thoroughly it thrived I didn't find out for another few years. The truth is, I never really found out.

I think there might have been a gag order involved. At any rate, one weekend Sam visited Duke and discovered that the BOG's had been banned from campus. And nobody would say why, only that they had been so thoroughly banned they weren't even allowed to speak to each other if they passed on the street in downtown Durham.

Weren't allowed to talk to each other on the street? That didn't even sound constitutional, so Duke must have been serious about the banning.

As far as Sam knew, pedestrians were still dodging furniture flying out of Kappa Alpha on Saturday nights. For that matter, as far as any of us knew, the KA's were still getting little shots of morale-boosting encouragement from whatever was left of the North Carolina Klan. The KA's hadn't been banned, but BOG's couldn't even speak to each other on the street? And nobody was allowed to say why. Whatever we'd been father to all those years ago when we were trying to discover where sex came from, it gave me a little thrill of pride.

Nothing at college was more boring than leaving it. In the tedium department, Duke pulled out all the stops. Graduation was scheduled to run from ten in the morning until five in the afternoon.

My family was perched somewhere in the balcony. As were both of Sam's fiancées, the one who'd come all the way from Columbia to watch her beloved graduate, and the one right there at Duke who'd stayed on after the end of her junior year so she could celebrate his great day alongside him. They were scheduled to come running up at the end of the ceremonies, throw their arms around him, and discover each other for the first time, and Sam...well, nobody ever found out who was responsible for what came next, but certain suspicions hang in the air until this day.

Ten o'clock came, "Pomp and Circumstance" fired up on a continuous loop, and brigades of professors in gorgeous academic robes trimmed in velvet and fur, sporting odd soft caps and medieval hoods, paraded down the aisle. It was a fine and evocative sight and the high point of the ceremonies.

After what seemed like hundreds, maybe thousands of professors, speakers mounted the pulpit and filled the air with the wisdom of distilled platitudes. I slipped into a stupor and lost track, but there must have been a valedictorian and various deans. I know the president of Duke put in his two cents' worth. More like twelve dollars' worth, seeing how long he took. The governor of North Carolina got a turn but, luckily, it wasn't an election year, so what he had to say only ran on for a day or two. When he finally stood down, it was early afternoon and nobody had graduated yet.

Those proceedings kicked off in academic pecking order with PhD's making their stately way down the aisle one at a time, their names and the subjects of their dissertations and their academic adventures called out for all to admire. They would shake hands with rows of professors and deans and dignitaries, then head all the way back down the aisle before the next newly minted doctor would set out on the long, proud voyage. I had never realized what a center of academic accomplishment Duke had become. There were scores of these guys, the afternoon droned on, and we were hours behind schedule.

When the PhD's finished, they started in on the masters' candidates, and things didn't speed up. I'd thought there were a lot of doctorates, but Duke had been churning out masters by the carload.

Finally, the time came for undergraduates, and there were thousands of us. Each called by name, but, mercifully, none of us had any achievements to brag about, and we streamed down the aisle in an unbroken line, grabbed our degrees to prove to our parents we really had been going to college all these years, and shook lots of hands. First the arts majors. Then the science guys. Then the engineers and on through the different departments. At least that was the plan.

We'd gotten through about "R" in the arts majors when "Pomp and Circumstance" fell silent, the line of arts graduates stalled, and the president mounted the pulpit and started in with, "In these turbulent times...." Somebody had phoned in a bomb threat.

He knew there wasn't a bomb, we all knew there wasn't a bomb, but nobody was going to argue with an anonymous phone call. Not to worry, though, we would all reconvene in the basketball stadium.

Whomever that "all" was intended to cover, the people who formed up in the basketball stadium didn't seem to include PhD's or those with master's degrees or any of us arts undergraduates with names starting anywhere previous to "R," no matter what the president tried to tell us to the contrary.

Sam was a science graduate, and he didn't show up, either. I think plenty of science graduates really did find their way to the basketball stadium, but Sam was long gone by then. And his fiancées remained long gone from each other, and Sam was off the hook. In these turbulent times...all you had to do was pick up the phone and mumble something about a bomb.

Damn! If I'd thought of that, we would have been out of there before the governor stood up.

10

Giving Peace a Chance

I always supposed they'd have a war for me when the time came, and Vietnam showed up right on schedule. Still, I thought I'd like to see a bit of the world first, so I went down to the draft board and told them to keep their war warm, I'd be back in a couple of years. I was going to Kenya. "Born Free" had been playing on the radio a lot, and I'd signed up with the Peace Corps.

My draft board didn't have a problem with that. They knew they'd still have a war when I got home and sent me off with their blessings. The problem was the FBI.

Who would have guessed they ran background checks on Peace Corps volunteers? Background checks were for diplomats and army officers, not recent college graduates heading off to teach English in rural villages in Africa. Shows what I knew. The FBI came by Buckhead asking whether I was the kind of guy who might attend a Klan rally. It turned out it wasn't just beaten-down farmers and frightened mill hands in the picked-over cornfield that night. G-men had been there, too. Jotting down license numbers.

Maybe my neighbors were smart enough to tell them it sounded like something I might do out of curiosity. Or it could be that some Good Ole Boy in the Atlanta office thought it would be fun to see how far one of our own could get in the Peace Corps. Mostly, I think, the FBI knew enough about that gang of would-be nightriders to realize they didn't pose a danger to anything more animate than a couple of telephone poles lashed together. In any event, they gave me a clean bill of health, patriotism-wise, and off I went to an out-of-season resort run by Greeks in upstate New York.

I'm not clear on how the Kenyans who taught us Swahili got stuck in the United States, but it had something to do with being invited here as part of an exchange program and Congress cutting the funding before they had tickets home. A win-win as far as the government was concerned, because when the Peace Corps cast about for language teachers, there they were, a whole group of Swahili speakers frantic for money. And that was the ethical part. What the Peace Corps wanted us to do once we learned Swahili was a good deal more sketchy.

During the first couple of years after independence, the government in Nairobi had replaced the colonial administrators with Kenyans, staffed the officer corps in the military with Kenyans, launched government bureaus and departments, all populated by Kenyans, and for that couple of years, any Kenyan with a college degree, and plenty who'd barely scraped out of secondary school, grabbed the brass ring in ways that had been unimaginable three years earlier. People noticed and began demanding education for their own children.

The government set up schools for them, but it was a bad idea. The jobs weren't opening back up until the twenty-somethings who had them began dying off. The ambitious new grads couldn't go back to their villages, there weren't places for them there anymore. Mostly, they went to Nairobi or Mombasa and wound up driving taxis. If they were lucky. And if they were male. Working the streets, if they weren't. Everybody would have been better off if they'd just stayed on the farm, so the government did the responsible thing: it shut down the schools.

And the people did the human thing. They got together and created Harrambe schools, We-Will-Work-Together schools, to provide the education the government wouldn't give their children. That's where we came in. We were slated to teach English in those schools. Not English as a second language, which would have been immensely useful, but English lit. Milton and Shakespeare. The Kenyan government didn't want any part of it, but saying no to Lyndon Johnson was not something a hopeful third-world government did easily.

So there you had it. Our government was using indentured Kenyans to prepare Americans to teach Shakespeare to kids whose own government knew better than to do any such thing. And at least some of us were willing to go do it because it was our ticket to Africa to see the animals we'd heard about in a song.

Making me sit at a desk eight hours a day learning Swahili wasn't good psychology, and it wasn't what I had in mind. Peace Corps would have been better off handing me a pick and giving me a dead hermit to molest. Still, I stuck with it because of the animals. One afternoon I got hauled out of class and handed a letter.

Odd, I thought. Everybody else picks up their mail at the front desk and started back to class. But acting as my personal messenger wasn't the reason the person had brought me the letter. A theological emergency had arisen, he'd dropped what he was doing, bounded up two flights of stairs, pulled me into the hall, and thrust the envelope at me. As far as I know, that was the only crisis during the entire five weeks in upstate New York serious enough to bust somebody out of class for.

"Tell your friend to be more considerate of the people who run this hotel," the person said, making it clear that from now own, the social sensitivity of my Cracker buddies would be one of the deciding factors as to whether I would, in fact, get to see animals.

I looked at the letter. Sam had lost track of where I was staying and had written my name on the envelope, followed by the words "AT THAT HOTEL RUN BY GREEKS NEAR MONROE, NEW YORK." That was enough to get the letter to Monroe, where the local post office knew who was whom, hyphenated American-wise. And that had been enough to get the letter into the wrong hands. The problem, it began to dawn on me, was that Sam had used the word "Greek."

Everybody else knew the people who ran the hotel were Greek. I was pretty sure they knew it, too, so it wasn't like Sam was revealing any secrets. It had to be something else. Being Greek must be like having an uncle who's light in the loafers or a father who faked a heart condition to avoid fighting in the Second World War, something nobody mentions out loud so as to avoid embarrassment. "They're ashamed of being Greek?" I asked. That didn't turn out to be the right question and I didn't get a thoughtful response.

It was a time of great certainties, only nobody seemed able to articulate why they were so sure. You were just supposed to know.

❧

You'd think a genuine African folk tale would go over big on Tell-a-Story-in-Swahili Day. And it did, with the lovely Kenyan teacher. She doubled up with delight at the antics of Br'er Fox and Br'er Rabbit. The fact is, I think she'd heard the story before, or some version of it as a girl, because when I didn't know the word for tar, she said, "Gum." Back home, it had been a gum baby.

I had the story from when I was a kid, too, from three degrees of separation from genuine African storytellers. From Jake Harris, who'd gotten it from his daddy, Joel Chandler, who'd tapped directly into an African tradition still going strong in Plantation, Georgia. And given our teacher's reaction, I'd gotten it right.

That kind of authenticity didn't have a place in the Peace Corps, and, well, the Tar Baby had been black. "You want to make fun of black children, why don't you just call them pickaninnies and be done with it?"

"It wasn't a black kid," I tried to explain. "It was made out of tar."

"Gum," the teacher said. "It was a gum baby."

"If anybody in that story was black..." I was groping here, but I knew I was onto something "...it was Br'er Rabbit."

"Now you're telling me black people are animals?"

"I'm just saying that he was a powerless, disenfranchised rabbit." It wasn't for nothing I'd spent four years analyzing English literature at Duke. "That makes him black, per se."

"Percy?" the charming Swahili teacher said. "His name is Kisungura."

"Powerless? You think black people don't have any power?"

"I'm saying, in the Plantation South, black men didn't exactly..."

"The gum baby wasn't a man," the teacher sounded puzzled.

"You told your teacher that black men are children, is *that* it? Boys, perhaps?" The representative of All That Is Decent glared at me.

"I think that a very clever rabbit managed to talk his way out of a tight spot by being a lot smarter than the forces of oppression that enslaved him." I would have raised my fist in a Black Power salute, but I was already on shaky ground, racial consciousness-wise, and wasn't sure how that would play out. "This isn't a story of oppression. It's an allegory of survival, triumph even, over the forces of racism and repression." I was beginning to feel like Br'er Rabbit myself, talking my way out of trouble.

"Brother Kisungura was stuck to a Gum Baby," the teacher said. "It was the Gum Baby who was doing the oppressing." Given the right opportunities, that lady would have done well for herself in the liberal arts department at an American university.

"You know, you really do need to be more considerate of those around you." My moral instructor gestured at the teacher so I'd know exactly whose feelings I needed to be more considerate of. Clearly, he'd not been a liberal arts major.

One bright morning while I was sitting in Swahili class dreaming of animals, word reached us that the Bolivian army had run Che Guevara to ground. Somehow, he'd convinced himself that a bearded Argentine could disappear into a sea of smooth-faced Indians speaking a language he could not comprehend and holding ideals he couldn't imagine.

The Bolivians sent his hands to Argentina so his fingerprints could prove they'd gotten the right guy. Then they dumped the unamputated parts of Che, and six other people, into an unmarked hole next to the airstrip at Vallegrande. Had they marked the spot, our Cuban governess would have packed her dancing shoes and bought a ticket to Vallegrande. Then cha cha cha'ed for hours next to the tarmac.

I would have gotten along better with the other trainees if they'd had the opportunity to know that brave, driven, outspoken lady. But when I tried to tell them about her, they weren't interested. Che lives, they said. "Comandante Guevara died a hero's death freeing the Indigios in the jungles of South America." Lofty ideas were what they cared about. Actual people didn't have anything to do with it.

The day was coming, and not so far away, when the Swahili lessons would be over and I was going to have to know how to be an English teacher. The only problem was that How To Be a Teacher wasn't part of the syllabus.

"So..." I sidled up to a Peace Corps honcho at the close of one of the lectures on cultural sensitivity, "...how does one go about teaching English?" From the stare he gave me, I might as well have asked if he knew where that Africa place was.

"I mean..." I tried to articulate something that never seemed to have been articulated in his presence before. "Teaching is a profession. People must know how to do it."

"Sometimes," the honcho looked thoughtful for a moment, "teachers pick out the rowdiest kid in class and make him hall monitor."

"They have halls in Harrambe schools?" From the pictures, it looked like most of the schools were circles of kids sitting beneath trees.

"Nothing like having the rowdy kid on your side if you want to restore order." He had the satisfied smile of the successful mentor who has passed along a hard-won nugget of wisdom to a not-so-bright protégé.

So, I thought, we're on the right track here. People do know something about how to teach, and I asked another question. "Where do lesson plans come from?" Somewhere along the line I'd gathered the impression that teachers worked from something called lesson plans. I just didn't know what a lesson plan was or where you got one. Professors at Duke had piles of notes they lectured from. Maybe lesson plans were like notes. Or a script, I thought. "Maybe if we got hold of some lesson plans we could...."

"Lesson plans?" the honcho gave me a puzzled look. "You want to know about lesson plans?"

"That and, you know, how teachers..."

"This guy wants to know about lesson plans?" one of the secondary honchos walked up.

"Lesson plans," I nodded. "And what teachers..."

"Let me handle this," the primary honcho waved away the secondary honcho, then turned back to me. "You graduated from college, right?"

"Sure," I nodded. "Duke. I went to..."

"And high school? Can't go to college if you don't graduate from high school."

I nodded again. I was getting the feeling my name was about to be added to a list, and it wasn't going to be a good list.

"Did you skip class a lot or something?"

"No more than the average..."

"How could you sit through all those classes and not know how a class is put together?"

I've sat on airplanes, too, I thought, but nobody ever invited me to take the controls. I knew enough not to say that, though.

Then, "Not to worry." He gave me a benevolent smile, "We're going to get you some kids to practice on."

He paused a moment as if he wasn't sure whether to let me in on the wonderful surprise the Peace Corps had in store for us. *What the hell?* he must have thought, and decided to let it all hang out. "They'll be black kids, so you can get all the practice you need." Then he turned his back and fired up a new conversation with somebody else.

As far as anybody could tell, there weren't any black kids in Monroe, so the Peace Corps found us some in New York City. A week later I was in a place called Hell's Kitchen, trying to puzzle out how to teach Shakespeare to rural Africans in a school that was so famous for gang violence it once starred in a movie called *Up the Down Staircase.*

On the immersion-in-Africanness front, the Peace Corps pulled out all the stops and found an African woman for me to stay with. She was a courtly, middle-aged immigrant from Alabama, a model of Southern womanhood whose family had been in America since before the Revolution.

It was all wasted effort. A couple of days before we were slated to fly to Nairobi, Peace Corps management called me into the office. I wouldn't be going.

The reasons were...well, they weren't too direct about it, but it had something to do with a popularity contest. Not that they'd told us we were in a popularity contest at the time. What they'd said we were doing, along with filling out a lot of forms, was writing down a list of people we wanted for roommates. They didn't tell us that if enough people didn't want you for a roommate, you didn't go.

Now Swahili, I could have understood. If they'd asked the roommate question in Swahili, they could have told right off I was the kind of guy who would walk to the head of a village and puzzle out the name from a stop sign. But whether enough people wanted me as a *roommate*? We'd all be in different villages. In different villages, we wouldn't have roommates

The thing was, it wasn't just me. When the plane took off, every single person who wasn't from the South climbed on. The ones waving goodbye, well, we were the ones the rest of America didn't want to room with. The white Southerners. Every one of us. And nobody ever showed us the poll results so we could see for ourselves who actually wanted to room with whom.

11

A War of My Own

What white Southerners did get to do was go to war. But we had to ask.

At a time when draft boards everywhere else were having trouble filling their quotas, ours had backlogs. I'd have to wait nineteen months if I wanted to get drafted. An entire hitch was only two years. And what was I supposed to do in the meantime? So I told them to move my name to the top of the list.

If there hadn't been a draft, I would have signed up anyway. Vietnam was what was going on in the world and I didn't want to miss out. But there was more to it than that. Our family had been going to war for generations, including both sides in the Civil War. It wasn't just the young Confederate soldier slipping through Yankee lines to visit his wife and baby girls who fought in that one, Uncle Wesley did, too.

Wesley graduated from West Point in 1860. By 1863, he was a major general on Phil Sheridan's staff, his promotion backdated to make him one day senior to George Armstrong Custer, also one of Sheridan's boy generals. Even at that early date, Sheridan knew that Custer needed a grown-up in the room. And Uncle Wesley was nothing if not grown up.

He made a reputation for himself at battles with liquor-related names like Todd's Tavern, Brandy Station, Wilderness Tavern, and Yellow Tavern. He also systematically burned every home and every barn, every shop and silo and mill, and all the crops in the Shenandoah Valley. War crimes were a dirty business, but somebody had to do them. The family never talked much about that part of Uncle Wesley's career.

When President Lincoln was murdered, Uncle Wesley served as one of his pallbearers, then, after the war, reverted to lieutenant colonel and spent almost two decades commanding Buffalo Soldiers on the Texas frontier. He broke loose only once, at least legitimately, when the army sent him to France to observe the Franco-Prussian War. Paris must have looked good, because he seems to have spent his remaining years in Texas remembering whatever it was he left behind.

Eventually, he was re-promoted to full colonel, presided over the court of inquiry that tried to figure out what went wrong at the Little Bighorn, and departed Texas to be superintendent of West Point, where he invited his friend Sam Clemens to come play with one of the new machine guns, thereby planting the seeds that grew into *A Connecticut Yankee in King Arthur's Court.*

During the Spanish-American War, Uncle Wesley commanded at the Battle of Manila, sending Arthur MacArthur to attack the city from one side while Philippine rebels attacked from the other. When the Spanish surrendered, he became the first American military governor of the islands, much to the surprise of the Filipinos who'd been under the impression we'd come as liberators. A few months later when Emilio Aguinaldo launched a war against us, Uncle Wesley was safely back in Paris, where he'd probably wanted to be all along, representing the United States at the Peace Conference that ended the Spanish part of the American War.

With a record like that, somebody from the family was going to have to follow in Uncle Wesley's footsteps. My grandfather drew the short straw and entered West Point two years behind Arthur MacArthur's son, Douglas. A new generation of Merritts and MacArthurs mobilizing together. Grandfather was a lover, not a fighter, and was lucky to graduate. When he did, the army sent him to the Philippines, where he was lucky to escape with his life.

By the time he arrived, Douglas MacArthur had already made a name for himself. He'd been leading a patrol through enemy-infested jungle when a couple of guerillas stepped onto the trail in front of him and started shooting. MacArthur gunned them down with his service .45 and returned to camp covered in glory.

Grandfather led his own patrol into the jungle, but the guerillas had changed their tactics. They went for the last guy in line. Then picked off the new last guy. When Grandfather came out the other side, he was alone, and when his hitch was up, felt no need to reenlist. Instead, he used his engineering degree to travel around the South building mills.

Huntsville must have needed a mill, because that's where he met my grandmother, and her sisters who refused to talk to him.

World War I was Uncle John's war, and it taught him to be Uncle John. Not that he wouldn't have been Uncle John anyway, that's the way he was made, but being in charge of a mule train across the Pyrenees when one of the mules plummeted over the side gave him room to develop his potential. Uncle John probably knew what was on that mule, it's the kind of thing officers are paid to keep track of. But as the war dragged on, that mule began carrying more and more stuff. Every time something disappeared from the supply depot or the mess tent, it got loaded onto the mule. By the time the Armistice rolled around, that mule was carrying a whole battalion's worth of supplies.

The Second World War came just in time for Dad. He graduated in June 1940 and went straight into the army. With a master's in business administration, he was assigned to the Quartermaster Corps...which sent him back to school. The same school he'd just graduated from. Harvard Business School. The army was going through one of its periodic fits of trying to modernize, and civilian universities were filled with officers taking crash courses in modern.

Dad landed in the same classes with the same professors he'd graduated from a few weeks earlier and looked like a Supply Corps genius to the generals and colonels who were struggling with the whole concept of modern. On test days, he'd pull the test he was about to take from his notes, glance at it, and ace the thing. When he finished up at Harvard Business School a second time, he was sent straight to the Pentagon.

Modernizing or not, the army still clung to its courtly ways, at least when officers were involved. And courtliness required new officers to pay their respects to the commandant. In Washington, DC, the commandant was the Commandant-in-Chief. Franklin Delano Roosevelt.

No shave-tail would ever have been under the illusion that the president would actually receive him. The protocol was to drop by the White House, hand your card to one of the guards, and go on about your business. Which Dad got around to doing one particularly muggy afternoon on the way back from a tennis match.

Who knows what authority White House guards have? Dad sure didn't. When the guard told him to wait, Dad stood politely outside the gate while the guard made a phone call. And came back with the news, "Mrs. Roosevelt will receive you now."

I have never heard Mrs. Roosevelt's side of this story, but according to Dad, it was not a comfortable half hour for a junior officer in sweaty tennis clothes, sipping tea, and making small talk with the wife of the president of the United States.

By June 1944 Dad was—at least in Mother's estimate, and, perhaps, in reality—the youngest major in the United States Army. He was sure the youngest looking. I've seen pictures. He was so baby-faced he looked like he would have needed parental permission to even be in the army, and here he was in a major's uniform. Which led to some smaller brushes with the law in the persons of various military policemen who were under the impression that seeing is most likely believing.

The brush with the law that almost got him hanged involved another round of tennis. On the day after the Normandy invasion, somebody noticed that June 6, 1944, was circled on Dad's wall calendar, along with the words, "Today we take it to them."

That particular red circle and note had been on his calendar for a month, and the wall being at the Pentagon, there was a good chance Dad had picked up some advance word about D-Day. The very least army security could imagine was that he had some loose lips on him. The most they could imagine had to do with enemy agents and nighttime meetings on park benches that led to our boys getting pinned down under the cliffs at Omaha Beach. And don't give us that crap about tennis tournaments, we've heard that before. As it worked out, Major General Leroy Lutes had heard it before, too, back in May when they organized the tournament, and Dad beat the rap.

Korea was Cousin John's war.

He was a company commander up near the Ch'ongch'on River when hundreds of thousands of Chinese soldiers Douglas MacArthur promised weren't there came swarming through the American lines. It was Cousin John's job to stop them.

Even though Doughy was sliding into matrimonially induced senility, she knew what the telegram from the Secretary of the Army meant. It arrived in early afternoon, and for blocks, and all through the night, her neighbors could hear her screaming.

Weeks later, a letter from John showed up, saying, "They're sending us into a very tight spot tomorrow. Frankly, I can't see how we'll get out of it." It was after reading that letter that Aunt Doughy began stashing wads of money under the carpets.

While I was waiting to take my turn in the army, Rachel and I went down to the Memorial Arts Center to see *The Royal Hunt of the Sun*.

It wasn't just Andy Warhol who'd cashed in on the disaster at Orly. The Atlanta Art Association had been marketing the shit out of it for years. Now, half-a-decade later, they'd turned all those dead wives and mothers into a fine new center for the performing arts.

You'd have thought they would have plastered the lobby with prints of "129 Die in Jet," but kindred-spirit Andy Warhol wasn't anywhere to be seen. Instead, Hebrew prophets lined the walls. An Atlanta artist named Ben Smith had done a series of woodblocks—life-size prints in tones of black and orange, of white and flesh—of gaunt, spooky-looking men with hollow eyes clutching robes about themselves. There are a lot of prophets in the Old Testament, and Ben Smith had done most of them. In the spirit of the City Too Busy to Hate, the prints weren't just for decoration. They were for sale.

At intermission a crowd accumulated in the lobby, talking and laughing and working its way toward the refreshment stand. And whispering. Not pointing, that would have been discourteous, but gesturing with their chins, or saying quietly, "To your left. In the corner. It's him."

The corner wasn't bustling and crowded. Just three or four men, well dressed in conservative suits discussing something among themselves. Colored men.

It took a moment to realize who they were, at least who one of them was. It was Martin Luther King and a fistful of his aides having a private conversation among themselves, and God, and the Old Testament prophets.

I tried to imagine four well-dressed colored men hanging out on the ramshackle wooden walkways that had been torn down to build this place. I didn't believe, even in the 1950s, that anybody would have told them they weren't welcome. Black man, don't let the sun set on you in the art school. But I think enough people would have gone up and asked, "Yes? May I help you?" that they would have gotten the picture.

It was different that night. Nobody approached them. Not because they were colored. Because they were Dr. King. Whatever he was discussing was too important, too intimate, too...godly, almost...for any of us to break in on. I wondered about that later, if that was the way people started treating him toward the end of his life, as some kind of saint you weren't supposed to approach too closely. It must have taken a lot of the fun out of jostling in crowds and chatting with strangers.

For a moment, I was seized with the desire to walk over and say something, but it was hard to think what. "Hi there, Dr. King. How's this racial-equality dream coming along?" That didn't seem right, but anything else would have sounded just as silly. Besides, that probably wasn't what he wanted to talk about. What he probably wanted to talk about was football. Or how his kids were doing in school. Anything but this racial-equality dream that was consuming his life.

Malcolm X had had a different dream, the dream of Americans forever kept from one another by the color of their skin. His was the same dream I saw in the flaming cross in a frozen cornfield in North Carolina. Where Mr. X's hatred and fear of Crackers turned lots of us into Crackers, Dr. King assumed we were all children of the same God and let us forget about being Crackers long enough to see one another as brothers.

Dr. King created us, but we created him, too. If black Americans needed a leader, white Americans needed a saint, and he became our anointed. He was a brave, flawed, charismatic man. A man America was supremely lucky to cast up for herself in a time of such turmoil and distrust. But it wasn't God who made Martin Luther King into a saint. We did that for ourselves.

Less than four months later he would be dead. Shot down by a white man who held fast to Malcolm X's dream. Now, the bulk of my lifetime later, when I think of the hollow-eyed portraits staring from the walls of the Memorial Arts Center, I don't see woodblock prophets. I see the faces of a past we would not choose to live again.

A few nights later, Ceci showed up in my bedroom. It was a chilly evening, and she said she was too cold to sleep. I could see why, what with not having anything on except her most seductive wig.

Years earlier something had gone wrong with her follicles and her skull was as bald as if it had been boiled. She said it was from absent-mindedly chewing on a brush while oil painting. She'd been using white paint, had swallowed lead, and her hair fell out. That seemed like an odd bit of bad luck since white paint is made with titanium.

She was only fifteen years older than me, but naked, she might have been some pickled corpse left over from the time of Ramses II. She stank of cigarette smoke, she was wobbly from vodka, and because I didn't drink vodka, carried a twelve-ounce ice-tea glass filled with bourbon she expected me to down at a single gulp. Then, before I could scramble out of the way, she grabbed me in the crotch and demanded, "Stick it in."

I have been in more seductive situations, and I could think of all sorts of reasons not to stick it in her. I can think of more now that I have the leisure to reflect upon the offer. At the time, what I thought was, *how soon do I get to leave for the army?* In the army, you have a gun.

In the army you get to see a bit of the world, make friends with your old army buddies, run around and yell, shoot rifles, and throw things that blow up. The army was fun, if you didn't take it too seriously.

The army sure didn't take itself seriously. They trained us in Missouri. In February. In the snow. For the jungles of Vietnam. Sometimes we didn't train at all because the snow had gotten too deep. They had a rule about that. Also, when the weather was too cold. They had a rule about that, too.

That winter was cold and snowy and we spent a lot of time indoors, shining boots and polishing brass. When we could get outside, we practiced marching in case we were called upon to stage a parade for the Viet Cong.

Of the eight weeks of basic training, we spent an entire week running around with sheathed bayonets on our rifles yelling, "What is the spirit of the bayonet? *Kill.*" And poking bags of sawdust in case we were sent over the top in a mass attack with sheathed bayonets against bags of sawdust.

The rifles we trained with had wooden stocks and long barrels so we could bash in doors like in World War II movies, then toss in a grenade while we flattened ourselves against the building. The only guy I ever heard of who tried that in Vietnam got blown away when fragments from the grenade blasted through the bamboo wall he'd flattened himself against. Over there, we used M16's with short barrels and plastic stocks which would not bash in doors and which we had not trained on.

The one weapon we did train on that I actually used in Vietnam was hand grenades, but that day I was on KP, so I missed it.

They had us memorize the chain of command all the way up to President Johnson, which, given how far down the chain we were, took some memorizing, but they never mentioned anything about the tactics the enemy employed or showed us their weapons. The enemy, as I understand it, got an entire year of training, including lots of time on our weapons and our tactics.

Since we all pulled KP sometimes, or spent a few days laid up with respiratory infections, or just got snowed in, none of us actually came out of training with the training we were supposed to come out of training with. When the Inspector General came by to make sure we'd gotten it anyway, we were ordered to lie. We were, as the brass constantly reminded us, the best-trained, best-equipped army in history.

All that was a bastion of sanity compared to what was going on in the world outside. By then, the war in Vietnam had stopped being a matter of foreign policy and turned into a question of conscience. The problem was, consciences differed.

Some people claimed the whole idea of war was immoral and began marching around in the street singing sappy ballads about peace. Other people weren't against war in general, they just thought we were on the wrong side of this one and insisted we bring the army home. People who thought we were on the right side of this one couldn't see the morality in abandoning the good people in Vietnam who trusted us to be on their side. The people who thought we were on the wrong side didn't believe there were good people on our side and took to calling those who thought there were, fascists. Millions of the people who got called fascists had risked their lives a generation earlier fighting real fascists and didn't take kindly to being called that. They said the moral thing was to do whatever it took to win. But doing that involved the draft, and a lot of people thought the whole idea of conscription was immoral and started burning their draft cards. The people who got called fascists suspected the ones who burned their draft cards didn't really care about the draft, they just didn't care to get drafted. A few really did care about the draft. Or peace. Or something, and started bombing recruiting offices to prove it. People opposed to bombing anything launched a campaign against napalm, while still others said it was immoral not to back our troops with everything we had. And we had atom bombs.

The whole thing got balled up with race, and some people started claiming the war was nothing but a scheme by white Americans to send black Americans to Vietnam to kill brown Asians. Other people thought that was a racist thing to say. Why, they wanted to know, had it been okay to go to France to save white Europeans from Nazis, but it wasn't okay to go to Vietnam to save brown Asians from Commies? Those of us who were willing to actually do the saving stopped being patriotic young men and started being drug-addled baby killers. The whole thing was enough to make a body want to go hunt up some babies.

The army didn't have any doubts about why we were fighting, though. One evening, when we were worn out from a long day of poking sheathed bayonets into bags of sawdust, the company commander came by and spoke to each one of us individually. "Private," he said when I stepped into the office, "we are fighting in Vietnam to stop Communism."

He paused to let that sink in. Then wound up with, "Communism looks good on paper, but it doesn't work in the real world."

Hold the phone, I thought, remembering all those people at Duke who'd imagined the same thing. "Not to me," I said. "Communism doesn't look good to me."

"Communism," the company commander reinformed me, "looks good on paper."

"No, Sir," I said. "Communism does not look good on paper."

"Private," he tried again. "Communism most certainly does look good on paper."

"Communism," I said, "is a terrible idea. How could anybody think Communism looks good on paper?"

Because that's what the script the Colonel gave me says, I could almost hear the company commander thinking. "Communism looks good on paper." Then, after he'd thought it over a bit, "*Very* good."

"You want me to go to Vietnam to fight Communism," I said, "because it looks good on paper?"

"That's why we need to stop it," he said as I saluted and turned to leave. Then, "Communism sure does look good on paper."

In the barracks we pretty much stuck together, black soldiers stuck with blacks, white soldiers with whites, and got along when we had to. After all, we had a common enemy. And he'd be coming by at 4:30 in the morning, rattling our beds and making sure we didn't miss one minute of being in the snow.

Then, one day, Martin Luther King was murdered and the army canceled our weekend passes and sealed us inside the post. Outside, America was burning, and inside, race became something to huddle around. Most of the black guys knew where the white guys had been when King was shot, so they were pretty sure we hadn't actually pulled the trigger, but they couldn't help suspecting we might have had something to do with it behind the scenes. Other black guys weren't so analytical about it and thought it didn't make any difference who actually pulled the trigger, all you Crackers are guilty. As for us Crackers, we didn't feel very good about it either. The ghosts of our sins had come down from the attic and were stalking through the house.

One day, when I wasn't expecting good news, Andy Warhol was assassinated. I was probably the only person in the army who cared.

It happened on June 3, 1968, six years to the day after Mother burned alive on the banks of the Seine and was a good opportunity to have gotten a newspaper and traced a photo of Warhol's body. I could have made a name for myself with "1 Dies in Studio." Unfortunately for the future of fake art, the assassination didn't pan out. Like everything else in Warhol's strange, hollow life, there was a lot more hype than substance to his death, and he pulled through.

Toward the end of training, a sergeant loaded a squad of us onto a truck and off we motored into the gathering twilight.

That was the night our company was going to learn to establish a perimeter, and send out guards, and set up listening posts, and defend ourselves from the Viet Cong. We seven were the Viet Cong, and it was fun. Hands down, the most fun thing I did in training.

The other hundred and thirteen guys in our company never had a chance. We stole their rifles, made off with their packs, counted coup, and in a single devastating move, took the company commander and first sergeant prisoner. Seven of us without any training in insurgent tactics, with no experience working together, without even a plan, we did that. It was exhilarating and made me feel like I was in northern Alabama running Yankees to ground with Nathan Bedford Forrest. And scared the shit out of me.

In a few weeks, this would be real. And our side, no matter what my private inclinations on the matter, wasn't going to be Nathan Bedford Forrest. In Vietnam, we'd be Yankees.

When most Americans get sentimental about our boys at war, they think of embattled farmers beside a rude bridge. Or marines raising the flag at Iwo Jima, and rangers going up the cliffs at Omaha Beach. They think of the brave, tenacious, doomed defense at Corregidor and Petersburg. And the courageous successful defense at Cemetery Ridge and Bastogne and the Seven Days. They conjure up images of opened-faced, smiling GI's passing out Hershey bars to people who'd learned to expect nothing but rape and terror, murder and looting from teenagers in foreign uniforms. But for me, it's something different. When I get sentimental, I think of our boys marching onto troopships. I love the idea of that.

Generation IV, if I've got this generation business straight, sailed away in wooden ships to watch from the foot of Chapultepec while school-age cadets wrapped themselves in Mexican flags and plunged to their deaths

When Generation VII fancied the time had come to do something about the Kaiser, troopships were made of iron and lit by electricity, but the kissing sweethearts and tossing children into the air one last time—forever in a lot of cases—was the same.

For our parents in Generation VIII, it was Gen VII all over again, even the same ships, sometimes, and the enemy the sons of the same enemy.

Then it was Generation VIII (a), and off to Korea.

We should thank our lucky stars, because there's another way we could have fought our wars, a way that haunts the memories of people who did their fighting closer to home. Those are the memories of bleary-eyed high school kids who should have been worrying about prom dates and algebra tests, stumbling out of bed to man antiaircraft guns. Of children and sweethearts cowering in bomb shelters. Of sirens blaring night after night, and people too old to fight walking the streets as air-raid wardens.

Memories of bombed-out cites, of starvation, of cold. Of ruined factories and burned homes. Of beaten armies and last, desperate defenses. Of whole populations trying to get out of the way of enemies too powerful to fight. And too numerous to be avoided. And too hated and feared ever to be given in to.

Fighting our wars on the other side of the world, that suits me just fine. At least until we can arrange to do the whole thing on the moon, preferably the back side. When that happens, we can salute our gallant young blasting into space to defend our old people and children and loved ones as far from our sweet land as ever we can manage.

The day came when it was my turn, and I marched onto a Flying Tiger airliner along with a hundred-and-some other guys and a bevy of stewardesses, and flew in style to Tan Son Nhut Air Base in South Vietnam, helping carry the latest of our wars to a place very far away, indeed.

We took a bus in through Saigon, through a shimmering kaleido-scope of noise and smells and unrecognizable sights. Through old men staring at us from unreadable faces. Past motorbikes putt-puttering by. Past women in gorgeous silk ao-dais. Past ancient French automobiles and trucks spewing diesel fumes amid the beat-up pastels of decaying colonial buildings. We rode past smoke rising from cooking stalls, people lounging in doorways, past babies and mama-sans screeching like cats in a strange language. Past hands reaching toward our bus. Past garbage and rubble and traffic and potholes, each isolated and disconnected, nothing forming into a recognizable whole.

Was the man in the yellow shirt hiding in the shadows because he didn't want us to get a good look at him? Or was it the police he was avoiding? Or his wife? Or maybe he just wanted to get out of the sun. Or do a drug deal. Or hawk a fake watch.

We had friends in those streets, lots of them. People who hated the Communists and wished us well. But which ones were they? Some of the people outside the bus had already killed Americans. Others, probably most, just wanted us to go home, and the invaders from the north, too. And leave them to manage their own lives in their own ways.

In a land where knowing how to see could save your life, where not being able to read a face or a situation or a warning could get you and everybody around you killed, we were overwhelmed with sights. People and objects, light and color, sounds and smells and movement. And we could see nothing.

❧

I spent a few weeks pulling guard duty at Cu Chi.

Cu Chi was a huge base camp north of Saigon, the home of the Twenty-Fifth Infantry Division. It was one of the most heavily defended spots in the entire country, a place to get introduced to the war without having to be part of it. Or to get away from the war without actually going anywhere. Not having any rank to speak of, my introduction to the war was to help defend Cu Chi, which meant I spent a lot of time out on the bunker line.

Cu Chi was ringed by bunkers with interlocking fields of fire, chain-link fences, coil after coil of razor wire, and free-fire zones carefully zeroed in and waiting for human waves of North Koreans to come screaming across the open fields, like happened in the last war. I was assigned to bunker twenty-seven.

To the rear of bunker twenty-seven, and bunker twenty-six, and bunker twenty-eight, was the helicopter pad. It wasn't the people in Cu Chi our bunkers were protecting so much as the big Chinook helicopters behind us. We could hear them at odd hours, taking off or coming in. The enemy didn't have anything like them. As far as I knew, nobody had anything like them.

Chinooks were a marvel of American technology. Fast and mobile and unbelievably powerful. They were the way we dropped hundreds of troops on the enemy and how we supplied our guys at lonely firebases. They were the way we delivered mail and medicine and brought our wounded and dead back to us. Chinooks were how we were going to win the war, and it was good knowing they were on our side.

❧

Three guys rotated through the bunker with me, two at a time. One, whose name I never caught, or, at least, can't recall, spent a lot of time lying on the shelf in back, Zenning away the hours until he could go home. Someone whose name I do remember was Nikiyama.

Nikiyama had ambition. He was Hawaiian, a beautiful golden color and astonishingly handsome. He kept his boots shined and his jungle fatigues starched and pressed when everybody else took pride in dressing like grizzled veterans. Nikiyama was the best-looking soldier I ever met. I think his plan was to become Trooper of the Year and get reassigned to an office where the colonels could show him off to visiting congressmen. Until that happened, he spent the nights he was in the bunker polishing his brass to the sparks raining down from Raymond's cigar.

He was permanent party in bunker twenty-seven. So were Raymond and the Guy on the Shelf, although, where Raymond was concerned, nothing felt like it would stay permanent for very long. They'd all three pulled strings to spend their tours at Cu Chi pulling guard duty, rather than out in the field where people would try to kill them.

None of the three were committed housekeepers, and things that should have been stored away were as jumbled together as toys in a child's bedroom. Rockets leaned against the walls. Magazines preloaded with rifle bullets were scattered across the floor like spilled playing cards. So were fragmentation grenades, white-phosphorous grenades, concussion grenades, rifle grenades, smoke grenades, TNT bombs, and claymores.

Machine-gun belts hung from the ceiling like dirty laundry, as did the hammock where Raymond spent most of his time. The hammock was held up by detonating cord, a high explosive fashioned into what looked like clothesline. You could chop down trees with it. One turn around the trunk and, whammo, cordwood.

It's dark in a bunker when the sun goes down. You don't want to ruin your night vision, so the only light we had was from the sparks cascading from Raymond's cigars onto the grenades and TNT bombs and claymores kicked beneath his hammock. A few years earlier, the surgeon general had made a big deal about smoking being hazardous, but not enough people had internalized it yet.

Besides, there was a friendly village lurking out front and nobody wanted to go outside for a smoke with a friendly village nearby. If you lit up within rifle shot of a friendly village, a slug from an AK-47 would catch you in the face, so Raymond did the prudent thing and confined his smoking to indoors.

Late one rainy afternoon, I slipped out of the bunker looking for a place to relieve my bladder. I walked a hundred yards toward the Chinooks, then over in the direction of bunker twenty-six trying to scare up a little privacy and came to a spot, blind to both bunkers, where nobody could see me.

I've always liked to aim at a target and found a waist-high bush flapping like a signal-flag in the rain. And discovered a hole, maybe a meter in diameter, sunk into the ground behind the bush. And rungs descending into the hole like steps on a ladder.

At first the hole didn't seem all that deep, just a yard or two. Then it snapped into focus. A great, round chimney plunging at least ten meters down. The rungs were on both sides, cut into the clay and reinforced with wooden planks. It was a tidy, professional-looking hole. At the bottom, a secondary tunnel headed off toward the friendly village.

Here we were, protected by miles of twisted barbed wire; by mines and mortars and machine guns; by artillery; by napalm and attack helicopters that could lift off within seconds; by bunkers filled with rockets and fragmentation grenades, white-phosphorous grenades, smoke grenades, concussion grenades, claymores, TNT bombs, and men with rifles; by the wealth and technology and might of a supremely powerful nation; and none of it would do a thing to stop an enemy who'd come crawling out of that hole. The day after that happened, all those beautiful Chinooks would be scratched from the equipment roster, and the names of whomever had been in the bunkers twenty-six and twenty-seven and twenty-eight would become entries in the morning report.

The sergeant of the guard came by at sunset and asked whether we had anything to report. I told him about the tunnel, but it was nothing he cared to hear. No tunnels out there, he told me.

"I saw it, Sarge. Just now. I got a good look. It's a tunnel."

"It's a well, Troop. Been checked out. It's a well."

"It's got steps, Sarge. And a secondary tunnel heading off toward..."

"It's a well. I told you. A well."

"So who dug the son of a bitch? Army's been here for years and we don't use..."

"Maybe it was already here."

"There's no water at the bottom, except rain. And hard clay all the way down. And steps and..."

"Listen, god damn it. It's a well. A fucking well. If that fucking bothers you, climb the fuck down and check it the fuck out."

Like a lot of reasoning where the army is concerned, there wasn't any answer to that. I sure wasn't going down those steps. The best I could do was wait for morning. And hope I made it to the field before whoever was at the end of that secondary tunnel came climbing out.

There's something called jungle eyes, and it's easier to do than you think. It's just that it can be hard to stop doing, sometimes.

The trick is to forget about color and just look at shapes. Color is easy to disguise. Paint your face green and black and wriggle under a bush and you become one more bit of background...as long as the people looking for you pay attention to color. But you can't do much about your shape. You can curl around or recede into a low place with only your head sticking out. But you still look like a curled-up person, or a head, to anybody who sees past the colors. Jake Gyre could do it from the middle of a river on a speeding boat.

From Cu Chi the army sent me to live under a bridge on the Saigon River: the Song Saigon, the Vietnamese called it, thirty, maybe thirty-two river miles downstream from the Parrot's Beak where Cambodia juts into Vietnam.

The Song Saigon isn't the Chattahoochee. It's a big, broad tropical river, yellow with mud and almost level with the fields and villages it runs through. And fast-flowing. So fast that if you fell off the dock at the wrong time, you couldn't swim back, but had to climb out on the shore.

In both directions. We were hundreds of miles upriver from the South China Sea, but twice a day, the moon sucked the water upstream quicker than a man could swim. This was not familiar landscape to an American.

There were others there with us, but nine in our squad: eight white Southerners, enlisted men under the command of a black staff sergeant. We had three boats, and Jake and I shared one—taking turns motoring up or down the river or through the canals that cut across the fields. Looking for the enemy or taking infantry to drop-off points. I was very good at killing bags of sawdust with bayonets, but riverboats were something I had not been introduced to.

The boats weren't armored. And they weren't armed. But with a pair of hundred-horsepower Chrysler Marine inboard engines, they could move. And with a squad of infantry onboard, we had firepower.

The infantry guys felt vulnerable on the river with no cover and no place to dig in if we got ambushed. But that's not the way it seemed to me. One shot, I figured, that's all anybody would get. And then I'd pull back the throttles, the boat would stand high in the water, the props would throw a rooster tail that would capsize any sampan we passed, and we'd be out of there. But mostly there wasn't going to be a first shot because I'd already have pulled back the throttles.

Driving that boat was fun and made me proud. For a few weeks of my youth, I *was* the United States of America, ten thousand miles from home, and the baddest thing on the water. I was Fort Ticonderoga and Chapultepec, Manila Bay, Midway, and the Great Marianas Turkey Shoot, and the reason nobody, nobody anywhere, wanted to try conclusions with the United States of America.

The bridge was a classic piece of American engineering, big, concrete and steel, as imposing and solid as a bridge on an interstate highway. It was our gift to the Vietnamese people, and the enemy wanted to blow it up.

Proving they couldn't was my job, and Jake's, and the job of the other six guys who drove the boats. It was our sergeant's job, too, and the job of the man in the jeep who ran the mobile searchlight. It was the job of the guys who sat on the bridge in the M60 Patton tank, barrel lowered menacingly toward Cambodia. It was the job of the Wolfhounds and the ARVN's sandbagged four to a bunker in the piers beneath the bridge: two soldiers from the Army of the Republic of Vietnam buddied with two Americans from the Second Battalion, Twenty-Seventh Infantry. Eight bunkers. Thirty-two men tossing grenades into the water. Those grenades, somebody in headquarters calculated, would stop a diver from planting explosives on one of the piers.

There may even have been something to that. I was in the water once, a couple of hundred yards away, when somebody dropped in a casual grenade. And I really got slapped. I wouldn't have wanted to swim up through a cascade of that, especially not while towing a load of high-explosive.

At night, Jake and I waited beneath the bridge in one of the boats in case a diver swam up anyway. Our problem was the guys in the bunkers. With nothing to do but toss grenades over the side, nights up there were long and tedious. The cure was primo, Southeast Asian bud, which made things down where we were plenty exciting, what with the grenades from dope-addled goofs going off around us.

One night, when we were tied up beneath bridge pier number two, a grenade landed in our boat. It rattled around a bit before rolling over the side and blowing a hole in the hull. Jake, didn't have a sense of humor about that, grabbed his M16, stormed up the substructure and into the bunker, and waving the rifle at all four occupants, demanded to know who dropped it. "You tell me right now or I waste every one of you fuckers."

From the pointing and cowering, it was pretty obvious that the ARVN hugging himself on the far side of the bunker was the one to go for, and Jake put the rifle to the man's forehead. "You die, Mother."

And pulled the trigger.

Click.

The man moaned and fell back.

"Next time, Fucker, there'll be a round in the chamber."

We didn't have any more trouble with grenades coming out of pier number two, and that's where we tied up from then on.

❧

The man in the jeep who ran the mobile searchlight was named Tony Paradise, and he was from Brooklyn. He was tall and rangy and had the same prescription for boredom as the guys in the bunkers. Dope in Vietnam was so plentiful and so good that when his tour was up, and he returned to Brooklyn, he felt short-shrifted and re-upped so he could spend another year in Vietnam puffing his brains out.

He was also a Rosicrucian and spent hours studying the Secrets of the Ages from a mail-order course the Brothers of the Rosy Cross had sent him. In the jeep at night he practiced controlling things with beams from his mind. One of the things he could control was a strip of paper balanced on a pin stuck in a cork and placed inside a milk bottle. He could make the paper spin around. Then he could make it stop and spin the other way. Tony was very entertaining company.

"Do that," I asked one night, "make paper spin around inside a milk bottle."

"We're in Vietnam," Tony said. "Where am I supposed to get a milk bottle?" By then, he'd been in-country seven months.

"How long you been taking this Rosicrucian course?"

"About six weeks," Tony said. "It arrived six weeks ago."

"There any milk bottles in Vietnam six weeks ago?"

"It was lesson number four," Tony gave me a what-planet-are-you-from sort of look. "I can tell the future, too. That's lesson three."

"You can tell the future?"

"Plenty of people have the gift. Just look at my sister. One time she was watching television, and she got this feeling something was wrong and she went downstairs, and, sure enough, our brother was mushing up the goldfish with a spoon. You tell me she didn't..."

"How long was your brother down there?"

"I don't know. Few hours maybe. He's not right. That's why she was home, to keep an eye on him." Tony exhaled a cloud of smoke. It was like having a conversation with a burning bush.

"Only predictions I ever heard," I said, "people don't tell you until later on. I can do that. A year ago, you're going to get drafted. How's that for something that came true?"

"Why didn't you tell me? You should have..."

"Didn't know your address."

"You have the gift. I'll sign you up." Tony rummaged through some scraps of paper on the floor of the jeep. "There's a form here, somewhere. They come in the back of Incredible Hulk comics and..."

"Predict something, first."

"What do you want me to predict?"

"Whatever. Just tell me before it happens so I know it's true. Then I'll sign up."

"You mean that? Just one prediction and you'll take the course? Just one prediction? You really mean it?"

Sure, I meant it. It didn't seem like anything to worry about.

Another night I was on the far bank, tossing back shots with one of the Wolfhounds. His whiskey wasn't very good, but it was better than any I'd brought and I gulped it like he was about to snatch it back.

Under the single bulb I could see him for what he was. Gray skin. Sunken cheeks. Veins and tattoos and scars slatting over reptilian muscles. A recruiting sergeant had found him shoveling coal at the bottom of one of the rattiest freighters on Lake Erie and had promised him a better life. He'd almost gotten it.

"Weren't no big thing," he told me. "I was just sitting on this little piss-ant of a hill, rolling a toke. Didn't have nothing to do and weren't anybody nowhere around. Just water, silver in all the rice fields. Then I saw, way off to one side, these black pajamas bobbing up and down: a little old mamasan stooping through her paddy, working straight toward where I was. Just me and her and all that water.

"I started thinking, the way we were, the two of us, what if I zapped her? Who'd ever know?

"She never turned around or nothing, just kept sticking those bright little plants in the mud. And coming toward me. Just step and bend. Step and bend." He poured three more fingers into a partially uncrumpled paper cup.

"Hell. My weapon was right there and she wasn't offering much resistance, if you know what I mean. So I tried sighting in on her. Didn't mean nothing by it, just wanted to see what it looked like on her.

"She just kept stepping and bending. Black on silver. We were like that for a long time, her thinking about rice, and me thinking about the best time to squeeze off a round being just when she starts up from a bend and how when I get back to the others, I'm going to tell them I saved this mamasan's life today when I had her dead to rights and didn't squeeze the trigger, and, just then, some sweat dropped in my eye and she began to stand up and I blowed her away.

"She tumbled back in the water. Splashed a lot at first, but after a while she quit. Time came I finished the toke and headed back to camp.

"Just one shot. Ain't that something? Always was good with a rifle. Got a sharpshooter on the M14, but I still think about her some. Like maybe I shouldn't have done it. But I can't see no reason why not.

"Like I said, weren't no big thing." He gestured at the bottle of whiskey. "Another shot?"

Back home, the war had turned into bad politics. A presidential election was coming up, and every time voters switched on the evening news and were treated to a new set of numbers about dead Americans, the politics became worse. Maybe...you can just hear some hack saying...if we quit pestering the enemy, they'd leave us alone. That way, our boys would stop being killed so much and the news would look better. At the bridge, we were ordered to pull in our patrols.

No more Fort Ticonderoga. No more Chapultepec or Manila Bay or Midway. No more Great Marianas Turkey Shoot. Our job was to keep ourselves safe by paddling around inside the string of logs that protected the bridge from floating debris. From then on, we spent our days swimming and sunning ourselves and drinking beer, and Jake and I spent our nights tied to pier number two, safe beneath the one bunker we were certain a grenade would never tumble out of again. And the enemy was left to himself.

Because Tony Paradise was up all night running the searchlight and smoking dope, he slept during the day. One afternoon he had a daymare and woke up screaming.

"They're going to blow the bridge," he said. He was pale and shaking and genuinely terrified.

"Who?" we all wanted to know. "Who's going to blow up the bridge?"

"They. The enemy. On November fifth. Lots of guys are going to get killed. It was horrible."

"You saw that?"

"There was a full moon. I saw everything."

"Me," somebody said. "Did you see me?"

"And me? What about me? Did I get killed?"

"How should I know? Guys were hanging all over the rail. I couldn't see who they were."

"How about you? What happened to you?"

"I don't know. I wasn't here."

"You weren't here? How could you not be here? You're *always* here."

"All I know is I'm not going to be here, and a lot of guys are going to be killed, and...." It was surprising how dignified Tony sounded.

But, still, he wasn't going to be here? Tony had been at the bridge eight months. He was going to be here another four, then he was going home. And now he was trying to tell us the bridge would be blown while he was somewhere else? That wasn't going to happen. Tony Paradise had made his prediction, and the prediction he made just went to show he couldn't predict anything at all.

The man in the bunker, the ARVN Jake didn't shoot after he dropped the grenade on us, died anyway. A few weeks later, Jake and I were in our boat tied up at the usual place when somebody yelled, "OH, SHIT," and three figures plunged out of the bunker.

The shadows along the piers flashed black while the concrete facing us glared a hateful gray-white. A fragmentation grenade burst overhead and a hard noise slapped our ears. Jake was out of the boat and toward those people before the sound reached the far bank.

He came back with one of the Wolfhounds, dragging an ARVN. They had their arms around him. His head lolled forward, his knees were bent, and his toes scraped along the concrete. They were moving in and out of the shadows. I couldn't see him well, and I couldn't tell what was wrong, at least from the front. No marks. No blood. He looked like a drunk being helped to bed.

They lowered him onto the deck of our boat, face down like a drowned man, and I saw his back. It was dark with blood. He'd been running like the others when the grenade went off.

I rode with him while the boat slammed across the river to the chopper pad on the far side. Holes were burned in his uniform at his neck and shoulders, his arms, his spine, his kidneys, his buttocks, his genitals. Blood welled everywhere, a hundred wounds too deep to staunch. His trouser leg had been blown off, and his calf was mostly gone as if it had been eaten by crabs. He squirmed a little and opened and closed his hand on the deck. He might have been trying to tell me something, I couldn't tell. I wanted to take his hand in mine, but I hesitated.

Then we were on the bank and he was unloaded and I lost my chance. I wish I had him back, now. After he was gone, I rinsed the deck with river water. It didn't take much.

Later, I went up to the bunker. It was a mess. Piss and dried puke. A small wooden table blown over and as full of holes as a rural stop sign. The sandbags were all leaking. Liquor and glass puddled on the floor. An ARVN was shrieking at a Wolfhound, and they were both screaming at another Wolfhound. The one who'd dropped the grenade. After all those nights on the river, it was us who hurt them.

"Dead. Died twice on the pad, and they brought him around. Then he died again," one of the other boat drivers climbed into the bunker.

"They cut his clothes off and you could see his back good. You should have stuck around."

After a while people returned to playing cards and dropping grenades in the river. The bottles and baggies came out and things got back to normal. The odd part was that nobody important ever seemed to notice anything had happened. No officer took charge. No sergeant came, and, as far as I know, none ever thought he should have.

The Wolfhound who dropped the grenade was still in a fog. I think I would have been, too. He kept holding his right hand—his grenade hand—in front of him, making squeezing motions the way the dying man had on the boat. Then he turned his arm over and a dark trace of blood ran down his wrist. "Look at that, I've been hit." He hadn't noticed before. "Ain't that some shit? Think I'll get a purple heart?" I guess he needed something to think about. And medication, just like the ARVN he'd killed.

He kept opening and closing his hand, squeezing blood into his palm. He needed more than medication, but I don't see how he could have ever gotten it.

One morning, the sergeant called us in for a briefing. An update, really, on the status of the enemy. We got these from time to time.

The North Vietnamese had a sapper battalion that specialized in bridges, and they were very good. We'd first heard about them when they blew a bridge in I Corps. Then vanished into the countryside.

A few weeks later, they were in Hanoi, hanging out at bars and with girls and catching up on their sleep. A bit of R & R before heading back out.

The next time our sergeant called us over, they'd disappeared from the bars. Nobody knew where they were, but there were only four bridges in the whole country worth their trouble. Three were on the coast. Ours was inland. "They show up on the Ho Chi Minh Trail, only place they going is here."

A few days later, they were in Laos. On the Ho Chi Minh Trail.

A week or two after that, they were in Cambodia.

The last time our sergeant called us over, they were in the Parrot's Beak. Thirty, maybe thirty-two miles upstream.

Artillery, I was thinking. B-52's. A few 500-pound bombs ought to do the trick.

"You know better than to say somethin' like that," the sergeant gave me a sorrowful look. "Nobody's gone bomb nothin' in Cambodia...." We had all the airpower in the world. We had a bridge to protect and scores of Americans. Lots of Vietnamese, too. We knew what the enemy was planning and where they were. And no politician in America wanted to take the heat for sending bombers to Cambodia.

"Maybe we could make a mistake," Jake said. "It's all jungle up there. Bombs could fall in the wrong place and..."

"That's what I tried sayin'," the sergeant said. "Wouldn't work, anyway."

"Why not?"

"They're not in Cambodia anymore. They're comin' down the river to check us out."

"Hot damn! Then we've got them. All we've got to do is wait for them to..."

"Ain't none of you troops gone shoot no fishermen, that's the orders I got."

"Fishermen?"

"You think they gone come marching up here in North Vietnamese dress greens and singing the 'Internationale'? You think they stupid?"

None of us thought that. In this war, stupid was like C-rations. The United States had a monopoly on the entire supply.

It was a pretty morning, a couple of mornings later, when we headed down to the water. There wasn't much to do except lie in the sun and drink beer and listen to the radio. Tomorrow was Election Day, and the Armed Forces Radio Network filled the air with the details.

All that day, groups of fishermen in twos and threes drifted beneath the bridge. Dozens of them in sampans floating past pier number two right below our tank, past two platoons of Wolfhounds, dozens of

ARVN's, and thousands of hand grenades, past machine guns and white-phosphorous grenades and scores of men with automatic rifles. Past artillery and gunships that could arrive within minutes from a single radio call.

They were draft age and looked hard and confident, like soldiers who'd seen a lot of war. They smiled and waved, friendly fishermen, although I never saw any of them cast a net into the river. And until they tried to kill us, friendly they would remain. That was our orders. We wouldn't win their hearts and minds by shooting them.

Election-Day night was Jake's last night in Vietnam. Tomorrow he'd head to Cu Chi and then onto an airplane back to the States. The airplane we called the Freedom Bird and the States we referred to as the World. Jake was going back to the World, and he started celebrating a bit early, seeing as how he'd still be in Vietnam that night, and when the time came to guard the bridge, I was out there on the boat alone.

Even headquarters must have gotten wind something was up, North Vietnamese-sapper-battalion-wise, because around midnight, a captain none of us had ever heard of materialized in bridge pier number two, yelled down to where I was tied up, and ordered me to do something about that god-damn diver. I hadn't noticed any divers, but somebody must have, judging from all the yelling and gesturing.

I took the boat to the shadowy place out on the water where everybody was pointing and motored around for a few minutes, giving ineffective pokes into the darkness with a boat hook. Then came back and tied up at the usual spot. The captain was still there, and he eased his frustration by ordering me to put on my mother-fucking life jacket. Now, Dick Brain.

None of us boat drivers wore life jackets, they interfered with our sprightliness. At least that's what we told the people who tried to make us wear them. Truth is, they interfered with the knowing, worldly image we wanted to project.

Image or not, the captain seemed like he was looking for something to make an issue out of, so I rooted around the bilges until I came up with one. That was the first and only time on the Saigon River that I ever wore a life jacket. Twenty minutes later, he was back on shore and I was calculating how soon it would be safe to take the thing off.

Before I could make my move, the bridge went up in a huge explosion, just like Tony said it would. There was a beautiful full moon that night, but he wasn't there to admire it. Something had gone wrong with a searchlight somewhere else in the war, and Tony had to go see about it.

The diver had planted high explosive on the pier directly beneath my boat, probably because it was the only place he didn't have to worry about grenades. Lucky for me, because it put a good Detroit-steel deck between me and the blast, and I just expanded along with the rest of the shrapnel, splashing down fifty, sixty meters away on the far side of bridge pier number three. It was hard to figure the geometry of that since I would have had to punch through meters of solid concrete before I came down in the water. Also, through sandbags and barbed wire and steel girders, but there I was. And here I still am, all these years later.

I bubbled to the top with what the World War II movies call a million-dollar wound. Other guys weren't so lucky. The tank came to rest, still buttoned up, in eighty feet of water. The men inside never had a chance. Neither did nineteen others, ARVN's in the substructure, Wolfhounds buddied with them. Guys on the banks crushed by falling concrete or speared by flying steel. Twenty-three men gone, defending a bridge that could not be defended with automatic weapons and tanks, with white phosphorous and grenades and machine guns and TNT bombs and air power we weren't allowed to use.

I suppose I should feel bad about not enlisting in the Rosicrucians, but somehow I could never bring myself to do it. Some signs, I think, are better off ignored, no matter what promises you may have made back when you thought you wouldn't have to keep them.

Dawn came, and I was cranked up in a hospital bed, head canted to the side, watching a television at the far end of a long ward lined with wounded soldiers. It was yesterday back home, and the election returns were just coming in. Where Vietnam was concerned, America was always a day behind; it was built right into the system.

The election was a squeaker...Nixon versus Humphrey versus Wallace...and the returns ran on for hours. Through the day and into the evening, until our necks were paralyzed from being turned too long in one direction. Nixon versus Humphrey versus Wallace. Just thinking about that election has given me a great sense of comfort over the years. Whenever our system throws up an unsavory choice of candidates, I remember those three and think, we've had worse. We've *survived* worse.

When the television finally called it for Nixon, I turned away, got my head straight, and relief flooded through me. Finally, the darkness that had engulfed our nation since President Kennedy was murdered was coming to an end. I wished the new president well with all of my heart.

There was a lady at the 106th General Hospital in Yokohama, a Japanese lady. A civilian employee, I think. Or maybe just a visitor. She wasn't wearing a uniform.

She was middle-aged, mid-forties, I'd guess, which meant she knew a lot more people killed in my parents' war than my parents ever did. Ship after ship of young men sent off to lonely islands with no plans to bring them back. Brothers and cousins, her first boyfriend, perhaps, and the man she would have married if enough men had come home. And others who stayed home, old people, grandparents, maybe, aunts and uncles, teachers, her mother and father, shopkeepers, acquaintances she waved to on the street, her own children, possibly, burned alive in the fire-bombings or simply vanished at Hiroshima and Nagasaki. A woman with every cause to go to her grave hating Americans. Hating, especially, American soldiers. A woman who saw me fumbling in the chow line, unable to manage a tray and crutches at the same time.

And came over and asked in the kindest way if she could help, then took my tray and led me to a table and made a place for me. Then bowed and walked away.

I thought of Mother, and how proud she'd been of the men of her generation, how whenever she introduced me to one, she bragged on what he'd done in the war. Mother had the right to be proud of those men and to keep alive the memory of the ones who never came home.

That lady in the chow line would have been proud of her men, too. And would have wanted to keep alive their memories, and the memories of those who'd stayed home and still been caught up in the war. But seeing her notice such a little thing as an out-of-place half-kid struggling with a cafeteria tray, I couldn't help but feel—I still can't help but feel—she had found some way to remember the heroism and put the rest out of her mind.

My grandmother discovered the same secret, the truth that it is better to hold some things more closely than others. To show in the light only the memories that bring more light.

When she told how the Yankee captain warned the family that our Confederate soldier had been seen slipping through their camp, and please ask him to stop because we would hate to have to shoot such a fine-looking young man, she left out the ending.

It wasn't until the close of her life that she told me the rest, the bit she'd been holding back. The part about how her mother's mother ended the war as a widow with two little girls forced to grow up without a daddy, because their daddy had loved them too much to stop coming. And the Yankees shot him. Close enough to the house, I'm sure, for his young wife and little girls to hear the whole thing.

A day or two before heading back to the States, I got a letter from my own dad. An old army buddy had found his address, thought about him for the first time in twenty-three years, and written from the other side of the world.

He had stayed in the army, was a full colonel now, had been assigned to III Corps in South Vietnam, and had tucked a picture of a blown bridge in with the letter. No particular reason. Thought Dad might be interested.

Dad didn't know it was the bridge I'd been at, just thought he'd pass along the photo. A curiosity. Something he imagined I might be interested in.

12

Dancin' on a Rubber Leg

I spent five months on an amputee ward at Fort Gordon in north Georgia, at least that's what the records say. In real life, I spent most of those months on convalescent leave because nobody could see any reason for me to take up a bed. Least of all, the doctors. The doctors had actual missing limbs to take care of, and all I had was a smashed foot in a walking cast. That would heal just fine somewhere else.

The ward was long and open with beds on both sides and windows behind us. Except for the boxed-in nurses' station at the front, we could have been in Richmond, and it could have been the Chimborazo Hospital a hundred years ago, lined with Confederate soldiers getting used to doing without legs. Or arms. A ward filled with men who remembered the way they had been in their youth, strong and virile, two weeks, a month before. Men worried about how they could earn a living, what their lives would be like, how they would seem to wives and lovers and to those they had yet to meet.

Disease was on the ward, too, the same disease that had been in Richmond every summer. Along with his wound, the man in the bed next to me had brought home malaria. And a hundred-and-five-degree fever.

Nobody in authority would believe him, although one look at his sweat-soaked sheets and I didn't have any trouble. I don't think the nurses were used to malaria, and the doctors, well, the doctors were orthopedic surgeons. Besides, they'd already done their rounds and weren't about to come running back just because some enlisted man wanted an excuse not to mop the floor.

Mopping the floor was part of our rehabilitation. "Be good for the men. Make them feel useful. First step to a new life." Like most of us, the doctors were draftees putting in time until they could go home and start their own new lives.

A sergeant came through three times a day to roust us out of bed and get us rehabilitating. And when the guy next to me wouldn't roust, the sergeant began to insist. Even for an army sergeant, it's not easy to make somebody swimming in and out of consciousness mop something.

After a while, the sergeant called for backup, but having two sergeants yelling didn't change the situation. When they started shaking the malaria guy, he just rolled his eyes back in his head and ignored them.

They ran it up the chain of command until a gaggle of brass was shoved in next to my bed, demanding the guy get his sorry ass in gear. *Now*, Dick Brain. Finally, at about the colonel level, they came up with somebody who had actually seen malaria or at least recognized the fact that a man sweating himself to death might need more than the psychological boost he'd get from running a mop.

One guy who did pop out of bed and grab a mop was a lanky black kid from Athens. He was minus an arm above the elbow and a leg below the knee, and he swung his crutches and juggled the mop like a circus performer. It was a thing to see.

"Mop?" he said. "You want to see me *mop*? You come back next month and see what you see. I gone get me a rubber leg and I be *dancin'*. You just wait. You see."

I was at Fort Gordon waiting out my time between convalescent leaves when the ward was raided.

The nurses' station was a little walled-off room at the entrance to the ward where whatever nurse was on duty could keep track of us while not actually having to spend much time with us. And hanging inches above her head when she looked out the window was Miss December.

Miss December wasn't wearing much, but she did have a small white teddy bear between her thighs. And, according to the magazine she'd been torn from, had a thirty-nine inch bust and weighed a hundred-and-nineteen pounds—which made her pretty spectacular, even by centerfold standards. As fitting a welcome back to the pleasures of the

World, to the joys of youth and promises of the sixties burgeoning around us, as a body could wish.

I don't know who posted that picture, but I've got a pretty good idea what he was like. Young, for starters. Very young. The average American soldier in Vietnam was nineteen. An amputee, most likely. Almost everybody on the ward was, and groping with body-image problems a lot more severe than any of the nurses had to deal with. At the very least, that picture took his mind off his own misshapen self and let him fix his thoughts on the pleasures waiting outside. More than that, looking at Miss December's unlikely figure was an inspiration, a vision of what modern prosthetics in the hands of a skilled surgeon could accomplish.

But by then, the victim bandwagon was crowded with newly discovered grievances. The feelings of the patients weren't the feelings the people in charge cared about, and the picture had to go.

Wars and rumors of wars filled the headlines, but never anything I cared much about. Until one morning, there was.

The *Atlanta Constitution*, 23 January 1969, on a far inside page. "American and South Vietnamese casualties are reported heavy as 250 to 400 Communists overran the Twenty-fifth Division base camp at Cu Chi. Their immediate objective is thought to have been the helicopter pad located directly behind..."

Bunker twenty-seven and bunker twenty-six and bunker twenty-eight...

"At this time it is not known how many of the big choppers were destroyed, but a spokesman for the Twenty-fifth stated that the loss would have no effect on..."

...Raymond and Nikiyama...

"...also not known how many are still at large within the compound, and the base remains on full alert..."

...and the Guy on the Shelf.

"...investigation has already begun into how so many enemy soldiers could have passed undetected through the wire."

I never saw the list of the people who made the morning report the next day, but one thing I'm certain of. The sergeant who refused to know about the tunnel wasn't on it. And neither was anybody else, all the way up to Williamson, Ellis, W. Major General, Commanding, who had more important things to do than take time off from the war for the sake of a hole in the ground.

Spring came to Atlanta and I was there to see it. Bright orange azaleas burst into the sun. Dogwoods turned pink or white. Wisteria dripped from rooflines like soft purple icicles. Great billows of rhododendron lined the edges of yards. This was Buckhead at its most unreal, painted with colors as vivid, and as alien, as any in a box of kids' cereal.

And always, lying just out of sight, was the battlefield Buckhead had once been, filled with yelling and running and confusion, back when warm weather meant tangles of blackjack, stands of pokeweed, and briars tearing at your uniform. I kept finding myself scanning the shadows, trying to make out the shapes lurking behind the flowers.

What those shapes might be, I couldn't have said. Whoever they were, they weren't Vietcong. Or divers come to blow me up. They might have been Yankees, I don't know. Or Confederates, now that Buckhead had become strange. Except it would have seemed even stranger to them.

Sometimes I would go to the mall and stump along on my cast, trying to make sense of all the goods stacked in the windows, trying to see past the confusion of color and pattern, when somebody would call my name and I'd wheel around, blood pounding, feeling alarmed and vulnerable that he'd spotted me before I'd seen him.

"What's with the leg?" That was pretty much always the first question. "Golf injury?"

It was a joke, and we'd both laugh. The way I twisted my body around when I hacked at the ball, it had been a matter of time before I pulled something loose.

"Vietnam," I'd say. "I was..."

"Good one, Ole Hoss." Nobody from Buckhead went to Vietnam. That was for country people. For people who dropped out of high school. For people who didn't know any better. "What really happened?"

There had been Chinese soldiers in Vietnam Uncle Sam didn't want the folks at home to know about. No point telling Americans we were in Asia fighting a land war against China. It would discourage them.

We had long-range patrols in Laos and Cambodia doing more, I was pretty certain, than counting trucks on the Ho Chi Minh Trail.

We had teams of assassins operating in North Vietnam, and the government didn't want people knowing about them, either. It would cause trouble. But when the time came, they sent us back to family and friends and never told us to keep our mouths shut. It was all very strange.

"I was..." it was hard to think what to say.

"Dumped off your bike, that it? I've been wanting to get my hands on a Harley. Not too bunged up, is it?"

I shook my head. I didn't have a bike.

"Why don't I come over Saturday and check it out and...?"

"It was a boat. I was on a..."

"Not that little rowboat you and Shelby took out on the Chattahoochee? That thing was a drowning waiting to happen. Don't see how it could break your leg, though."

"Foot. It's my foot." Meanwhile, I would be scanning the shadows, making sure nobody else was sneaking up on me. Jungle eyes are a hard thing to lay aside.

Sometimes I'd run into people who knew I'd been to Vietnam. Friends I'd had for years and were glad to see me back. Friends with whom I'd spoken a common language since kindergarten, in some cases. Buddies who'd shared secrets about parents and girlfriends, about troubles at school. One or two I'd run from the police with on warm nights. None of whom I had the words to tell what had happened, what it had really been like.

It all came out as funny stories. The time the general flew over in his chopper while I was pulling a water-skier. The guy with the one-armed monkey. The time the sniper fired back at us from the other end of the rifle range. Nothing about what it was like to be there, how the people were, the feeling of standing the boat on its stern and tearing along the Song Saigon, how it was, for a little while, to *be* the United States of America, and I realized why the army didn't tell us to shut up about what the rest of the country wasn't supposed to know. It didn't make any difference. We couldn't tell it anyway. At least, not to anybody who hadn't seen it for themselves.

Things hadn't always been that way. A hundred years ago, plenty of Southern boys came home to places where everybody knew about war, where farms had been ruined, homes burned, families scattered. To a place where the things that had happened to you had happened to everybody. Those boys wouldn't have had any trouble telling what they'd been through.

It was good to return to a country so drenched in peace that people didn't believe war was real.

∽

It wasn't just my friends who wouldn't believe I had been wounded in Vietnam. Other, more worldly people, wouldn't either.

Sam and I invested some of my leave in a trip to Cape Kennedy to see the rockets that came from my family's land.

I'd taken to wearing my army field jacket when I went out because it kept me warm. And because it looked macho without my actually having to do anything macho. And because I was proud of it. It was olive drab with my name over one pocket, US ARMY over the other, a Twenty-Fifth Infantry Division Tropic-Lightning patch on the right shoulder, and a Third-Army patch on the left. When I went out in that jacket, I was looking fine.

At the Cape, we got off a tour bus at one of the launch pads and trooped around trying to imagine what a rocket would look like fueled up, tethered to the derrick, shedding ice and mist, then rising into the sky on a tower of flame. When the other tourists hopped back onto the bus, I clumped up behind, my cast thumping the steps.

A few minutes later we came to the Vertical Assembly Building. The empty space inside was more than five hundred feet high and so big it had its own weather. Feeling appropriately small, I clumped back onto the bus.

While I was in mid-clump, the driver growled at me in a whisper nobody else could hear. "Get those US Army patches off that god-damn jacket."

At first I thought he just objected to my wearing scraps of uniform in public. The army has rules about that sort of thing. He was ex-military, I'm almost certain of that, and I didn't see the point in arguing. Now I think it was something more personal. He thought I was making a political statement.

If this had been 1942 and I'd been hobbling around in a cast and wearing an army field jacket, people would have bought me drinks. In 1969, it didn't work that way. In 1969, nobody wore army anything in public, at least if you were in the army. Wearing army things was something you did to prove you *weren't* in the army. I think that old soldier took uniforms seriously and people who made fun of them even more seriously. He was on my side on that one. Looking back, I should have said something. We had a lot in common.

A few days before I shipped to California, I went down to the hospital to see Dr. Garrett. I would do that sometimes. Because I loved him. And because I thought I should. And because Dad wasn't allowed to. Ceci wasn't comfortable with anything that had to do with Mother, and she put her foot down where visiting Dr. Garrett was concerned.

They kept him in a melancholy little room in a narrow, uncomfortable-looking bed. Over the years when I visited he would talk about Dad. I'm pretty sure he wanted to talk about Mother, but didn't have it in him, and Dad was as close as he could get. Then, that last visit, he thought I was Dad and talked about me.

In a way, it was like old times, Christmas Eve at his house while the grown-ups chatted about us kids playing in the other room. Only, this time, I got to be a grown-up.

I think it was Christmas Eve for Dr. Garrett, too. He'd forgotten he was in the hospital and was looking forward to his daughter coming in and joining us. Try as it might, sometimes, evil can't get the grip on you it wants.

And, sometimes, it does. Instead of Mother, a nurse came in and began to draw blood.

Dr. Garrett shrank into the narrow bed and tried to hold his arm away from her, but he was old and wasted from strokes and too much time in the hospital, and she just pulled his arm out and stuck the needle in.

And he began to cry.

That's almost my last memory of him, a strong man who believed a man showed his strength by ignoring pain. The one person in the family who'd had the courage to say what happened the day Mother was killed. A man who wouldn't show his tears, even when his daughter died.

"Now, now," the nurse said. "It's just a test." The same pointless test, it seemed to me, they had run on him every day I'd come to visit, and every other day, too, for years.

An endless line of needles stuck into an old man who couldn't remember he was in a hospital or what the tests were for. Only that his life had become a parade of strangers sticking needles into his thin, old arm. When he wanted love and comfort, when he wanted his daughter, he got pain.

"Why do they do this to me?" he asked, and I had no answer and left. He died before I saw him again.

One of the upsides of being wounded in combat is that you get to come home early. Another is that you get to pick your next duty station. I picked California and the Summer of Love.

Technically, the Summer of Love happened while I was in the Peace Corps, but I figured there might be enough love left over for me to scoop up some. So when I marched out of the hospital at Fort Gordon, it was to Fort Ord.

To 28,000 acres of beachfront along the curve of Monterey Bay. Cool in the summer, temperate in the winter, whales and sea lions and otters playing in the surf, an easy drive down the coast to Big Sur or up to San Francisco. Just about as far from the blizzards of Central Missouri or the Georgia heat as you could get. The only thing wrong with Fort Ord was that it was run by the army.

The commanding general was a fool who spent his afternoons being chauffeured around, busting enlisted men who neglected to salute the general's flag on his car.

Drugs were everywhere, and the soldiers split right down the middle on the question of intoxicants. Those who did drugs thought the rest of us weren't cool and made a point of saying so. Those of us who put our trust in alcohol thought they were bigger fools than the commanding general but kept our mouths shut about it. There were more of them than there were of us, and they looked a lot more unstable.

Acid-fueled parties and loud, monotonous music went on all night in the barracks. Scary-looking guys shot heroin in the shadows, and then, right out in the open. The huge, brutish thug in the bunk next to mine was Lieutenant Smith. That was his name, not his rank. His mother had wanted people to treat him with respect. Private Lieutenant Smith was on edge a lot. He was awaiting trial for rape.

On post, lots of us got along pretty well, whites clowning around with blacks or drinking really cheap, really bad wine together. But when we went out, we went out with our own kind. Everything in America had taken on a racial charge, and a black guy caught fraternizing with whites had to worry about getting beat up by his brothers.

This being California, there were whole new races to not offend. Friendly, smiling Mexican-Americans transmogrified into militant Chicano farmworkers when they stepped outside. Then stepped back inside and announced that none of us would be eating grapes anymore.

After one of the guys in the barracks showed up dead from a heroin overdose, the first sergeant began patrolling the corridors at night with a twelve-gauge. But he had the misfortune to be white, and a group of black soldiers, probably after drinking too much wine they would have been better off boycotting because of the grapes, decided he was gunning for them and made a racial incident out of it. By the following afternoon, the first sergeant was reassigned far from Fort Ord and, I believe, very shortly afterwards, invited to leave the army.

Drifting through it all was a single, lonely Eskimo named Friday, probably the only nonwhite on the entire West Coast not to make an issue out of his race. Like the rest of us, he was just wanted to go home.

After sowing a whole prairie of wild oats, my sister Anne concluded the time had come to lay aside the ways of a maiden and turn into a respectable matron. The only hitch in her plan was that the boy she wanted to turn respectable with wanted to be a marine. No way Anne was going to wait while her intended was off serving his country, so she went searching for a new one.

She shared Mother's talent for finding what she was looking for, and right then, what she was looking for was a husband who wouldn't show so much spirit. What she found was a nice, safe boy whose ambition ran no further than serving in the National Guard, a boy who would do his serving right here at home because his daddy was a general in the Georgia Guard and had prepared a spot for him. Then, once he'd completed his patriotic chore, he'd go to work for Daddy in a nice, predictable business he was scheduled to inherit some day. You'll do, Anne said, and he bought her a ring. The news must have come as a huge relief to Dad.

Unfortunately, Anne wasn't as sensitive as she should have been when it came to choosing the date and planned the wedding for the same summer Ceci turned forty. It was all just too much. To take some of the indignity out of the situation, Ceci set Marti on fire at the rehearsal dinner.

While Marti had her head turned, Ceci crept up and placed a candle beneath her hair. Marti didn't notice until she smelled burning. When she did, the only way she could put herself out was to douse her head with her companion's drink. She spent the rest of the evening in a wet dress with a large chunk of her hair singed away and smelling like a crematorium.

Out in California, I discovered one of my best friends from Duke was at Travis Air Force Base up near Fairfield. The Fairfield Airfield, he called the place. For a jet-jockey, Al wasn't particularly gung-ho. It was just that money had been tight when he was in college, and the hundred-dollar-a-month scholarship the Air Force waved in front of him had been important.

Still, being a pilot with a bachelor pad was a lot better than being an enlisted man in a chaotic, drug-filled barrack—and I spent as much time with Al as I could swing. Which is how I wound up in his backyard before dawn one summer morning staring into the sky.

The moon hung in the dark like a beautiful, ancient coin lit by a spotlight—electrum, maybe, from the silvery way it shown—while Al's television glowed blue through the open window. "That's one small step for man," the television said, "one giant leap for mankind."

Those were the words, "One small step for man." Not "a man" or "one man." Not even "this man." Just "man." With maybe a billion people listening, Neil A. Armstrong, American astronaut and first human being to set foot on the moon, tripped over his own tongue.

I don't know whether he'd been told what to say, but I wouldn't put it past NASA. Nobody wanted a hot-shot test pilot casting about in his subconscious and coming up with, "Well, I'll be dipped in shit. Those candy-assed engineers got me here after all. And Yuri and John and Alan and all you other peckerwoods down there on Earth, whose name do you think the kids will remember now?" However he came up with it, it was a vacuous little sentiment calibrated not to offend anybody—just enough to trip over when the moment came.

And in tripping over it, what he said was much better. What he said was: "I can't fucking believe I'm here. All those years playing the game, all that discipline and politics to get this ride, and I'm so knocked over I can't even remember what I was supposed to say." It was eight years almost to the day since Anne and I stood on Grand Bahama Island while Gus Grissom sailed overhead in *Liberty Bell 7*.

When I was sixteen and the infinite reaches of my life stretched out in front of me, or six years later in a hotel in DC watching the news about Gus Grissom and Ed White and Roger Chaffee, or two years after that in Al's backyard, so much seemed possible. Back then, I knew the day was coming I'd be soaring overhead, too—that it wouldn't be just a dozen men on the moon, but thousands. And women and kids, too. Families and cities. Factories and farms and vacations—and anybody who really wanted to go, could go. Because that's what people do. That's what it means to be human—to dream huge dreams and to wonder and speculate and to go *see.* And to take the wife and kids and the old folks along so they can see, too.

I know the truth about those ancient *Australopithecine* ancestors of ours. All that talk about being pushed out of the trees by better monkeys, monkeys who could climb faster and snatch the kumquats before we could get them, that talk is wrong. It wasn't because we were pushed out of the trees that we turned into humans.

It was because we were already turning into humans that we skinned down the trunks, just to find out what was on the ground. Then ambled off to visit that other clump of trees across the endless ocean of grass for no better reason than to find out what was there, too. And then to reconnoiter the hills in the distance. And to pack the bags and wander up to Europe to check out the Ice Ages and find out what woolly mammoths were all about.

There were saber-toothed cats there. And cave bears in the living quarters. And the mammoths had a way of lurching forward and stepping on you when you really didn't want them to. And a lot of our parents burned up in their capsules before they ever had the chance to be fairly launched. But some got through, and it wasn't just sheets of ice and stone tools that journey led to. It was Oxford, as well. And Beijing. It was Galileo and Cervantes and the Valley of the Kings. And a man named Armstrong walking on the moon.

There was a time...the summer of 1493, probably...when word about the Bahamas got around, and people all over Europe gathered on the far shore of the world, burghers and peasants on the cliffs at Brittany, Yeomen and small-holders gazing west from Cornwall, straining to see for themselves the shining fish and the reds and rich purples and creamy whites of the shells whirling through the sparkling water forever hidden below the horizon.

When I stand on our shore on a clear night, I am not trying for glimpses of worlds I'll never see. I don't have to imagine the beautiful colors shining through the darkness. I can look all the way to my own islands sparkling overhead and imagine my children voyaging there and catching them in their hands.

Ceci showed no more talent for dying than Andy Warhol.

After Anne's wedding, she went home and killed herself by downing a bottle of witch hazel. She had been under the impression, she said later, that she was shooting harmless slugs of vodka.

Dad rode with her in the ambulance and Marti followed in the car, under strict instructions to slip out of the neighborhood with the headlights off so the neighbors wouldn't cotton to what was going on. There weren't any maids around that time of night and, if played right, even the Grapevine Line wouldn't find out.

"*Shit*," Marti said when the doctor stepped out of the emergency room and announced Ceci would live. Marti had been hoping for better.

When Ceci got out of the hospital, Dad packed her off to a drying-out facility, and she loved it. Dying was just the tonic she needed. From then on, every time she wanted to catch up on her sleep or be pampered for a week or two, she would kill herself.

With love guiding the planets and peace steering the stars, Fort Ord went into lockdown every now and then to keep harmony and understanding from coming inside and inflicting bodily harm on us.

Locked in with me was my buddy George from Mississippi. George was a Druid. A secular Druid, but a Druid nonetheless. Unlike the California Druids and earth-goddesses rioting outside the gates, George was the real thing. He came from a long line of Druids...a line, to hear him tell it, that went back much farther than any claimed by us nominal Christians.

The matter of George's religious affiliation came up when I got to talking about the horse bones and empty coffins we'd unearthed at Winchester Cathedral. "Seemed odd," I said. "Burying the hind leg of a horse in sacred ground. Besides, protein didn't come cheap in the Middle Ages. Why would anybody...?"

"Druids."

"Druids? What do you mean Druids?"

"I mean Druids," George said. "Like in *Druids*. When Druids want to bury somebody, they take him out onto the heath at night and do it right."

"This was a graveyard. Besides, there weren't any Druids in Winchester. In the Middle Ages, Winchester was..."

"That's what you *would* say," George said, "if you were Christian. You guys put monks in charge of the records. You think a Christian monk would write about Druids?"

"You're saying there were still Druids in England during the Middle Ages, and they carried their dead out on the heath and..."

"Not right away. Nobody wanted to get burned at the stake, so they had a show burial first. If they had enough pallbearers so everybody was a Druid, they'd lower the coffin in empty. Otherwise, they'd put something big and meaty inside and bury that. When night came, they'd go out on the heath and give the departed a proper send-off."

"So..." I said, "...why do you know so much about Druids...?"

"You think you Christians were the only people to immigrate to America?"

"You telling me..." I was starting to have an odd thought about George, "...*you* are Druid? Do you go out on the heath at night and..."

"Do you go to church?"

"Not so much."

"Same here. Grandfather was pretty serious about it, but I don't pay much attention to religion myself."

We don't smoke marijuana in Muscogee
We don't take our trips on LSD

"Bummer," one of the dope-heads said when he picked up Merle Haggard on the radio instead of the acid rock he'd been dialing for. "Who are these hate-filled people who say things like that?

I'm proud to be an Okie from Muskogee

Okies from the Smokies, the word ran around the barracks. Crazed, moonshine-addled rednecks with shotguns and ropes.

"They're everywhere," another dope-head said.

"Okies are violent, racist people. And they're looking for us."

"Okies from the Smokies," the first dope-head said knowingly and flopped on his bunk, strewing burning ash across the blanket. "Man. Okies from the Smokies."

"I've never even been to the Smokies," a fourth dope-head had regained consciousness enough to track the conversation. "And now they want to kill me? What's with the Smokies anyway?"

"Yeah, if there's anybody we don't need, it's those Okies trying to make the rest of us do their thing."

"Well, I ain't fucking my sister, I can tell you that."

"Me neither, bro." Then, maybe unwisely, "I've met your sister."

But the first dope-head didn't notice. He was too busy worrying about Merle and his hate-filled lyrics. "Man. All over America people are listening to this...this racist garbage."

"Solidarity," a pale white guy who looked like he didn't get out much raised a clenched fist in what might have been a Black-Power salute. "Damn, I need a hit."

"Here you go, Man. We got to stick together on this."

"Yeah. Turn the channel on that mother. Find us some Janis. I can't stand listening to this shit anymore."

Until the scare wore off, the dope-heads kept the noise and the drugs a bit more private. They didn't want to call any more attention to themselves than necessary. Not with Okies on the prowl.

If the Russians ever invade California, I thought, I'm going home and cutting a star out of my flag.

"An old army boot," somebody yelled from the audience, and the comedians magically produced a combat boot. That was the deal. Yell out an unlikely object, and they could turn it into something funny. On weekends, Al and I would head into San Francisco to enjoy being Americans.

One of the actors placed the combat boot on the fake mantelpiece at the back of the stage. "It's my souvenir from the Nam." What made the skit funny was that the boot still had his foot inside.

We were at an improv club in what looked like a converted brick warehouse in a suddenly artsy district of the city. But from the easy way they pulled out the boot, and the practiced look of the skit, I had my doubts about the improvness of it all.

On stage, one of the comedians limped around being an amputated veteran who was stupid enough and patriotic enough to be proud of what he'd done. Stupid automatically, because he'd been in the army. Even stupider because he was patriotic. Stupidest of all because he was proud and expected the rest of us to share his pride. It was a tedious skit and not humorous, but the audience laughed anyway, the mean way people laugh when the joke is on somebody they don't like.

I don't remember what Al thought of the show. He'd be heading to Vietnam in a few months, but pilots didn't come home carrying one of their feet in an old army boot. Pilots vanished over the Red River. Or parachuted into years of beatings and starvation, isolation and torture, at the Hanoi Hilton.

"Mop?" I kept hearing a lanky, young black man swinging his crutches between beds at Fort Gordon. "You want to see me *mop*? You come back next month and see what you see. I gone get me a rubber leg and I be *dancing'*. You just wait. You see."

> Creative and sensitive, Virgos are delicate people who, like rare and special orchids, require individual treatment to fully blossom into their true unique beauty.

In the Age of Aquarius, Virgos from California were the most creative, the most sensitive, the most delicate, the most special-orchidy of all. At Fort Ord hundreds, maybe thousands, of Virgos showed up, entire training battalions of sensitive, delicate, special orchids, all arrived on the same day. The draft lottery had kicked in and the first birthday drawn was September 14.

"Hey, lemme see that," you could imagine a drill sergeant turning an astrology magazine over in his hand as if he were examining the Jap ear he'd taken prisoner on Guadalcanal when all thirty shitheads, as he referred to the new draftees in his platoon, announced that it was a bad day to go outside. The sergeant wouldn't have been from California. As far as anybody could tell, drill sergeants came from Arkansas. And he wouldn't have been a Virgo. No drill sergeant in the history of the world had ever been shy and delicate, especially not shy and delicate in the special-orchid way.

The day came when a drill sergeant had had enough and did something he shouldn't have done. He confiscated one of the astrology magazines, ripped it into pieces, and began rifling through lockers for more of this ass-trology shit. And tore those up, too. In a platoon of thirty shitheads, he destroyed 267 pieces of astrology-related literature and banned the import of more. Unfortunately for the drill sergeant, one of the shitheads had watched too much Perry Mason, and a few days later, he was in the office of the Judge Advocate General.

It should have been a no-brainer. The First Amendment doesn't have anything to do with the army and neither does the Thirteenth Amendment against involuntary servitude. Even the Second Amendment doesn't apply. In the army you're allowed to bear arms, but you don't get to keep them. The army keeps them for you. The lawyer knew that, but it didn't change the advice he gave.

He wasn't a Virgo, either. The chance of being a trial-lawyer born under the sign of the Virgin wasn't much greater than being a drill sergeant. Sensitive, delicate, special-orchids aren't attracted to either profession. What the lawyer was attracted to was money, which he'd been expecting in considerable amounts as soon as he passed the bar. But instead of genteelly arabesqueing into his father-in-law's white-glove firm in downtown San Francisco, he'd been struck down by the draft and was spending his days looking for opportunities to strike back. When the shithead showed up in his office, the first thing out of the lawyer's mouth was, "What have they done to you?" When he found out, the lawyer picked up the phone and called the drill sergeant's company commander.

"I don't mean to tell you how to run your company, but I can't see how a court martial could find anything pornographic or seditious about the magazines your drill sergeant has been destroying, if you take my meaning."

The company commander wasn't certain whether the court martial in question applied to him or the drill sergeant or the shithead, but either way, he took the lawyer's meaning, had a few words in private with the drill sergeant, and by that weekend, the barracks had filled back up with astrology literature.

Come Monday, his entire company refused to go to the grenade range because one of the magazines said, "Beware of accidents," and everybody knew how bad an accident with hand grenades could be. The fact that thirty-five other magazines all said it was a good day to learn a new skill didn't cut any ice with the shitheads. They were sensitive, astrology-minded shitheads, and they knew which magazine took precedence in a conflict of that kind.

Having a horse is going to make Marti into a lesbian, Ceci announced, and began telling Dad that his daughter was about to take a U-turn, sexual-orientation-wise, if she didn't start spreading her legs around something besides an English saddle, and quick. So Dad told Marti to get rid of the horse.

The horse was an expensive thoroughbred she'd traded up for when she discovered a little rich girl whose daddy had given it to her for Christmas. The daddy should have checked with the girl first, because she was afraid of horses. She wasn't afraid of ponies, though, so Marti bought a ten-dollar pony and swapped for the thoroughbred. Or, that was the plan.

Even with Marti's gifted eye for horseflesh, she blew it. The pony turned out to be another horse. On the short side, as horses go, but still a horse. So Marti taught it to squat, measured it in front of the rich girl, and traded it straight up for the thoroughbred. The rich girl got a pony and Marti got the thoroughbred. Value-added all around.

Months later, when Marti still hadn't gotten rid of the horse, Dad cornered a friend with a daughter and sold the horse to him. That would have been the end of things, if the daughter had known how to ride. But she didn't, so part of the deal was for Marti to teach her. Soon enough, Marti had convinced the girl that a thoroughbred wasn't the horse for her, bought a twenty-five-dollar horse, swapped it for the thoroughbred, returned the thoroughbred to the barn Dad had moved it out of, and began giving riding lessons to pay the board.

When word got around the horse community that Marti was in the business, one of Mother's friends sent her a young Arab mare to train, and by the time she graduated from high school, Marti was spending her afternoons with a horse she wasn't supposed to have, training a second horse Dad didn't know about, giving lessons, mucking stables she wasn't supposed to be at, and riding her thoroughbred in whatever time she had left. In a more orderly household, this would have come to light.

In ours, Marti would arrive home from a long afternoon teaching, training, mucking, and riding, looking like she'd spent the afternoon teaching, training, mucking, and riding. Mary would meet her at the kitchen door with a kimono, Marti would kick off her boots, roll up her jeans, slip the kimono over her clothes, splash water on her face at the kitchen sink, run her fingers through her hair to get out the bigger pieces of straw, and step into the dining room. Dressing for dinner was one of Ceci's firmest rules.

When Marti headed off for college, Mother's friend sold the Arab mare for a lot of money, split the proceeds with Marti, and Marti used her half to buy a string of horses. She had so much demand on her time she almost flunked out, but Dad just chalked it up to her not being a very good student, which she wasn't.

A few weeks before my army career was scheduled to end, Bing Crosby dropped by Fort Ord with a wad of tickets. He was putting on a golf tournament at Pebble Beach, and there would be a lot of famous golfers there. Also, a lot of famous movie stars. The tickets were for the people in the hospital and the soldiers home from Vietnam. He entrusted them to Headquarters Company.

Headquarters Company actually gave some tickets to hospital patients and guys back from Vietnam before the higher-ups caught wind of what was going on. Tickets for the Bing Crosby National Pro-Am Golf Tournament at Pebble Beach were much too scarce a resource to go wasting on the likes of hospital patients and vets.

The first that most of us vets and hospital patients knew about the tickets was when an order showed up on company bulletin boards:

> No later than 16:00 hours this date, all enlisted personnel in possession of tickets for the Pebble Beach Pro-Am Golf Tournament will return said tickets to their company commanders.
>
> No later than 17:00 hours this date, each company commander will provide this headquarters with a full accounting of all such tickets in his possession.

Before we saw that order, it never occurred to any of us enlisted personnel that a golf tournament was something we might care to attend, but the more we thought about it, the more it seemed like just the thing.

It wasn't long before going to the Bing Crosby Pro-Am turned into the sine qua non of everything we'd been fighting for in Vietnam, everything we wanted out of life. And since we couldn't go, we did the next best thing. We wrote our congressmen. The army might not be a democracy, but America was. Or, kind of a democracy, if you came from Georgia.

Lots of congressmen didn't seem to care, at least not very much. Weeks after the tournament, letters were still drifting back from congressmen saying how much they cared but not actually promising to do anything. My congressman was different. My congressman really did care. In the first place, my congressman was from the South, and Southern congressmen care about things military.

In the second place, he wasn't a congressman at all. He was Richard Russell, and he was chairman of the Senate Armed Services Committee.

Before Senator Russell had a chance to take matters in hand, Mr. Crosby solved the problem. We'd been rooting for him to show back up and say the kind of things to the commanding general we were better off not saying, but when he motored out to Fort Ord he did something much more handsome. He came to the hospital and personally handed out a second batch of tickets. This time, directly to patients. Then he made sure a third batch of tickets got to the soldiers home from Vietnam.

A week later, we were out at Spyglass Hill, gawking at the celebrity golfers.

And the golfing celebrities.

And at the generals and colonels in their fine uniforms. It was a beautiful day and a sight to remember. And a study in elegance from Mr. Crosby.

The weekend before I left the army, I drove up to San Francisco and stayed in the same fleabag hotel I slept in on every visit. Around midnight, I went for a walk.

It was a bad neighborhood, and I didn't know my way around very well. But something was up. A few blocks away, red and blue lights were flashing. As I got nearer, I could hear the froggy honking of fire trucks.

Big canvas hoses were looped across the street, spraying fountains of water from brass fittings. Firemen were running and yelling, and people were crowding to see what was going on.

Get your ass back, somebody shouted. A fireman or maybe a cop. "This ain't a show. These men got a fire to fight."

I backed my ass into the shadows in an open doorway leading to a dark flight of stairs. Water was all over the street. Lakes of blue, then red, as the lights flashed. And yellow and more red from the sign over a Chinese restaurant.

Something moved behind me. Something I hadn't...all that alertness, all those jungle eyes I'd brought home from Vietnam, I was losing it. Not so long ago, nobody could have slipped up on me like that.

"Beautiful, isn't it?"

An Oriental lady in a white dressing gown, a woman three times my age, a woman whose life had no congruencies with mine at all except those single few moments gazing onto a wet street, was seeing the same things in the dancing colors and the practiced minuet of the men fighting the fire as I was seeing.

She was right. It was very beautiful.

My last day in the army, the troop commander called me into his office. Headquarters was in a flurry, and it was my job to do something about it.

Our commanding general was up for promotion. He would be taking a break from his rigorous schedule of being chauffeured around the fort busting enlisted men who didn't salute the flag on his limousine to appear before the Senate Armed Services Committee. The chairman had sent him a packet of material he was going to be questioned about, and not to put too fine a point on it, the general needed a retraction. From me. Now.

"Your letter," the troop commander informed me, "reflected upon the integrity of a great American." Then he made it clear that I wouldn't be leaving the army until I got things sorted out for the great American in question.

"He can *do* that? Keep me in the army?"

"Just write the letter," the troop commander said.

Reflected upon the integrity of, I thought, as I composed the retraction. "I understand I have reflected upon your integrity. I am sorry your integrity can be reflected upon."

I dropped the letter into the mailbox on the way out the gate and into civilian life. My timing turned out to be pretty good.

I drove up to Mount Spokane to pick up Al from survival training. Before going to Vietnam, aircrew got survival training in case they were shot down over the jungle.

At the time, America had some pretty persuasive jungles to conduct that kind of training in. We had jungles at our bases in Thailand and the Philippines, we had the entire Panama Canal Zone, and we had Fort Polk, Louisiana, conveniently fitted out with bayous and snakes and alligators. With all that to choose from, the Air Force found the perfect place to teach jungle survival skills: on the side of a mountain in Eastern Washington, maybe a hundred miles from the Canadian border.

In February.

They taught Al and a group of other guys to build shelters out of pine boughs and to snare snowshoe rabbits, then dropped them far up the side of the mountain. In three feet of snow.

It was their job to not get captured. They did not want to be captured, their instructors informed them. If you are captured, you will be interrogated. And you do not want to be interrogated. The way to not get interrogated was to get off the mountain without getting caught.

The tactical problem was that the only one way off the mountain was down a steep draw where their interrogators were waiting for them.

And that all the snowshoe rabbits had been snared generations ago by previous aircrew learning to survive in the jungle.

And that you couldn't walk anywhere without leaving three-foot deep trenches in the snow to show where you were.

On the other hand, it was cold up there, the escape-and-evaders were dressed in lightweight flight suits, and nobody could think of anything better to do than trudge downhill. It wasn't long before they were rounded up and dragged to a typical, snow-covered Vietnamese village for some instructive beatings and a day or two shivering in tiger cages.

The experience didn't bolster Al's confidence in his ability to survive in the jungle. It did, as he put it when I picked him up, remind him that he did not want to be shot down. Which had been his opinion all along.

A few weeks later I was motoring through Monterey and thought I could save a couple of bucks by spending the night at Fort Ord. When I showed up at the barracks, I got an earful. "Whoo-whee," my old army buddies said. "What did you *do*?"

I hadn't been out of the army six hours before a squad of military police came looking for me. "They weren't going to let you leave the army," my old army buddies said.

"They can *do* that?" I said."

"Had the papers all filled out. Something about the commanding general and a letter and..."

Six *hours*? Who knew the army post office was that efficient?

I don't know whether my by-now ex-commanding general ever got his promotion, but I've always hoped for the worst. He'd certainly fallen into the right hands. Senator Russell was not one to be intimidated by military brass. He'd chaired the committee that ruled Douglas MacArthur violated the Constitution when he sent his troops up to the Yalu River and got my cousin John killed. Carl Vinson wasn't the only good man Georgia's corrupt electoral system kept in office.

13

The South before the Civil War

Ceci never recovered from Anne's wedding.

For months, she brooded on getting old. She dove into the women's magazines and reviewed all the literature about menopause. None of it sounded like something she wanted any part of, and she hatched a plan.

The science was pretty simple. All that really happened in menopause was that your body stopped making the drugs it needed to keep itself young. But that didn't mean the drugs weren't available, not in this day and age. The problem was menopause itself, with its hot flashes and mood swings. With a hysterectomy, Ceci began to realize, she wouldn't even have to go through that.

With the right drugs and a hysterectomy, she could short-circuit the aging process and go striding into the twenty-first century always young, always the most beautiful woman in the room, regaling generations of admirers with tales of the stodgy, unimaginative matrons who'd lived in Atlanta decades ago. Dried-up old crones now, if they haven't already blown away.

The womens' magazines hadn't told the whole story, though. When the nurses wheeled her out of the operating theater, it wasn't just her aging plumbing Ceci had left on the table. It was her sexual appetites as well. From that morning on, for the remaining twenty-eight years of his life, Dad never had sex again.

It's hard to know how he felt about that, because he wasn't the only one who'd been cut off. Entire cohorts of men locked away in the Atlanta federal prison had to go without, too. Along with her interest in sex, Ceci lost her ambition to become a prison psychologist.

Months earlier, she'd decided to re-up her psychology credentials and get a job at the federal pen. None of us knew the specifics of what that would involve, but the fact she would most likely be spending her days locked in private rooms with very horny, not very socially restrained men, hadn't escaped us.

❧

When Marti was in her forties she got Dad alone on an airplane. At 35,000 feet he couldn't escape, so she asked him what happened to Mother's body.

And he couldn't tell her.

It wasn't that he didn't know, he did. It was just that he couldn't talk about it. "It's too painful," he said, and that was that. Three decades after his wife was killed, he couldn't even bring himself to tell his adult children where she was buried.

❧

Ceci invested in a Doberman and tortured it until it was insane. During the day she kept it isolated in a cage. At night she released it in the yard to a solitary life of snapping at the fence, trying to get its teeth around something. Insane dogs make the best watchdogs, Ceci said.

My sister Anne brought the same unbridled commitment to being a matron she'd once shown for being a girlfriend, had three baby girls, and became a doting mother. The girls were the apples of Dad's eye, but he didn't get to see them much because Ceci thought they were immature.

One Sunday he invited Anne and the girls over to lunch. When she'd parked in the driveway, had her arms filled with bottles and blankets and the youngest, and was leading the other two across the gravel, Ceci loosed the Doberman.

After that, the girls weren't allowed to visit. The whole idea was just too dangerous, Ceci said. And because you never can tell about Dobermans, Dad wasn't allowed to see his granddaughters anywhere else, either. Ever.

As the girls got older, he'd call one or the other of them from the office, set up a clandestine liaison, and take her to lunch at an out-of-the-way little place Ceci didn't know about.

❧

The day came when Ceci's mother died, and Ceci not only inherited the Merrill Lynch fortune, she inherited her mother's station in society. She and Dad left Atlanta, moved into the big, empty house in Gulf Stream, took over her mother's position at the Palm Beach Club, and set about making their mark among the crème de la South Florida crème.

Ceci had finally made it. The Palm Beach Club was as high as you could climb, high-society-wise. According to legend, they refused to admit John Kennedy when he was president. Not because he was Catholic, plenty of rich people are Catholic. Not even because of the tainted rum-running money. Pretty much everybody's money was tainted. But on account of his profession. Palm Beach Club people just couldn't feature hobnobbing with political riffraff.

Sunny times at the Palm Beach Club lasted for a while, but the day came when Ceci insulted the wrong wife or made too much of a point out of wearing the wrong outfit or threw up on the wrong pair of feet, and she was invited to find a new social club to make her mark at. By then, she'd outgrown Florida anyway.

She and Dad headed further south, found an ex-pat community in Mexico, and built a house in a classy barrio. They installed a bronze mermaid out front and named the place *La Sirena* in the mermaid's honor. Or, maybe, Ceci's. Mermaid isn't the preferred way to translate *sirena*. The better translation is siren, so it's just as likely they named the house after cannibalistic maidens who lured Greek sailors to their deaths.

The house had three stories and was bigger than the one in Gulf Stream. The upper floors could be sealed off with steel gates in case of revolution. The place was surrounded by a wall twelve, maybe fourteen, maybe sixteen feet high, like the house Ceci came from on West Paces Ferry, only the wall in Mexico had broken glass on top.

They had a large patio in back and a lawn devoted entirely to croquet, which Ceci didn't play and Dad made up the rules for so that not only did nobody else ever win, they didn't even get to step up to the ball. Cages with male canaries were scattered about, and while Dad swatted his lonely way around the yard, he was serenaded by very angry, very horny birds who couldn't get out of each other's personal airspace.

There was a fully fitted-out cantina on the far end of the third floor where Ceci comforted herself late into the evening without having to socialize with anybody, especially Dad. Her room, where he was also not invited, was across from the cantina. She spent most of the day cranked up in a hospital bed in front of a television, gazing at a financial channel she picked up on cable, hypnotically watching the stock-ticker crawl across the bottom of the screen.

Dad had a pleasant bedroom on the other end of the second floor where sun streamed through his window and was as distant from Ceci as possible without being downstairs in the revolution zone. The ceilings were held up by endangered timbers illegally logged from the beautiful forest outside Acapulco Shelby and I bused through all those years ago. The forest is, I have been told, completely gone now. During the day, the house was filled with servants.

"I know this can't last," Dad once told me, "but Mexico is a lot like the South before the Civil War."

My sisters and I flew down for his eightieth birthday. We'd brought along the sort of small presents you can carry on a plane. A sweater, a box of preserves, books we thought he might enjoy.

I found him sitting alone, dressed in khaki slacks and a blue sports jacket as if he were at a yacht club instead of a small room with a three-story high, vaulted-brick ceiling. It was strange to see him there, like visiting your father at the bottom of a mineshaft he'd been cast into.

I told him that Mother's sister, Susan, had died of throat cancer in an ex-pat community not too far away. He hadn't spoken to her in years, hadn't known she was ill. Didn't even know she was nearby. It was sad. He'd always liked Suzy. He was sorry he hadn't spent more time with her.

Then I mentioned his own sister, the one Marti had been named after. She'd died, too. Several years ago. Dad hadn't known about that, either.

Anne and Marti located Ceci upstairs at her dressing table, her scalp still boiled and naked like some kind of horrible, wrinkled homunculus, her body shriveled and frightening, her breast misshapen by cancer. "I am still," she was muttering to the mirror when they came in, "the most beautiful woman in the room."

"It's your father's fault," she said when she caught sight of my sisters. He'd gotten old. "Dave Dillard is the same age as your father, and he looks great. How could your father do this to me?"

Then she launched into a monologue about a lady down at the market, a witch who'd sold her a bottle to help out wives in situations like hers. And given her the name of a doctor who'd come right away and declare what happened a heart attack. As the next of kin, Ceci could have Dad cremated without an autopsy. It would all be so simple. This was Mexico. She had money. She could do anything she wanted. Behind her, a row of wigs was lined up on stands like bloated, shrunken heads.

She came downstairs and sat next to Dad at the bottom of the mineshaft, as if it were her birthday, too. And in a way, it was, because instead of opening the presents we'd brought, he reached into his sports jacket and pulled out a small elegantly wrapped box. "I didn't want you to feel left out," he said. Remembering, perhaps, the night Ceci hadn't been the bride at Anne's wedding rehearsal.

Inside was a gorgeous, jeweled bracelet that she barely glanced at before slipping into the pocket of her dressing gown. Then gave Dad a curt nod, followed by, "Stop slumping. You look like an old man who shits in his diapers." Dad gave my sisters and me the same sheepish smile Beauchamp used when his wife embarrassed him about that Europe place.

After he'd opened his presents, Ceci stood and headed for the elevator and her private bed, her nipple leaking poison from the cancerous breast the most beautiful woman in the room refused to have removed. Then turned to Dad, "Why aren't you like Dave Dillard? He still looks good."

One Saturday morning, Ceci's son left a message on my answering machine. Dad was dead. The son was visiting Cuernavaca, had gone into his room, and found the body. From what the doctor said about the time of death, Ceci had been on the patio making out with the gardener.

At least that's the story, picked up through the parallel society of maids and butlers, cooks and chauffeurs, who permeated upper-class homes in the South-before-the-Civil-War. If it weren't for the hysterectomy thing, it would be an easy story to accept, given a gardener terrified of losing his job. It's also the kind of thing Ceci would have thought I'd believe, which made it a pretty good line to feed into the stream of gossip if she, or the gardener, needed to be somewhere else at the time.

I didn't make it to the funeral. None of us did. Ceci didn't invite us, and she held it the evening of the day the body was found, as soon as she had it cremated and before any of us could buy plane tickets.

When it came time for Dad's will to be probated, it turned out he hadn't owned anything. Not his wedding ring. Not the pictures in his wallet. Nothing. His will mentioned plenty of stuff, but he didn't have any of it when he died. He'd given it all to Ceci a few hours before. The judge had her word on it.

The dust hadn't settled when Sabino Gama called. Sabino was Dad's butler, and Ceci had fired him for asking too many questions about Dad's death.

He'd gone to the cops, and now the police, the FBI, and Mexico's most important newsmagazine were looking into the matter. Would Marti and I please come down and tell them what we knew?

We met them at a fancy tourist-villa in Cuernavaca: a dozen cottages scattered about a grassy lawn, huge flowery trees, a three-story hotel on one side, and the other three sides sealed behind an impassable wall. Marti and I sat on the porch of her cottage with five Mexicans, all men. Sabino Gama, a burly cop from the Morales State Police, an even burlier cop from the Mexican Federal Police, a reporter from the newsmagazine, and an undercover guy from the FBI.

The man from the Mexican Federal Police told us his name was Espino. Then he showed us his ID, but it was odd-looking. Not the official government-stamped card people all over the Developing World are so fond of, but a laminated scrap of paper with hand-scrawled words.

And not even squared off, but sliced at funny angles, as if whoever made it had been too cheap to use a new sheet of paper and just cut it from something pulled out of a wastebasket. Then Señor Espino reached into his briefcase and flipped a switch on a tape recorder.

There wasn't any reason to record the meeting, not that I could see. Whatever Marti and I had to say, we'd say in much more solid form when the time came. There was another thing. Señor Espino didn't want us to see that he had a tape recorder, he was just clumsy when he switched it on.

"Somebody came into Señor Merritt's room in the middle of the night," he said, "and forced him to drink something." There had been a struggle. Spilled liquid was all over his bed the next morning and the headboard was cracked. Yes, Sabino Gama nodded in agreement. "This is how it was."

Don't you think it odd, Señor Espino asked, that Ceci's son happened to be in town the very night your father died? Didn't the son work at a school in Texas? And hadn't that school been in session? "Have you ever known him to visit Mexico while school is in session?"

Marti and I shook our heads.

"Señor Gama tells me there was no other man inside the house the night your father died."

Sabino nodded.

"Which makes the son the only person who could have overpowered him and forced him to drink from that glass."

"What happened to the glass?" Marti asked.

"And the headboard," I said. "I'd like to see that headboard."

There was a quick conversation in Spanish, followed by an explanation in English, that as soon as Ceci learned her husband of thirty-five years was dead, she'd ordered the maid to make sure the glass was washed and rinsed.

Next, she called a doctor who pronounced it a heart attack. Then got hold of the crematorium while her son went down to the land office and had Dad's name removed from the property rolls, putting *La Sirena* entirely in Ceci's name.

As soon as Dad was out of the house, she had the headboard removed. "Guests," she explained, "might want to stay in that room," and she couldn't have them sleeping in a bed with a smashed headboard. It was an open-and-shut case now that Marti had arrived to testify to what Ceci had said about the witch and the bottle on Dad's eightieth birthday.

There was only one hitch, Señor Espino explained. "This is Mexico, and I am embarrassed to say it, we will need to deal with the judge."

"What do you mean, deal with the judge?"

"The judge. We will need to take care of the judge before Ceci can be arrested."

"How much?" I managed to get out. Señor Espino was right, this was Mexico, but I hadn't been expecting to be hit up for a bribe. Especially not by somebody with a laminated scrap of paper for an ID who claimed he would carry the money to a judge I'd never met. "How much?" I asked again.

"*¿Cuantos?*" Señor Espino turned to the others. They had a quick discussion in Spanish, but nobody seemed to have thought about how much the judge might want. Then, before they could come up with a number, Señor Espino's cell phone went off.

He said something in hurried Spanish that, to me, sounded an awful lot like, "Not yet." Then unconsciously waved toward one of the hotel rooms across the way, as if he were talking to somebody in a window. When I looked where he was waving, I caught a glimpse of a man in a third-story room who looked very much as if he had a movie camera aimed at us. My Spanish never improved much from the days of Alto, and I might have fallen victim to a false cognate, but the longer I sat there, the more Espino began to sound like it meant something along the lines of "sting."

"Tonight Señor Gama and Señorita Marti will go to the police station and sign statements about what they know," Mr. Sting said. "And we will find out how much money the judge requires. Tomorrow we will meet back here and Mrs. Merritt will be fried bread."

The police station was not designed to instill a sense of comfort, especially at night. The building was shadowy inside and institutional, and, from time to time, policemen in combat gear and flak jackets ran past, yelling in Spanish and carrying M16 rifles. The burly cop from the Morales State Police led us up a flight of steps, summoned a typist, unlocked a darkened office, and Sabino began to dictate his statement.

The typist did not have the air of a woman who worked with typewriters very often. The statement was no more than eighteen or twenty paragraphs, and they were short paragraphs, just two or three lines each. But it took her two hours of hunting and pecking, backing and erasing, then hunting some more, before she had it finished.

Marti only had about twelve paragraphs to say, but she said them in English, so the typist needed three more hours before her statement was ready. By the time we made it back to the tourist-villa hotel, she and I were exhausted. And completely spooked.

At the meeting the next day, everything was in place. The tape recorder. The Mexicans. Mr. Sting's cell phone. The guy filming from the third-story window, everything. Maybe, even, the dozen or so very athletic-looking young men lounging around the grounds of the fancy tourist-villa hotel. They had regulation, military haircuts. None of them looked like tourists, and they were all keeping an eye on me. Every now and then, the cell phone crackled. Mr. Sting kept it switched on so that whoever was on the other end could track our conversation in real time.

"Señor Espino," I said, planning to squelch the whole idea of a bribe before the meeting got off the ground.

"*¿Espino?*" he looked blank. "*Me llama Valdez. Jorge Val...*" He shook his head. "*¡Me llama Espino!*" Then, "Two hundred and fifty thousand dollars," the newly reconstituted Mr. Sting said. "The judge will need two hundred and fifty thousand dollars."

"You are asking me for two hundred and fifty *thousand* dollars?" Boy, had these guys misjudged their mark.

"*Sí.* For two hundred and fifty thousand dollars we will have Mrs. Merritt in jail by the end of the..."

"I cannot dishonor Mexico's grand and honorable judiciary in such a manner," I shoved back my chair and announced in my most pompous and careful voice, so there wouldn't be any ambiguity about what I meant on the other end of Mr. Sting's cell phone. Or on his tape recording.

"You mean, you will give us the two hundred and fifty thousand dollars?" Señor Sting tried again.

"Señor," I stood up, making sure the tape recorder and the cell phone got the message, "I would never come into your country and offer a bribe to any official of your government." As high horses go, this one needed to be pumped up as tall as I could get it.

"You mean," Mr. Sting said, "you will need to go to America for the money?" On the table between us, the cell phone started to squawk. Somebody on the other end was yelling.

"No," Mr. Sting said into phone. "Not *yet*."

"No," I said into the phone and the tape recorder, "I will not go to America to get the money. There will be no money because there will be no bribe." Since I was already standing, all I had to do to end the conversation was turn and make my way past an unnaturally muscular Mexican standing at parade-rest on the lawn.

I grabbed my bag, walked past six more glaring Mexicans who spun their heads like owls as I went by, hailed a cab to the bus station, went to Mexico City, and was out of the country on the first plane. Marti followed, spent the night at the airport Hilton, and was home by noon the next day.

What was really going on during those couple of days we never discovered, but Sabino Gama provided a clue when he called a few months later. Because I hadn't come up with the bribe money, he hadn't gotten his cut and had been forced to go back to work for Ceci. But if I was interested, he had a line on a million shares of PeMex stock, and...well, it was hard to figure what I was supposed to do about the stock, because his English wasn't any better than my Spanish. I asked him to put it in writing and e-mail it to me, but I never heard from him.

Still, his *cut*? Why was Dad's butler expecting a cut of bribe money earmarked for a Mexican judge? That was the small question. The big question was, went back to work for *Ceci*? If there was one thing Ceci would never do, it was rehire somebody she'd fired. Or forget a grudge.

Sabino Gama spent two hours at the headquarters of the Morales State Police swearing out a statement accusing her of murder. Of all the strange bits of this strange story, his going back to work for Ceci was the strangest. It made me wonder who he'd actually been working for during those meetings with Señor Espino.

You can't keep a good man down, and Dad came home for a visit.

At least, that's what the Chihuahua said, and Chihuahuas know. Their bulging eyes can see ghosts, which is why Ceci bought herself one after Dad died. To warn her if she was in line for any supernatural after-effects.

The Chihuahua smelled a rat, and when she discovered it facing her bed, barking at nothing she could see, she moved to a new house on the far side of the ex-pat barrio. Then she donated the house Dad was haunting, the house they'd built with illegally logged endangered timber from the beautiful forest that once hugged the coast near Acapulco, to charity. If it was a charity for anything other than tax-deduction purposes. How Ceci even located that outfit, I can't imagine.

The people who supply trinkets for street-kids to hawk to tourists, and, I imagine, the endless supply of virgin sisters the street-kids also hawk, had gotten themselves registered as a 501 (c) (3), and Ceci gave them a haunted house. Whatever karmic implications there might be to that are way too complicated for me to tease out.

Not long after she moved, I got another call. This time from the Fagins themselves, and they were creeped out. Dad was still on the patio.

Ceci hadn't wanted him in the house, so she'd put his ashes outside where she wouldn't have to be bothered with them. Then, when she moved to her new digs, she left him behind...along with the old coat hangers and empty jars and dead plants that weren't worth keeping.

Despite having invested in a hysterectomy, she died anyway.

The way her son explained it, she turned up unconscious one morning after having downed a hundred sleeping pills under the impression it was diarrhea medicine. She'd had a lovely dinner with a dear friend the night before, had looked great, hadn't been depressed, the only thing wrong was a bit of tummy trouble, the diarrhea pills looked a lot like sleeping pills, she was old, and the light dim, and, well...in her son's mind, what his mother had meant to do was swallow a hundred *diarrhea* pills? Suicide by constipation wouldn't have been my first choice, not while I had sleeping pills in the same medicine cabinet.

And the person who found her? He was the dear friend she'd had dinner with.

The same dear friend who, somehow, let himself into her walled, burglar-alarmed, and heavily defended house seventeen hours later.

The same dear friend who would have been Ceci's lover if she hadn't neutered all possibilities of desire three decades before. And if he hadn't been a gay art dealer.

That was another strange thing. Ceci had filled her home with fashionable art. Art that was expensive, had a ready market, and lots of which wasn't there the morning the art dealer found her OD'ed on diarrhea pills. So here's what I like to think happened:

The gay art dealer didn't go home after the lovely dinner but stayed over, as he did lots of nights. Ceci wanted to talk. Talk led to more talk, Ceci didn't feel as loved and as supported as she should have, and went for the pills. She'd always had good luck with killing herself.

The problem with killing herself this time was that the art dealer wasn't Dad, Ceci had a house filled with art that only she had an inventory of, and seventeen hours was just about the time it took to fetch a truck, cherry-pick through the inventory, get the loot stashed someplace safe, and give the sleeping pills time to become irretrievably dissolved in her bloodstream.

I don't think Ceci was too concerned about an afterlife, she'd already bought herself a place in heaven. Her will left the house to the same Fagins she'd given the haunted house to. The fact that it wouldn't pay for as many trinkets and sisterly virgins as it would have when it still contained its most saleable art, that was something the art dealer was going to have to square with Jesus. It wasn't anything Ceci's soul had to worry about.

14

Could Be I Was Mistaken about that Slavery Thing

It isn't just our heritage we get from our ancestors, it's more like we are our ancestors. It just takes a while to notice.

I first began to suspect something was up in the ancestor department when my son turned three and started shrugging his shoulders when he didn't know the answer to something. Or he didn't want to talk about it. It was the exact shrug my grandmother shrugged when she didn't know the answer. Or didn't want to talk about something. I never saw it on anybody else, including me. My son didn't pick it up from her, either. They never met.

Seventy-two years after my grandfather died of a detached retina, I smacked my head into the overhanging portion of a camper trailer and dislodged a retina of my own. Not such a difficult thing to fix, in this day and age. The ophthalmologist injected nitrogen into my eye, the bubble pressed the retina against the back of the eyeball, and he welded it in place with a laser. Air and light. I was home the same afternoon.

In 1927 nobody knew about gas bubbles or lasers, but the best medical minds did have an opinion that a retina might be reattachable—with red-hot needles. Since my grandfather had access to the finest healthcare, that's what he got: a month in bed, head wedged between sandbags while doctors stuck red-hot needles in his eye. It was a bad idea. A red-hot needle will weld a retina in place, but it's still red-hot, and when you pull it out, the retina comes with it.

I have no idea whether my grandfather got his sight back, or how much, but when the month was up, the doctors had done all they could, including, as it turned out, leaving behind blood clots. A few days later, a clot broke loose and lodged in his brain and he died.

And that death—that one death that left my ten-year-old dad with no father to show him how to be a man around women—has rolled down through our family in ways that are not yet all felt.

Before Grandfather was born, Uncle Wesley vanished from the Texas frontier. After spending years out there, after serving loyally through the Civil War, after burning the Shenandoah, after serving as one of President Lincoln's pallbearers, after sailing to Paris to observe the Franco-Prussian War, Uncle Wesley didn't show up for work one morning.

What had become of him turned into a mystery that reached all the way to the war department. His personnel file is stuffed with handwritten memos, each one asking the same question: where is Colonel Merritt? Months later, somebody found him. He was back in Paris.

"I thought I was supposed to be in Paris," he replied in a very formal handwritten memo. "I was at a party with General Somebody-or-Other, and he told me, You know, we could use a man like you in Paris. So here I am." Nobody knew what to make of an excuse like that. In the end, the army just brought him back to Texas.

What he had going in Paris must have had a powerful hold, because years later, after he'd finally been reassigned from the frontier, after he'd been superintendent of the United States Military Academy, after he'd become one of the highest-ranking generals in the United States Army, he disappeared again.

Another search. Another exchange of memos—this time typewritten. Months after that, another memo, "We have located General Merritt in Paris." Followed by a carefully typed note from Uncle Wesley, "I thought I was supposed to be in Paris." Followed by the same question that had been asked years earlier. "What shall we do with General Merritt?"

This time, the directive came back from the secretary of war himself: "Cut General Merritt orders assigning him to Paris." Rank, as they say, really does hath its privileges.

Dad grew up not far from the house of Rafael Semmes and spent a lot of his boyhood looking at pictures of the admiral and the *CSS Alabama* and hearing stories of the sixty-three Yankee ships the two of them sent to the bottom. The call of the sea was strong, and Dad and his cousin spent their summers in college working merchant ships. The summer of thirty-six, they jumped ship in Hamburg and hitchhiked to Berlin to see the Olympics.

They weren't supposed to do that, not without papers, and not without tickets to the Games. But luck was on their side, or at least it was opposed to a couple of schoolteachers from Poughkeepsie who were called home for a family emergency. Dad and the cousin inherited their tickets and got to see Jesse Owens, an Alabaman who was there legitimately, pilfer four gold medals out from under Nazi noses. When he and the cousin hitched back to Hamburg, the Gestapo was waiting on the docks.

The Gestapo dealt with them on a case-by-case basis, cousin first. They stole his watch. They dumped out his wallet and took his money. Then they passed around his traveler's checks. "*Ach, vas isst das*?" they said in the Hollywood-movie German Dad always used when he got to the part about the traveler's checks.

"Just traveler's checks," the cousin said, trying to act unconcerned.

"Und vas isst dese traveler's checks?"

"They're like money. You sign them and..."

"Sign them," the Gestapo said.

With the checks safely signed and in their pockets, the Gestapo started the whole charade with Dad. They stole his watch. They took his money. Then they came to the traveler's checks. "*Ach, vas isst das?*" they demanded in their most innocent Nazi voices.

One thing about Depression-era Alabama, it taught a boy the value of a dollar, and Dad wasn't about to go handing his to a bunch of Nazi goons, no matter how black their uniforms. "Oh, nothing," he tore up the traveler's checks and flung the pieces into the Baltic. "Just scraps of paper." Which is how he and the cousin came to spend three days in one of Hitler's slams.

Dad was seventy-three when his mother died, and he'd still never told her what happened the summer he was nineteen. But it doesn't seem much different to me than what she did forty-two years later when she went to Angkor Wat.

In her late eighties, or her early nineties, depending on which birth certificates you believe, she bought a ticket and flew around the world.

There was lots of world she wanted to see, and high on the list was Angkor Wat. Unfortunately for Grandmother, Angkor Wat, along with the rest of Cambodia, had fallen into the hands of the Khmer Rouge. And the Khmer Rouge were nobody you wanted to visit.

They murdered a third of their own countrymen under the slogan "To keep you is no benefit. To destroy you is no loss." They murdered members of the former government, anybody who'd been to college, ethnic Chinese, ethnic Thai and Vietnamese, Catholics, Muslims, Buddhist monks, and anybody who wore glasses. Then they took the children they'd orphaned and taught them torture techniques using animals.

The Khmer Rouge didn't like Americans any better than they liked their own people, but my grandmother had cashed in good Coca-Cola stock to get there, and she wasn't about to let a bunch of Khmer Rouges spoil her trip. She chartered a small plane and flew up to Angkor Wat on her own.

I always imagined her climbing down from a Cessna or a Piper Cub in one of her summery pink dresses with a bold, floral print and walking around in the ruins for a day, maybe two, before heading back to Thailand.

When my son was seventeen, he went to Honduras as an exchange student. After he'd been down there four or five months, I received the only phone call I ever got from the exchange-student people.

The conversation sounded scripted, as if they weren't sure how I might react. "How's things in Portland?" the exchange person asked. "Weather's great here in San Diego. How about them Padres? And, ooooh by the way...would you happen to know where your son is?"

I didn't happen to know, but I did know how to find out. I called Western Union and canceled his money. He'd been mugged a while back and lost his bank card, so the little packets of cash I wired him were all he had.

He strung out his last fifty bucks for more than a week. When he finally contacted me, it was by e-mail, starting with, "Dad, it is not okay to abandon your son in the jungles of Central America."

Maybe it's okay, I thought, *Maybe it's not okay*. We'll discuss this when you get home, and took longer than I should have to answer the e-mail. After days of slow-motion negotiations, I agreed to send the money for a bus ticket to Tegucigalpa. Then I asked where to send it.

"San Cristobal de las Casas."

San Cristobal de las Casas? I thought. That's *Chiapas.*

Suddenly he had my full attention. "Son, the Mexican government can't get into Chiapas sometimes. How did you get there?"

"On the bus."

"Pay attention here. There's this guy. Subcomandante Marcos. Wears a ski mask. Smokes a pipe. Don't have anything to do with this guy."

"I know all about him, Dad. His picture is on every telephone pole." To this day I don't know whether those were wanted posters he saw or recruiting posters.

One Saturday, the kids and I were motoring along the parkway from Baltimore to DC when we spotted the turnoff to the National Security Agency. It's on, no kidding, Canine Road. Who could pass up something like that?

We were mugging and taking pictures of ourselves in front of the big, sky-blue, circular concrete seal with an out-of-sorts looking eagle perched on a skeleton key when half-a-dozen squad cars came screaming out of the gate, slammed to a stop, and buff-looking guys with pistols strapped to their sides took my camera and erased the pictures. Then they started demanding ID. They were the National Security Agency's security people, and they ran smack up against my mother. If you don't like being bullied, then it's up to you to do something about it. That's the way Mother saw it, and she was never one not to do something about it. Those guys didn't have a chance.

Channeling through my daughter she never met, Mother announced that she wouldn't be showing any ID, thank you very much, or tell them her name, either. What she would tell them was, "I'm an American citizen minding my own business in a public place. I don't have to show you anything."

That was news to the NSA, and they had a little huddle about it. Important principles were at stake. When they'd figured out how to protect those principles, they told my daughter they'd keep her in a holding cell until she rethought her opinion of what Americans can and cannot do in public places.

"So," Mother asked in my daughter's chirpiest voice, "I'll see a judge on Monday?"

This resulted in another huddle. Then one of the security guys climbed into a patrol car and made an emergency radio call. When he climbed back out, nobody mentioned holding cells again. Instead, an unmarked car sped up. Then an unmarked—at least, an ununiformed—middle-aged white guy popped out. He was, I think, the head of security at National Security, and he knew what to do. "We'll handcuff her," he said with a straight face. "For officer safety."

My daughter is a relatively short, very curvy, sweet-faced, soft-spoken young lady, while every one of the men who needed protecting could have bench-pressed the patrol cars they drove up in. They all had guns, one was sporting a brass badge that said PISTOL EXPERT, while another had his PISTOL EXPERT patch sewn permanently onto his uniform, and I started laughing.

"Who knows what she has in her purse?" the head of security said.

"You have my permission to search my purse." My daughter tried to hand it to him, but he wouldn't take it. So she placed it at their feet and stepped back.

The purse was the size of a paperback book, if paperback books came with shoulder straps. Lying in the street, it didn't look threatening, but those guys couldn't have stepped around it more gingerly if it had sprouted rattles and fangs. "Pick up your purse, Lady," they told my daughter. "Lady. *Pick up your purse.*"

After a while she did.

That ended the threat of attack-purses. Instead, the National Security people decided to write her a summons. That way, she could come back Monday and explain to the judge why she thought she had the right to be in a public place. All they needed was her name.

She agreed to give it to them. On two conditions. First, they had to guarantee they'd use it only for the purpose of filling out the citation, not to find out who she was.

Confronted with a legal hair the United States Supreme Court would have had trouble splitting, they called another little huddle. Before agreeing to any deals, they needed to know what the second condition was.

"Show me the statute you plan to base the summons on."

That led to a second emergency radio call.

Somebody inside the bowels of our darkest, most feared spy agency radioed back a legal opinion. The National Security security people nodded to themselves. Then one of them turned over his ticket pad and showed my daughter what was printed on the back.

What was on the back was a list of the eight things cops get to write tickets for, things like driving faster than thirty-five or parking too long or riding a motorcycle without a helmet. It didn't say anything about being an American in a public place. While they were discussing among themselves how to persuade her they really could give her a ticket, she pulled out a scrap of paper and began writing.

"Here," one of them handed her a legal pad. "No need to use that. You can write your name here." Then looked over her shoulder, hoping to be the first person at National Security with the scoop on who she was. "*Lady,*" he said in an almost plaintive wail, "you're supposed to write your name. Not *ours.*"

The reason you're reading this now is that it started getting dark, time had come to go, and she handed them her library card. The front of the card listed the branch libraries. The back had her signature accepting "responsibility for all materials charged on this card," but no picture. No printed version of her name. No birth date, address, rank, serial number, or anything else to tie the card to any particular American.

One of them took the card and disappeared into a patrol car. A few seconds later, he reported back with the news, "You can go now."

Anybody else would have gone. Mother wasn't so hot-footed. "Why," she demanded, "are you letting me go?"

"We checked you out." The head of security smiled. 'You're okay."

"You checked me out? What did you check me out *against*?"

"Our database. Now go."

"You have a *database* on American citizens?"

"No, Lady. Nothing like that." The head of security started to back up. "Not on Americans."

"No databases, unh *unnnh*," the other guys were coming to his defense. "Not on Americans."

"No, Ma'am. No databases here." By now they were all backing toward their cars. "No *way*. Not at the NSA."

"Not on Americans."

Thirty years after I moved away, the Olympics came to Atlanta. I took the kids to see, but the place wasn't the same. In my absence, the city had transmogrified itself into Hotlanta.

Instead of the Grapevine Line, we took MARTA downtown. The Metropolitan Atlanta Rapid Transit Authority: a light-rail system just about as sleek and modern as any in the world. The announcements about the stops, and standing back from the doors, and which seats were reserved for old people and pregnant women and folks on crutches were announced all over again in French. This probably had something to do with the Olympics but definitely gave the ride a cosmopolitan flavor the bus system never displayed—on par, now that I think of it, with motoring through rural Canada.

Peachtree Creek was gone, channeled into a concrete pipe big enough for a brigade of Billy Sherman's bummers to march down in parade formation. A creek that, when I was a boy, seemed unchanged from the time of John Bell Hood's cavalry, had been turned into a sewer.

Where once Shelby and I were the only people we ever heard of to boat the Chattahoochee, thousands do now. There's even a regatta complete with drownings and beer and Coast Guard helicopters.

The one-lane trestle bridge where a long-ago girl and I waited in Mother's Fiat to cross the river was gone, as was the two-lane blacktop, both paved over by an interstate highway. The big hickory trees and the ice cream stand outside Cumming, and the bitter woman who seemed so proud of the mass lynching that spring day when I was sixteen, had disappeared, too.

Buckhead remains, like a trip back in time. An island of antebellum fantasy surrounded by commerce and industry on all sides. A place with, as far as I could tell, every single house unaltered from the fifties. There didn't seem to have been a single fire, a single tree chopped down, a single change of paint color. It was as spooky and as out-of-time as Brigadoon.

I took the kids to the Memorial Arts Center, only it wasn't there. The Memorial Arts Center, built to honor the people killed at Orly, the newly opened theater where Rachel and I had gone to see *The Royal Hunt of the Sun* and seen Martin Luther King, too, had run its course as a civic monument and been renamed in honor of Robert W. Woodruff, the head of the Coca-Cola Company.

An actual memorial is still there, though. People tell me it used to be in a more prominent location, but times, like names, change, and the memorial had been shuffled over to a patch of lawn fronting a side street. The memorial was a waist-high wall, three-quarters of a circle with the names of Mother and her buddies carved into black granite.

I spent longer than my kids would have liked running my fingers over half-remembered names from my childhood, trying to put faces to the ladies I remembered from Mother's Coca-Cola parties, to people who came with their husbands for drinks in the evening, or drove me to school.

At the center of the memorial, enclosed on three sides by the black-granite wall, is *The Shade*, a gift from France. It is a bronze cast of one of Rodin's figures for *The Gates of Hell*, which, given the way the Orly people died, seemed appropriate.

As much as I admire Rodin, I was never much of a fan of *The Shade.* It seemed twisted to me and misshapen, which, I guess, Rodin intended but to my mind robbed the work of its power, as if done by a maudlin adolescent rather than one of the greats of Western art. It was another fifteen years before I had the chance to look at *The Gates of Hell* in person and discover that there was a reason *The Shade* looked misshapen. In the original there isn't just a shade, there are three shades twisting together like wraiths supporting one another in a single, brazen grouping. The French had sawn off the other two so that the figure that stands outside the Woodruff Arts Center is less a shade and more a passing shadow.

Before we departed, the kids and I picked some marigolds from the tidy flowerbed that ran next to the retaining wall that keeps the memorial from sliding into the side street. Then placed them on top of Mother's name.

Afterwards, we headed down to MARTA and on to the Coca-Cola museum. I glanced back a couple of times. The yellow flowers that I thought would look so fine against the black granite just seemed thin and spindly.

A few years ago I visited Ft. Lauderdale and came across a row of shops selling flamboyant, overpriced clothing. The shops mostly seemed to be run by foreigners. A Syrian, I think, specialized in baseball caps.

He had a baseball cap for every denomination a young American might care to espouse. NFL caps. NBA caps. American League caps. National League caps. Caps with the animal of every known college team. Industrial baseball caps for people whose patriotism ran to Harley Davidson or Massey Ferguson or John Deere. Baseball caps with marijuana leaves. And peace signs. And caps that swung the other way with American flags or patriotic assertions such as DON'T TREAD ON ME.

I knew this kind of shop, maybe this very shop. They'd been all over the South when I was growing up, back when you could walk into one of these places and come out equipped, headgear-wise, in the uniform of a Confederate general. Or a cavalry officer. Or an infantryman.

A Confederate hat, I thought. That would be just the ticket. Remind me of old times.

"A Confederate hat," the Syrian said. "Like in the Civil War?"

"That's it," I said. "A Confederate hat like in the Civil..."

"Sir," he took a couple of steps forward so his face was very close to mine. "We are Americans here."

I was always pleased that my people were mountain stock. Scots-Irish, moonshiners, maybe, but not slave owners.

The whole idea of slavery was so alien, so out of context with anything I could imagine, it seemed more like throwing babies into the flaming maw of a bronze statue in ancient Carthage than something practiced by anybody whose lives intersected with my own. It was especially hard to imagine with Southerners. With people who, of all Americans, valued liberty and rebelliousness. I was glad my family had had nothing to do with it.

A few years ago I made it to Huntsville for the first time. I wanted to check out our family land and brought along a map of Redstone Arsenal. There were creeks and bluffs back there with my grandmother's maiden name on them. There were cemeteries on the map, too, carefully fenced off, with family inside. I could have gotten a pass and, most likely, an escort to keep me from walking off with one of the rockets, and visited my ancestors if I could have shown I was related to them. But I couldn't, I hadn't inherited the name, and the guards at Redstone turned me away.

Afterwards, I drove around for a while, through second-growth pine forests planted in the thirties when the government was reforesting burned-out cotton land all over the South. No different than the trees Dad and I drove through in the fifties, only taller. All that land, all that human misery, returned to forest.

Then over to the Huntsville-Madison County Historical Society to see if I could find pictures of the way things had been and hit the jackpot: drawers of pictures, stacks of pictures, boxes of pictures.

Photography-wise, Madison County must be one of the most documented spots on the planet.

It was bustling, too, in the nineteenth century. Every autumn before the boll weevil, the city square filled with wagons bringing in bales of cotton: hundreds of wagons jammed together as closely as if the pictures were of street scenes in Shanghai. Ramparts of cotton stacked in warehouses and on railroad sidings and on plantations.

And fields of workers, hundreds of blacks, thousands newly freed from slavery, hoeing and picking and tending the plants, just like they'd always done. Had I had my mind on something besides my own family, I would have thought more about those pictures. My family, my ancestors, the people I loved, wouldn't have had any use for so much land if they hadn't had somebody to work it. Still, I didn't put things together. We were Appalachian South, yeoman farmers who worked their own fields.

Then I saw another picture. Not in Huntsville, but in Atlanta. My cousin Edward had been doing research of his own. Except his research wasn't generic. His research involved going through family documents.

The picture was of a slave, and it broke my heart.

He was an old man, and skinny, with a wrinkled face.

He looked like somebody I might have liked. And he was dressed in rags.

His shirt was split and falling off his back, and for months, all I could think about was those rags. An entire lifetime of producing wealth for my family, and that's what we gave him? Those rags are the total of what I know about that man, I don't even know his name, but they are enough. More than enough.

I don't know why the picture was taken. Surely not to include with that year's Christmas letter. The best I can come up with is that it was a mug shot. Not because the old man had done anything wrong but because, as old as he was, he might run. I like to think I would have.

Or maybe it had something to do with insurance, like documenting the silver so you can prove what the burglar took. I don't know.

And I don't know why, of all the people my family must have owned, the daguerreotype of that particular man came down to us. Was he especially beloved? But, then, why the rags?

Maybe he was the ogre, the famous Bad Nigger, the one mothers waved pictures of in front of naughty kids. "You girls settle down, or Uncle Rastus gone get you."

Whoever he was, he's gotten me, and he hasn't let go.

When I was old I met a man who grew up in Brunswick, and since he was old, too, I imagine he was one of the kids dancing for the nickels Dad tossed from the window as we drove through. He got out of Georgia and educated all four of his children. One of his daughters is a doctor now. A son graduated from Harvard, earned a masters at Princeton, and went on to become country director for the Peace Corps in Namibia.

Dixon Rawlins was Dad's best friend. He lived in Marks, Mississippi, in a walled compound. He owned thousands of acres of cotton land and soybeans and mills to process them and employed hundreds of field hands. His wife died at Orly, and he never got over it. He never married again, I'm not sure he ever dated. Ten years later, he blew his brains out with a shotgun. By then, one of his field hands had struck it big in Nashville. Country Charley Pride, with thirty-nine number-one hits on the *Billboard Hot Country Songs* chart, became the first black country music superstar and sold more records for RCA than anybody except Elvis.

At the only writer's conference I ever attended, my roommate was chairman of the African American Studies department at the State University of New York at Albany, a poet, and one of nine children from a dirt-poor family in a vanishingly small town in North Carolina, all of whom went to college.

When I lived in Botswana, I made friends with the American who ran the International Law Enforcement Academy. His job was to teach our policing techniques to Africans, make friends for our country, and instill our ideals into cops all over the continent.

When he was fourteen, he was alone on a lake in Oklahoma. Another boat rowed up, one with a grinning white guy in his thirties and his thirteen-year-old wife. The white guy pulled a gun and told him to get the fuck off the lake. He told the white guy to keep that grin on your face, because if you're not careful, I'm going to put you and Little Miss Jailbait, both, in hell, and you can spend your time grinning at the devil.

Four years later, he was in the army when his black sergeant warned him to break off his friendships with white soldiers. "There's about twenty brothers waitin' to beat the shit out of you, and I'm gone be at the head of the line."

"You be sure and do that," he told the sergeant, "because I'll want to find you so we can be in the hospital together. I will *damn* sure put you there." And went on being friends with whomever he chose.

When I was in the hospital at Fort Gordon, I met a lanky black kid. He could hardly wait to dance on a rubber leg.

We were right when we were growing up. We Southerners were of the stuff of heroes, filled with the courage, the grit and resilience, the rebellious spirit, the will to stand up to an unjust government, the faith in the possibilities of ourselves and our nation. We just didn't guess who among us the heroes would turn out to be.

Note to the Reader

The good news Malcolm X delivered about the Orly air disaster, that Allah had "struck down a planeload of crackers," has been emblazoned on my heart for more than half a century. Still, it seemed respectful to check his exact words. After all, who'd want to misquote a man who was always so careful in his use of language? This proved to be surprisingly easy to do. He spewed them out at a meeting of the Nation of Islam, they were caught on tape, then reported in the *Los Angeles Herald-Examiner* on June 6, 1962.

There was a lot more to what he said than I cared to go into, incitements to racial hatred, posturings of being the only courageous black man in America, sanctimonious gloatings about divine retribution. Someone close to the government must have been in the audience or, at least, read the papers, because this bit of good news is referenced in the FBI files on Malcolm X, Part II, Chronology, June 6, 1962.

My schoolmate, Taylor Branch, quoted as much of it as he could stand in *Pillar of Fire: America and the King Years, 1963-1965*. Simon and Schuster, 1999, ISBN 0-684-84809-0, p 14. But being a courtly sort of guy, Taylor cleaned up the language and had Allah merely strike down a planeload of white people; an example, to my mind, of the euphemization of all things Malcolm that culturally sensitive Americans have indulged themselves in since Mr X experienced his own divine retribution.

It seemed more authentic to me to quote the words he actually used. I took them from *The Victims of Democracy, Malcolm X and the Black Revolution*, Eugene Victor Wolfenstein, University of California Press, 1981, ISBN 0-520-03903-3, p 277. Wolfenstein had the effrontery to repeat what Malcolm X really said, but even he felt uneasy about the man's choice of words and set "crackers" off with quotation marks – despite the fact that nobody who heard the speech reported his making air quotes with his fingers.

The second part of the material I referred to, "we hope that every day another plane falls out of the sky," is from *Pillar of Fire*, p 14. Again, Taylor Branch has Mr X say "white people" when referring to the passengers and crew he hoped would fall out of the sky along with the planes. Again, I'm pretty sure that isn't what he really said.

Malcolm X was nothing if not steadfast in his hatreds, and refused to disavow any portion of his remarks to Alex Haley while being interviewed for an article published in *Playboy* in May, 1963.